Praise for
Safe House

"There's no greater joy than raising children. There's also no greater sorrow than when you don't feel like you have what it takes to do it. Using the transparency of his own story, as well as his experience as a family counselor and dad himself, Josh provides a road map for making our homes the emotionally safest places in the world for our kids. Most importantly, you walk away with a true sense of encouragement that you really do have what it takes to write beautiful stories for your kids!"

—CANDACE CAMERON BURE, actress, author, producer, and mom

"'Home, sweet home' is much more than a cliché; it's a critically important goal toward which we should all strive as parents. Making your home a safe house is one of the best investments of time and energy you can possibly make. Joshua Straub shows how in this insightful book."

—JIM DALY, president of Focus on the Family

"*Safe House* is a must-read and a humbling reminder that there's no safety outside of God's sovereignty. Thank you, Joshua, for reminding us that it's never too late to raise kids who live, love, and lead well."

—SHELENE BRYAN, founder of Skip1.org and author of *Love Skip Jump*

"In a humorous but candid approach, Joshua Straub uses scholarship and his own emotional pain to help us face and deal with our own stories. As a product of six broken homes and a lot of abuse, I know the urgency and the desperation to rewrite my story for my children's sake, and for heaven's sake. Many of us are familiar with panicked efforts to child-proof our homes, but after decades of training students, I often wondered if it was possible to parent-proof our children. This timely book, *Safe House,* is full of wisdom, examples, and appreciations of, most of all, hope for our most cherishable possessions—our children."

—DR. JAY STRACK, president and founder of StudentLeadership.net

"I wish I could've read *Safe House* before I raised my daughters. I'm sure it would've saved them many dollars spent on therapy. Thanks to Josh and this amazing book, I have a second chance. I am now embracing the principles in this book and applying them to my relationship with six beautiful grandchildren."

—KEN DAVIS, author of *Fully Alive* and speaker and communications trainer

"To the exhausted parent, these pages are filled with hope. To the insecure parent, these pages are filled with confidence. To the parent trying to win your child's heart before the culture does, these pages are empowering. Josh has created an insightful work-of-heart that will truly impact families for generations to come!"

—SHANNON ETHRIDGE, MA, life/relationship coach and author of twenty-two
books, including the million-copy, best-selling Every Woman's Battle series

"Parenting is hard. No doubt about it. We deal with insecurity and great frustration as we work through motives, parenting styles, and discipline strategies. Joshua Straub does a fantastic job in *Safe House* encouraging parents to stay focused on what's most important: the heart of the child. This book will help eradicate insecurity and insanity from your home."

—TED CUNNINGHAM, founding pastor of Woodland Hills Family Church
and author of *Fun Loving You* and *The Power of Home*

JOSHUA STRAUB, PhD

FOREWORD BY DR. MEG MEEKER

safe house

How Emotional Safety Is the Key to Raising Kids

Who Live, Love, and Lead Well

WATERBROOK
PRESS

SAFE HOUSE

All Scripture quotations, unless otherwise indicated, are taken from the Holy Bible, English Standard Version, copyright © 2001 by Crossway Bibles, a division of Good News Publishers. Used by permission. All rights reserved. Scripture quotations marked (HCSB) are taken from The Holman Christian Standard Bible®, © copyright 1999, 2000, 2002, 2003, 2009 by Holman Bible Publishers. Used by permission. Scripture quotations marked (KJV) are taken from the King James Version. Scripture quotations marked (MSG) are taken from The Message by Eugene H. Peterson. Copyright © 1993, 1994, 1995, 1996, 2000, 2001, 2002. Used by permission of NavPress Publishing Group. All rights reserved. Scripture quotations marked (NASB) are taken from the New American Standard Bible®. © Copyright The Lockman Foundation 1960, 1962, 1963, 1968, 1971, 1972, 1973, 1975, 1977, 1995. Used by permission. (www.Lockman.org). Scripture quotations marked (NIV) are taken from the Holy Bible, New International Version®, NIV®. Copyright © 1973, 1978, 1984 by Biblica Inc.™ Used by permission of Zondervan. All rights reserved worldwide. www.zondervan.com.

Details in some anecdotes and stories have been changed to protect the identities of the persons involved.

Trade Paperback ISBN 978-1-60142-789-2
eBook ISBN 978-1-60142-790-8

Copyright © 2015 by Joshua Straub

Cover design by Kristopher Orr; cover photography by Sergio G. Cañizares, Getty Images

Published in the United States by WaterBrook, an imprint of the Crown Publishing Group, a division of Penguin Random House LLC, New York.

WATERBROOK® and its deer colophon are registered trademarks of Penguin Random House LLC.

Library of Congress Cataloging-in-Publication Data
Straub, Joshua.
    Safe house : how emotional safety is the key to raising kids who live, love, and lead well / Joshua Straub, PhD. — First Edition.
        pages cm
    ISBN 978-1-60142-789-2 — ISBN 978-1-60142-790-8 (electronic) 1. Child rearing—Religious aspects—Christianity. 2. Parenting—Religious aspects—Christianity. 3. Families—Religious aspects—Christianity. 4. Mental health—Religious aspects—Christianity. I. Title.
    BV4529.S875 2015
    248.8'45—dc23

                            2015018773

Printed in the United States of America
2018

10 9 8 7 6 5 4 3

SPECIAL SALES
Most WaterBrook books are available at special quantity discounts when purchased in bulk by corporations, organizations, and special-interest groups. Custom imprinting or excerpting can also be done to fit special needs. For information, please e-mail specialmarketscms@penguinrandomhouse.com or call 1-800-603-7051.

To Dad, who's still sitting in the stands cheering me on,
and to Mom, who shows me to this day I have what it takes.

I love you both more than you know.

Dear Fellow Parent,

My beautiful Canadian wife, Christi, and I have two strong-willed kids: our son, Landon, and daughter, Kennedy. Christi and I had no idea how much a little line on a tiny stick would change our lives. My work life is no exception. Kennedy lived her first six sleepless months of life while I wrote this book—in a fog. When Landon became a toddler, he discovered that daddy worked from a comfortable, well-decorated home office overlooking the Ozark Mountains. From then on he wanted to "go to wook" too, which meant I had to go into hiding.

That's why most of this book was written in our frigid garage in the middle of winter with a screaming infant and a whiny toddler as background music. I complemented keyboard time with bouncing our newborn in an Ergobaby carrier while speaking into Dragon Dictation, occasionally interrupted midsentence to help Christi wrangle Landon into submission.

And you thought writers frolicked in cozy coffee shops to consoling downtempo?

Not this guy. At least not for this book.

I think that's God's sense of humor. To humble us in the very task we're called to do so as to make sure we don't pull our britches up too high, thinking we've got it all figured out. I often found myself writing on topics Christi and I were struggling with in the moment. I'm convinced nothing has the power to simultaneously enliven and exhaust a person more than parenthood. Becoming a dad is the most rewarding task I ever signed up for, but it's also the most difficult.

And if you're like us, you don't need outside help to question yourselves as parents. The mainstream media, the so-called experts, and, yes, even family have that covered, shaming our every parenting move.

So as you read the pages that follow, know that my heart is to remove the judgment and instead for us to come together as parents in our local coffee shops, communities, and churches to encourage and support one another as we all strive toward the same goal: raising kids who live, love, and lead well. I think you'll be surprised that achieving this goal, though not easy, is much simpler than we might think.

I'm glad we're on this journey together.

—Josh

contents

Foreword by Dr. Meg Meeker ix
Acknowledgments xiii

Part 1: Why Emotional Safety—and Your Story—Matter

1 Can Parenting Really Be This Simple?. 3
2 You Are Home: A Safe House Begins with You 16
3 Your Story, Your Kid's Brain, and the Science of Safety 33

Part 2: Building a Safe House

4 The Four Walls of a Safe House. 53
5 Explore and Protect 70
6 Grace and Truth. 92
7 Safe Discipline 110
8 Nurturing Our Child's Brain from Infancy Through Adolescence . . . 127

Part 3: A Safe Village

9 The Bible and Safe Parenting 147
10 A Safe Marriage 164
11 Establishing Faith. 182

Notes. 200

foreword

After practicing pediatric and adolescent medicine for thirty years, I have come to consider myself a professional listener, if you will. I have tuned my ear to the hearts of five-year-olds who don't want to go to school, divorced husbands who feel pushed out of their children's lives by angry ex-wives, and seventeen-year-olds who feel they can't stand being alive for one more day. I can honestly say that I have never met a child or teen that I don't like, and believe me, I've worked with a lot of angry, hurting kids. Early in my career, I worked in a teen and tot clinic (yep, teen girls with toddlers) in the inner city. Then I moved to a wealthy area outside of Springfield, Massachusetts and took care of children whose parents were doctors or other professionals. I have visited parents, living in dire poverty in the most remote parts of the Andes, who struggle to succeed at the most elementary of parenting tasks—to feed their children.

I have learned one thing: a parent's heart is a parent's heart. Whether a parent is a struggling, single teen mother or a wealthy professional, parents ache for their kids. They want their children to be healthy, safe, and most of all, happy. And they want them to live a better life than they did, even if those parents grew up in healthy homes. The altruism of parents' hearts drives them to want their children to have more of the good stuff in life. They don't necessarily want their kids to make more money or travel the world; they just want their children to experience greater peace and greater joy. That's it. So simple but so terribly elusive.

There's another thing that I learned early in my career, and it is this: if I want to help a child, I must help his parents. Why? *Because one parent—better yet two—holds all the power in a child's life.* If I want to help a sixteen-year-old girl stop cutting her arms, I talk to her father. If I want an anxious second-grader to feel safer going to school, I work with his mother on ways to calm him and retrain his thinking. If I could scream anything from the rooftops that parents simply don't get, it's this: *YOU make or break your children!* Not Madonna, Miley Cyrus, pornography on the Internet, teachers, coaches, or peers. Conscientious parents who read many parenting books have been duped into believing that when a son or daughter turns thirteen, they must loose them into their peer culture because that's what kids want, even need. We plan to pick them up again when they're eighteen or so and they've "become less like aliens." Then we wonder why our teenagers are so rebellious and filled with confusion and angst. But why wouldn't they be? We create a self-fulfilling prophesy by communicating to them that they *will* be hard to manage, love, and live with when they are teens. So why shouldn't they be?

This, friends, is an American cultural phenomenon. It is not normal and doesn't need to be part of the experience of growing up in America. This is something that we have created because we buy into peer pressures of our own. This brings me to my point. In the cacophony of voices—friends, experts, grandparents, and culture—telling us how to parent, we need an infusion of sanity. *Safe House* brings this sanity.

The truth is, great parenting is quite simple. But it's hard. It requires that we love well so that our children learn to do so. It means that, as Dr. Straub eloquently elucidates, "in order to be understood, we must first understand." And, most important, it requires that we focus on parenting our children's hearts. That's really what this book is all about. It teaches us to keep our parenting focus where we really want it to be but don't know how—on the emotional health of our children.

We parents get so wrapped up in working hard to create great portfolios for our children so that we can "launch" them to mighty places that we fail to see them. Countless times I have talked to parents (Christian and secular) about the importance of making sure that their children mature into adults who have strong character, which, I tell them, trumps academic, musical, or athletic achievements. The irony is that 99 percent of the parents I tell this too nod their heads in agreement and leave the conversation with a strong conviction that they, unlike their friends, are succeeding at doing exactly what I said.

But sadly, they aren't. Why? *Because no one is teaching them.* Their hearts are in the right place, but their own friends are so entrenched in portfolio building that they too, fall into line lest their friends' children turn out "better" than theirs. Here's a case in point. I was recently talking with a friend whose son has a huge heart for God. He is nine years old and asks his parents to pray with him. After talking with my friends for a while and applauding them for encouraging their son's faith so well, they thanked me. They agreed that it was sad how many parents (unlike them) focus on making their children feel valued through sports, academics, and so on.

Not long after that statement, the father launched into a diatribe about how talented this same boy was at baseball. Really talented. In fact, this father boasted (he didn't really mean to but knew I would handle it as a friend) that the boy might have a shot at Major League baseball one day. He talked about the fact that his child liked to pray, but he bragged about his baseball talents. If I picked up on where his true pride in his son lay, how much more would his son? Was this father a bad dad? No, but he did do exactly what he had just denounced in other parents. Why? Because he had been trained to focus on helping his son be outstanding at something. The problem was, he simply didn't know how to deviate from the parenting paradigm that his friends used. He didn't know how to find a different, healthier direction in parenting.

My plea to you, friends, as you read through this remarkable work, is that you ask yourself hard questions. Dr. Straub will make you look inside yourself as you read, and that is a great thing. You need to. We all need to. Because it is only by serious introspection that we can better ourselves as parents. And isn't that what each of us parents really wants?

You will learn in these pages what *emotional safety* means. Then, you will learn how to provide emotional safety for your children. I am convinced that once you are successful at that—and any parent *can* be successful at it—then you will begin to sink deep roots for your child from which he can grow. Finally, learning how to provide emotional safety for your children helps you begin to parent the way you really want to parent. You will be positively anchoring the heart and soul of your child.

I am confident that as you apply the principles herein, you will change not only your child's life but also *your life*. I know this because Dr. Straub is a stickler for backing up his theories with excellent data. You won't just hear his opinions; you will see the rock solid research behind everything he says. There are hundreds of voices from "experts" clamoring for your attention, but there are only a handful who can honestly impact your parenting in a profound and positive way.

I am proud to say that *Safe House* is one of them.

—DR. MEG MEEKER, best-selling author of *Strong Fathers, Strong Daughters* and the co-host of *Family Talk* with Dr. James Dobson

acknowledgments

A book is only as powerful on the life of a reader as the stories it tells.

I'm indebted to my parents, wife, and children for permitting me the freedom of vulnerability with our own story, with the hope that it can help others.

Christi, words cannot describe how grateful I am for your allowing me to escape to the frigid garage or a warm coffee shop during some of the most difficult days of our lives to write this book. There's nobody else I'd rather be on this journey with than you. I love you.

From conception to completion, there's no one who invested more time and energy into this book than my mother-in-love, Lora Lee Wood. Mum, without you, I'm not sure it would be a reality. Equally so are the constant prayers, encouragement, and support from my father-in-love, Ray Wood. Dad, I hope I can be half the anchor you are for my own family.

Mom and Mike, Dad and Deb, thank you all for loving our family unconditionally and leading by example.

Landon and Kennedy, you show mommy and me a joy we didn't know existed. The fun is just beginning.

And to those who helped me conceptualize, write, and edit . . .

Bryan Norman, it's a privilege to call you not just an agent but a friend.

Laura Captari, thank you for coming in the ninth inning to close it out. You got the save. I appreciate your words. I value your friendship more.

Gary Sibcy, your mentorship and counseling influence on my life is written all over these pages. Thank you for teaching me, talking through so many of these principles with me, and molding me into the counselor and teacher I am today. Let's enjoy more boat rides in San Diego soon.

Paul Staup, Frank MacArthur, Tim Clinton, Dave Brower, my clinical supervisors through the years, and to all of the counseling leaders who have invested in me, I am paying it forward.

John Blase, landing you as my editor was a genuine gift from God. Thanks for your input not just as an editor but as a father.

Johanna Inwood, Charlene Guzman, Kristopher Orr, and the entire WaterBrook Multnomah team, your hard work, dedication, and belief in this message are deeply appreciated.

Linda Purvis, thank you for helping Christi with the kiddos to allow me time to write, and especially for loving our family like your own. We love you.

PART 1

Why Emotional Safety —and Your Story— Matter

Can Parenting Really Be This Simple?

Safe House: (n): a dwelling that is a safe place for taking refuge.

—Dictionary.com

The world can be very unsafe. Our homes shouldn't be.

Especially for our kids.

I have fond memories of my childhood. I'm sure there were unsafe moments, but nothing I vividly remember. My foundation for safety was pretty well set.

Until Monday, July 9, 1990. That's when the cracks in our home's foundation were exposed and our Safe House began to crumble.

We had just returned home from our annual family vacation in Wildwood, New Jersey. From my ten-year-old perspective, all seemed normal on the trip. Ice cream on the boardwalk. Football with my dad on the beach. Hours of riding in waves with my eight-year-old sister. I didn't want to go home.

As the next morning came, I was groggily awakened to the sounds of crying outside my bedroom. I felt my body sink further into the mattress as my mom entered the room and sat on the bed next to me. My weeping little sister followed right behind her. I lifted my head to check the time. With my glasses on the nightstand beside me, I squinted through my extremely poor vision to see a blurry 6:04 a.m. lit dimly on the clock.

Breaking me out of my foggy half-sleep, my mom looked at me and said, "I'm moving out today. Do you want to go along with me or stay here with your dad?"

I felt immediately numb. Even in my stupor I knew exactly what was happening.

The tears welled up. With a shaky voice I asked, "What's Jenna doing?"

"She's going with me."

Through the sniffles, I quickly made up my mind. "Then I want to stay here with Dad."

I didn't know how to process what had just happened. What child would? Rarely had I seen my parents fight. For goodness sake, we just returned home from a wonderful vacation—or so I'd thought.

Waking Up to a New Story

Denial can be such a wonderful thing—until you're awakened from it. For another thirteen years, 20/2000 vision didn't describe just my eyesight; it unknowingly became a metaphor for my emotional insight as well.

I failed to face the pain of my parents' divorce. I was the fixer in the family, and everybody came to me for answers. So as far as I was concerned, I had it together.

Besides, I didn't see my parents fight. My stepfather became one of the biggest influences in my faith journey. My dad, stepfather, and I would even hang out together occasionally. If anybody had reason to believe their situation was an exception, it was me. I honestly believed I came out unscathed.

Then it all came crashing down. The emotional wounds from my parents' divorce began to surface in my own relationships. Two years of counseling ensued. In that time I learned one principle—the past is not your past if it's affecting your present. I began to realize that one of the greatest dangers to my future family was my own unresolved baggage. That's when I made the decision to begin rewriting my story—and rewiring my brain without even knowing it.

Writing Our Parenting Script

Our homes reflect our story. For some, that story is defined by brokenness. For others, it's defined by love, laughter, and joy. For most, it's a blend of the two.

The beauty of it all is that no matter our story or family background—good, bad, or ugly—we have 100 percent control in writing a new script. And it's a good thing too. Research shows that as parents we're the ones writing our children's story—and wiring their brains as well. That's both a powerful and scary realization. Especially considering that most of us parent the way our parents raised us, for better or for worse, oftentimes without even realizing it.

Have you ever considered what kind of story you're writing for your children? Or what effect *your* story is having on those little ones you love most? It's a story you'll want to begin writing down. (We'll do this together in the next chapter.)

In spite of my parents' divorce, I have a dad who loves me unconditionally. Whether I went four-for-four at the plate or zero-for-four at the plate, whether I pinned my opponent in thirty seconds or got pinned in thirty seconds, I knew my dad was there for me. I can count on one hand the number of wrestling matches my dad missed throughout my seven years of wrestling, most because he couldn't get off work on time.

Because my dad chose to rewrite his story.

My grandfather (his dad) left my grandmother when my dad was twelve. His dad wasn't there for him very much. As a truck driver he was always on the road. Though he loved my dad, he was generally unavailable to him. My dad recognized it enough to rewrite his own story and intentionally become emotionally and physically available to my sister and me growing up. Today, my dad's rewritten story impacts our own parenting journeys.

BUILDING YOUR SAFE HOUSE

Thankfully, you're a parent who's passionate about the emotional and relational dangers coming against our children. Being aware now of these dangers makes it possible to be proactive about building a Safe House so that years later we're not fighting against the tide of rebellion, distance, and irreversibly poor choices. This doesn't mean they won't rebel or make mistakes, but it does mean we're setting ourselves up— biblically and scientifically—for a better chance of raising them to live, love, and lead well.

If you're an expectant parent or the parent of infants, toddlers, or preschoolers and you're reading this book, you're well on your way to laying a solid foundation for your kids by building a Safe House now. As we'll learn, the first year of life is critical.

If you're the parents of elementary school children, you're on your way to solidifying or intentionally adjusting the relational foundation you've already set. If you feel behind the eightball a bit, thinking you may have made a few mistakes along the way, don't beat yourself up. You'll be able to begin training your child's brain for empathy, self-confidence, respect, and love with the safety principles and tips in this book.

If you're the parents of middle school kids, well there's no better time for your home to be a Safe House. This is often the hardest and most confusing time developmentally and socially for kids. (Think acne, first kisses, school dances, changing voices, late bloomers, and on and on.) This season of their lives gives you an incredible opportunity to teach them the process of learning how to problem solve, make wise decisions, and relate with you as their parent through the process. What a great way to build the emotional and relational foundation for heading to the often tumultuous teenage years.

And for parents of teenagers, a Safe House will help you interact with your teens in a way that wires their brain to prepare them for romantic relationships, difficult moral decisions, and self-control through their young adult years. If you feel like a failure in this category already, please give yourself grace. In my fifteen years of counseling teens (many of them juvenile delinquents) and their families, I have helped many parents learn new ways of communicating with their teenagers in a way that establishes safety without giving up parental authority.

For grandparents either raising grandchildren or watching your children and wondering how you can be of better help, you, too, can establish a Safe House in a way that truly makes a difference in their lives. These are years you cannot afford to spoil your grandchildren, as most grandparents decidedly vow to do. Not to rain on your spoiling parade, but the definition of the word *spoil* is "to diminish or destroy the value or quality of; to harm the character of a child." When you seek to spoil your grandkids, you're not only teaching them that it's okay to disrespect their parents but you're also teaching them ways to do that. Grandparents, my prayer is that as you read this book, you value the relational, spiritual, and emotional health of the next generation by partnering with your adult children to offer a Safe House for your grandchildren.

Throughout the book you'll see charts and strategies for each stage of your child's development. You can apply these to make the most of your child's developmental level to make her feel safe, build her brain, and write her story.

Will we make mistakes? Absolutely. But realize this, *you* have what it takes to write a story full of beauty and joy for your kids. And it's a good thing, too, because nobody has the power to write (and rewrite) our children's life story more than we do.

Writing great stories for our kids is a matter of becoming aware of, first, what's really going on inside our own heart—that is, the threats coming from our own story—and, second, inside our home—the dangers influencing our children from outside our four walls.

WHAT WE'RE UP AGAINST

I'd like to think our four-walled brick home is like Fort Knox. When I go to sleep at night, I'd like to think that my family is safe inside, protected from unwanted intruders and the elements. But we aren't. And unfortunately your family isn't either.

Our four-walled homes are more like cheap nylon tents. Though we try to protect our children and our families as best we can, the culture around us is creeping in through the holes. And as parents, many of us are either too busy or unaware of what threats may already be inside our homes by the way *we* relate.

There are threats in our homes that didn't exist a generation ago. We're navigating a whole new world of raising children in the twenty-first century. New cultural norms, devices, social media, and an overabundance of information and conflicting messages have created a confusing and convoluted world for our kids and us. And the speed with which the culture is changing can make our heads spin.

That's why building a Safe House has never been more critical for a generation of parents and the kids we love and raise. Let's start from a thirty-thousand-foot view and consider what kind of story the broader culture is trying to write for our kids.

We're all products of arguably the most individualistic culture in the history of the world. We live in a society today termed by Dale Kuehne as the iWorld, a society that believes "an expansion of individual rights will lead to increased happiness and fulfillment."[1] Such a society prides itself on one value: *feeling better.*

Whether we admit it or not, everything we do, the people we spend time with, the things we spend our money on, what we give our time to, all of it is colored by the lens of this individualistic philosophy. We raise our kids through this lens. And our kids are experiencing the consequences.

> When we don't believe we have what it takes as parents, it's too easy to reach for the outward affirmation that'll prove to us, and everyone else, otherwise. So we end up valuing success over character. Feeling better over loving better.

Why? Because the ethos of individualism is hostile to relationships. The result of an individualistic society that values *feeling better* over *loving better* is relational bankruptcy.

In fact, a Harvard study published just last year showed that nearly 80 percent of kids stated that the primary message they receive from their parents is that personal achievement and happiness matters more than care and concern for other people. The kids in the study were also three times more likely to agree with the following statement: "My parents are prouder if I get good grades in my classes than if I'm a caring community member in class and school."[2]

It seems we're sending our kids the message that outward success matters more than inward character.

But why, you might ask? I think it's because we're giving in to parental peer pressure more than we're willing to admit.

A good report card is a more visible measure of my parenting skills to teachers than my son's random act of sharing a toy with another child in the corner—an act that nobody ever sees.

When we don't believe we have what it takes as parents, it's too easy to reach for the outward affirmation that'll prove to us, and everyone else, otherwise. So we end up valuing success over character. Feeling better over loving better.

I mean, heaven forbid one of my friends thinks I'm a bad parent because I don't send my three-year-old to a preschool prep program supposedly giving him an advantage for higher education. Or that I'm a bad parent because I, at the expense of my son's "happiness" (that is, feeling better), didn't cave in to him when he threw his wooden train as hard as he could at my face.

If asked, I would say, yes, I care more about how my kids treat others than I do their personal happiness.

But I have to wonder, *Do I live that? Do my own actions and how I respond to my kids relay this message?*

I believe we're facing two problems with the feeling-better culture we live in: we're raising a generation that's relationally bankrupt and we're blind to how it's happening. Here's a snippet of recent outcome research to help paint the picture. Today's generation of kids is

- more narcissistic and self-centered[3]
- less empathetic[4]
- more disconnected and lonely[5]
- scoring lower on achievement scores[6]
- displaying a poor work ethic[7]
- less able to reason (that is, getting dumber)[8]
- more depressed[9]

- more anxious[10]
- more stressed[11]
- more medicated[12]

Some people may argue with this. But the direction of the data is overwhelmingly consistent. That these traits are true *of a generation* gives cause for great concern. These relational effects are the by-products of a culture that values *feeling better* over *loving better*, and all of them are antithetical to raising kids who live, love, and lead well.

A Safe House is a place where parents keep the end goal of raising emotionally safe kids in mind. The more intentional we are at *creating values* in our homes, the more aware we'll be to the opposing, unsafe values our culture tries to project into our homes.

Can you imagine the legacy and society we could leave behind if a generation of parents like ourselves became passionate, bold, and unapologetic about raising kids against this cultural tide of *feeling better* and were committed to doing what they could to raising kids who *loved better*?

For some of us, it begins by grabbing a pen, reminiscing on our own story, and re-writing. For others, it begins by dreaming—dreaming about our kids and the outcome we envision for them—and writing. Whether you're writing or rewriting your parenting story, if it's done in a Safe House, the coherent narrative you weave will be beautiful. But I must warn you: it won't be easy.

Simple? Yes. Easy? Not so much. Anybody who tells you parenting is easy, run the other way. Their kids are probably in jail.

The Beauty in Being Safe

Speaking of jail, I had a few shocking revelations when I first became a parent.

First, as ill-prepared as we were for the chaos about to invade our home, I couldn't believe my wife, Christi, and I were allowed to walk out of the hospital with a living, breathing, screaming, hungry, sleepless, restless, 100-percent-dependent-upon-us human being. Second, I was overwhelmed by all the books written on sleeping techniques, discipline strategies, parenting styles, and on and on, many of them contradicting one another. Last, I was amazed that no matter what kind of parent someone was or how successfully they raised their own kids, everybody, including those who never tried it, had an opinion.

One day, after receiving unsolicited advice from a woman whose kids were either in jail or having affairs, I asked my mother-in-law what the deal was with all of the advice. She said, "Well, it's the one thing nearly everybody has actually done. So they believe their way was the best way, even if it wasn't."

I guess that's one of the side effects of free speech.

As I continued to read and research techniques and consider everyone's advice, I needed a filter. It was becoming all too complicated for me. I'm sure you can relate.

Parenting in the twenty-first century is filled with choices. I counsel with and talk to parents all the time who are trying to negotiate different points of view about raising kids.

- "Should our baby sleep in bed with us?"
- "Should we let our baby cry it out?"
- "Should we spank our kids, and if so, when?"
- "How do I respond to a temper tantrum?"
- "Should I stay home with the kids or put them in day care?"
- "Should we home school or send our kids to a private or public school?"
- "How much screen time do I let my kids have?"

How many of these questions have you wrestled with? If you're like us, probably most of them. That's because parenting in the real world is about the countless choices we make to give our kids the best chance to develop and grow.

But there's a problem.

We live in a culture where the latest sermon, data, research results, and trends present themselves as *the* way (and often the *only* way, if you really love your kids) to raise them right. As guilt-prone parents who genuinely want what's best for our kids, it's easy to fall prey to the latest marketing ploys, product biases, and contradicting messages that cloud our journey to finding the beauty in our parenting story.

Currently the parenting fads include gluten-free diets, essential oils, using only green products in our homes, and trying to feed kids all-organic foods. If you're a parent on a budget, good luck trying to keep the balance with this one—buying the healthy items we can and not feeling guilty for what we can't afford.

The same debates hold true for immunizations, the kinds of toys we buy our kids, the schools they attend, the rigid schedules we beat ourselves up over to get them to sleep, eat, wake, play, and learn.

I'm stressed just listing all of these issues. No wonder we're uptight and overwhelmed as parents. These debates are ongoing and will never quit.

Add to this the pressure of the choices we see our parenting friends make. A quick glance at Facebook or Pinterest, and you see their picture-perfect kids, DIY family activities, unrealistically joyful vacations, and gluten-free gourmet dinners. No wonder parenting insecurity is at an all-time high.

There's absolutely no beauty in striving for perfection or keeping up with the Joneses. I love what Anne Lamott says about this in her book on writing, *Bird by Bird:*

> Perfectionism is the voice of the oppressor, the enemy of the people. It will keep
> you cramped and insane your whole life. . . . I think perfectionism is based on
> the obsessive belief that if you run carefully enough, hitting each stepping-stone
> just right, you won't have to die. The truth is that you will die anyway and that
> a lot of people who aren't even looking at their feet are going to do a whole lot
> better than you, and have a lot more fun doing it.[13]

Let me encourage you, we don't have to struggle over all of these choices. What we need is an approach to parenting that's much less complicated and passes the test of trusted research. As a person of faith, I also value that how I parent is filtered through the timeless lens of the Bible. Where scientific research and biblical wisdom sync together, we can find confidence, not perfection, in how we parent.

Thankfully, in spite of all of the other parenting debates, there is one primary factor across all the domains of research (psychology, sociology, neuroscience) necessary for raising kids who thrive: *emotional safety.*

We're all very aware that physical safety is important for kids. But have you considered the importance of *emotional safety*?

If you're like a lot of parents, that's probably not a term you've even heard before.

It's not hard to see why: physical safety is a multibillion-dollar industry that can be resolved with products. In media and advertising we see an exorbitant focus on the physical safety of our children: electrical outlet plugs, childproof locks, stairway gates, BPA-free products, child safety seats, "no-touch" playground rules, green cleaning products, organic food diets, and all-natural toys. Emotional safety, on the other hand, is more elusive and requires just one thing: *parents.* No product on a shelf can create emotional safety in a child the way we—as her parents—can. Perhaps that's why the industry remains quiet on it. Though I appreciate the reasoning behind all of the physical safety measures, the time and attention spent on them is out of balance.

Emotional safety is related to outcomes in the following areas (all specifically listed in chapter 3):

- children's academic scores
- behaviors
- brain development
- social skills
- problem-solving skills
- relationship formation
- adult-relationship satisfaction
- healthy identity formation
- self-esteem
- athletic and extracurricular success
- a sense of morality
- established values
- a faith that sticks

You won't find either the breadth or depth of outcome research for kids in any other parenting philosophy or strategy. Simply put, emotional safety is the key to raising kids who thrive in all areas of life. Kids less likely to rebel, lie, and use drugs in their teenage years. Most important, we can raise kids who love God, love others, and lead others to do the same. All it takes is a place of emotional safety—or a Safe House.

What good is it if we have a child who never gets a scratch, bump, or bruise, was fully breast-fed, and is as healthy as they come, never being sick and always eating organic vegetables, if he's a narcissistic, self-centered, irrational, and perhaps impulsive and addicted brat who blames, criticizes, and is otherwise unloving? if he's a child who becomes an adult unable to engage in or know the joy of sharing in intimate relationships?

> It is the posture from which we parent, not the technique, that matters most.

Okay, that analogy may sound dramatic, but if my kids possess any of those traits, I'll be very sad. I'll take broken bones any day over a broken soul.

In order to raise children who love God and love others, do well in school, excel in extracurricular activities, handle anger and frustration, develop self-control, resolve conflict, establish a good career, give back to the community in which they live, and marry and raise their own families to do the same, we need to begin emphasizing more debate and added discussion in securing our homes emotionally.

That's because emotionally safe homes are the breeding ground for kids who live, love, and lead well.

Emotional safety becomes the filter for all other parenting decisions. If there's any one phrase you take away from this book, remember this: It is the posture from which we parent, not the technique, that matters most.

It really is that simple.

Do You Really Have What It Takes
to Be a Parent?

Parenting in the twenty-first century is ripe with challenges, many the result of the happiness culture we find ourselves in. If you question this idea of happiness in our culture, just listen to Pharrell Williams's hit song "Happy": a message proclaiming "happiness is the truth." Chances are you're singing it right now in your head. I am.

I love to be happy. We actually hold little family dance parties some evenings in our living room with our kiddos dancing around to this song. But when we allow happiness to be placed as the highest order of truth in a culture, and it becomes our ultimate pursuit, what happens when we're not happy? The marketplace capitalizes on it. For parents, the formula works something like this: create more choices for parents to enhance their quality of parenting and raise happy kids. When the natural frustrations that come along with parenting turn to exhaustion, and the initial of-

> Mom and Dad, stop exhausting yourself trying to give your kids an advantage. You are the advantage.

fering of choices overwhelms them all the more, offer more products to help them feel less overwhelmed by the choices they already have. As journalist Eric Sevareid wrote in 1964, "The biggest big business in America is not steel, automobiles or television. It is the manufacture, refinement and distribution of anxiety."

Nowhere is this more true than in the marketplace of modern-day parenting.

If our pursuit of happiness or our children's pursuit of happiness is our highest truth, we will not raise kids who live, love, and lead well. Happiness is a shallow truth that defies the most basic parenting principle: sacrifice. Caring about our child's life story means there are times (though not all of the time) we sacrifice happiness. If we don't, we'll sacrifice our kids' ability to live, love, and lead well.

That's because on the other side of sacrifice is joy, and joy is a much higher level of truth than happiness.

In fact, if we, as parents, focus on character, then higher achievement *and* happiness will follow. And there's nothing more powerful in instilling these values than *your* loving and safe presence. Especially *your* spending time with your children in face-to-face eye contact (particularly infants and preschoolers under the age of five). Will it be easy? Not always.

That's why it's important to remind ourselves that we have what it takes.

Research shows *you* build the brain and character of your children more than any electronic device or educational video on the market by simply

- reading to your kids (and infants)
- singing to and with your kids (and infants)
- talking to your kids about their day
- laughing and joking with your kids (creating a positive environment has an amazing impact on brain development)
- playing outside in the dirt with your kids
- eating dinner regularly with your kids
- roughhousing with your kids (especially dads)

Do we want our kids to get good grades? Of course we do. Do we want them to be happy? I most definitely do.

But I also realize that true happiness and joy stem not from personal success or feeling good but from the sacrifice of loving and caring for other people.

And the most powerful way for that to grow in our kids is to simply be with them.

Mom and Dad, stop exhausting yourself trying to give your kids an advantage.

You are the advantage.

THE STORY BEHIND YOUR SAFE HOUSE

Whenever I visit my parents, I often reminisce on places I frequented as a kid. On a recent trip, I was driving through my hometown late at night and couldn't help but notice the lights on in the house where I was raised until I was seven years old. As I drove past our old home, I noticed other houses I had spent time in with friends. I slowed down enough to take it all in. The farther I drove, the more I pondered the stories behind every window in each house I passed.

Some houses were dark and cold. Others were well-lit—curtains and decorations adding to their inviting warmth.

Where are the kids today that grew up in those houses? I wondered. *Do they have kids? What are their stories?*

What about the kids in those houses today? Are they safe? Or is the darkened house reminiscent of the emotional coldness they live in?

There's a story in every home. The quality of that story is a reflection of how secure we are as parents. The more secure we are, the stronger our Safe House will be. That's because the foundation of a Safe House is a secure parent, which is the focus of the next chapter. The more secure we are, the better we'll be at erecting the four walls of a Safe House—the walls of exploration, protection, grace, and truth.

To be a sturdy and secure Safe House, these walls must be balanced over time. If any one wall becomes bigger to the neglect of another, it could very well be a reflection of the insecurity of the foundation. The more insecure we are as parents, the more likely our walls will be out of balance and the less safe our home may be.

That's why we'll start with a story—your story.

━━━ Writing Your Story ━━━

1. Describe or write down in your own words what *emotional safety* means to you.
2. What parenting fads, products, or issues have been or are most stressful for you?
3. When do you feel most insecure as a parent?

You Are Home: A Safe House Begins with You

Who we are and how we engage with the world are much stronger predictors of how our children will do than what we know about parenting.

—Brené Brown, PhD

'm a simple guy. Grew up a simple kid in a small town in central Pennsylvania. A son to blue-collar workers, parents who still work in the same factories they did before I was born.

It's funny how times change, how generations evolve. After fifteen positions by the ripe age of thirty, I quit keeping track of my jobs.

One of the deeper conversations I had with my parents was about life purpose. Some people have the notion that working in a factory is somehow less significant than, say, a people-helping or philanthropic position. I hate that our culture glorifies certain professions as being more valuable than others when it comes to making a difference in the world. Such thinking ignores eternity.

Every one of our lives matters. Whether the daily grind is spent on a factory floor in a rural town, a skyscraper office in a big city, at home as a mom, or somewhere in between, making a difference is about following the two most important commandments of Jesus—loving God and loving others.

No job constrains love.

My parents are living proof. Though I began with a broken part of my story, this book and the way I choose to parent are a tribute to the beautiful setting my story takes place in. More important, my parents are a reflection of God's grace.

Were my parents perfect? Nobody's are.

Did I always listen? What fun is that?

Did we have our ugly moments? Who doesn't?

But in all of it, from the beauty of family vacations to the ugliness of divorce, I never questioned whether I was loved.

It's why I wake up every Saturday morning through the fall excited to play in the backyard with my son, jump in leaves, pick up acorns, watch college football, and give him the time and love my dad gave me.

It's why I can't wait until I can take my daughter fishing, spend a day with her on the water, just the two of us, and give her the adventures and love my mom gave me.

I want to embrace every season with my kids, both literal and figurative—fall, summer, winter, and spring. I want to experience the smells. Honeysuckle in the spring. Fresh-cut grass in the summer. Fear in the winter. You know, those moments when our kids are scared and turn to us for support. I want to smell the fear of their failure or disappointment, walk with them through it, and teach them the fragrance of love.

I want to embrace the flavors. Home-cooked Thanksgiving turkey and trimmings in the fall. Ice cream sundaes together in the summer, especially after a big win. Defeat in the winter. I want my kids' rejection to bitter my own palate, so they feel understood. Then I can teach them how to sweeten their plate by tasting the goodness of the Lord.[1]

I want to create a bank account of memories—their best, worst, and even most mundane moments—from which they themselves will one day parent, for the quality of my presence while they're under my roof will one day determine the quality of their presence under their own. When they become scared or unsure of what to do when their children are rejected, they'll *feel the security* they had with me and instinctively respond the way they were loved.

> The quality of my presence while they're under my roof will one day determine the quality of their presence under their own.

Talk about leaving a legacy and setting patterns; this is how my parents were there for me. These nostalgic memories are now short stories integrated into my brain as a completed narrative that makes up my life story—a story written in a setting of love.

What's fascinating is that both research and the Bible reveal that our capacity to love stems from experiencing, or *knowing*, we are loved. The Bible says that we love because God first loved us. You love because somebody else first loved you.[2]

Making an eternal difference in the world, no matter the job you hold, is directly connected to our ability to experience love. The more we know love, the more we share it with others—our spouses, kids, parents, extended family, friends, and coworkers. The more we share it with others, the more we model it for our kids.

But in order to do that we have to connect with our own stories. For many, that means redeeming broken moments as our family did. My parents' porch swing often served as a bench of reconciliation for past offenses. For others, it simply means reconnecting, talking about the nostalgic moments, and verbally thanking your parents for how you were and are loved. This happens most often in our home on holidays and around the kitchen table playing board games. There are also those whose parents, who were supposed to be the source of your comfort, were also the source of your pain. If you were abused or harmed by a parent, I'm sorry. You did nothing to deserve that kind of treatment. Finding a counselor to walk with you in navigating that pain may need to be your next step forward. Integrating our stories into a loving, coherent narrative is the focus of this chapter.

THE POSTURE FROM WHICH WE PARENT

Many parenting strategies have overlooked the power of raising safe kids. For instance, behavior modification, arguably the most popular parenting technique, is a one-directional way of relating to our kids. The focus is solely on the child's behavior. Reward positive behavior and it will increase. Punish negative behavior and it will decrease.[3]

The problem with this approach is that it focuses primarily on the child's behavior, not the parent-child relationship. Most researchers and parenting experts failed to understand or address the two-way relationship of parenting children.[4] As researcher and author Brené Brown writes about parenting, *"What we know matters, but who we are matters more."*[5] I couldn't have said it better.

The more I study the research and filter it through the lens of the Bible, the more glaringly obvious it becomes: it's the posture from which we parent, not the technique, that matters most. As neuroscience researchers Daniel Siegel and Tina Bryson state, *"Our relationship with our kids should be central to everything we do.* Whether we're playing with them, talking with them, laughing with them, or, yes, disciplining them, we want them to experience at a deep level the full force of our love and affection, whether we're acknowledging an act of kindness or addressing a misbehavior."[6]

Or consider how the Bible describes God as our Father: "The LORD is merciful and gracious, slow to anger and abounding in steadfast love. He will not always chide, nor will he keep his anger forever. He does not deal with us according to our sins, nor repay us according to our iniquities."[7]

Think about the parent-child relationship in relation to that passage: God as a Father is slow to anger. He loves us infinitely deeper than we could ever imagine. He shows mercy. He gives us grace. Blame and shame are quickly resolved. When he is angry, it's for a brief time and because he loves us. When we're in the wrong, his anger is about what could happen to us if we continue the behavior. He will discipline, but he does not punish. Neither does his consequence match our offense.

Our relationship with him is central to how he fathers us.

The same should be true in how we parent our kids.

SAFE RELATIONSHIP = LOVE – FEAR

Neither one of our children were easy babies. A combination of colic, acid reflux, gastrointestinal sensitivities, constipation, gassiness, and an inability to sleep without being held led to many sleepless nights in the Straub household. To provide a mental picture of how not easy parenting can be, imagine our daughter having a difficult time falling asleep because of terrible gas pains. Wailing ensues. Then, at the exact same time, our strong-willed two-year-old son, who didn't sleep well the night before or hasn't eaten his breakfast, has a meltdown. Ever been there?

Oh, the irony of writing a parenting book.

Our son (generally) has a very sweet spirit. More often than not he's running around the house yelling, "Hap-Hap-Hap-Hap-Happyyyyy!" The more he winds up, the happier he is.

But he's also a toddler. Who throws temper tantrums—and sometimes screams with a voice that makes me want to curl up and start sucking my thumb.

No wonder it's so easy to give in to our kids. They can be little monsters.

Christi has shed many a tear in moments like this. Sometimes she records them on her phone to capture the humor and reality of it all. Moms, you're not alone.

Moments like this are stressful and exhausting enough even for the most secure parent. But imagine carrying into these moments unresolved pain and broken moments from your own childhood relationship with your parents. Research shows the more fragmented our stories are, the more insecure we're likely to be as parents. And the more insecure we are as parents, the more likely we are to write our kids' stories in a setting of fear.[8]

That's why I like to use this equation as the basis for how we parent in a Safe House:

Love – Fear = Safe Relationship

Think about it. The opposite of love is not hate. The opposite of love is fear. The Bible says, "Perfect love casts out fear."[9] To put it simply, an unsafe environment instills fear. A safe environment rids itself of fear.

Just think of the fearful ways we *react* to our kids in stressful moments when they act out. Yelling. Blaming. Punishing. Shaming. Maybe even spanking out of anger.

These *reactions* in such overwhelming moments tend to be fear-based. Look at the rest of that same verse in the Bible: "For fear has to do with punishment, and whoever fears has not been perfected in love."

When we *react* to our kids out of the insecurities from our own stories, we do so from fear—fear of our kids turning out a certain way, fear of treating our kids the way our parents treated us, fear of losing control as a parent, or perhaps even fear of being seen as a bad parent. *Reacting* out of fear often leads to *punishing* our kids for their behavior in these moments rather than disciplining them, a difference we'll get to later. For now, it's important to understand that reacting out of fear usually places the primary focus on our kids' behavior before the relationship.

> The opposite of love is fear. The Bible says, "Perfect love casts out fear." To put it simply, an unsafe environment instills fear. A safe environment rids itself of fear.

When we as parents react to our kids out of fear, it's not their misbehavior our kids are thinking about, it's the fear of disconnection they feel from the person who is supposed to be the emotionally safest in their life.[10] This is how the tendency to recreate the cycle of fear is rooted in our own stories.

Biblically speaking then, from what we've learned so far about God as Father, the equation **Love – Fear = Safe Relationship** goes something like this:

Perfect love drives out fear.

God is love.

God, as love perfected, fathers us in a setting of love, not fear.

God as a Father is safe.

Remember, research shows our capacity to love others comes from first having a loving relationship with a safe parent. If you're a person of faith, the Bible clearly reveals that person is God.

The same is true for our kids. They need us to be safe. What's fascinating is that scientific research reveals that the condition necessary for the brain to understand and grow in relationship to others is defined by, and I quote, "love without fear."[11] Here's a summary of the research, "In attachment, we need to be open to our child, feeling that *safety* in ourselves and creating that sense of 'love without fear' in our child."[12]

I AM NOT GOD

One of my closest friends, who is both gifted at and loves starting businesses, regularly discusses micro- and macroeconomics with his sixteen-year-old son. Yes, his son is wicked smart. As the safe and present father that he is, my friend uses business projects to train his son for the real world.

Recently, while on a yearlong mission in Costa Rica as a family, he decided to help his son earn money with a microfinancing project using an incredible woodworker in a local village. Not only would this project teach his son how to earn money; it would help the local economy as well.

As he told me about it, I could hear in his voice the excitement for his son. The further involved they got, the more passionate my friend became.

About a week later, my friend called me sounding unusually depressed. He said, "Josh, you know this project we've been working on? Well, my son looked at me and said, 'Dad, this is your project with my name on it. If you want me to learn, let me do something that I'm passionate about.'"

I asked my friend how he responded. He said they went for a walk along the beach, and after listening to his son's point of view, he looked at his son and said, "You know, you're right. I'm sorry."

My friend continued, "I asked him what *he* wanted to do. No rules applied. He told me he wanted to build a hotel in space. So that's where we started."

What my friend realized was that even though his intentions were so incredibly goodwilled, he actually did his son a disservice by overstepping his bounds and quarter-backing the project for him.

"I went from teaching him a lesson to letting him watch a lesson," he concluded. "I realized how imperfect my actions can be even though my intentions for my kids may be pure."

If you read the last section and were left with the lingering thought in your mind, *All of this perfect love and "parenting without fear" stuff is great, but I am not God,* that's right where you need to be.

If we try to be perfect, we'll parent out of fear.

If we think we should never make a mistake, we'll make parenting choices out of fear.

If we ebb and flow with the latest parenting technique and strategy, choosing to give timeouts this week and not give them the next, we'll parent out of fear.

So let yourself off of the hook now, you won't parent perfectly. You won't love your kids perfectly either. You are not God. Neither am I. Like you, I'm an imperfect parent trying to do the best I can to raise my kids to live, love, and lead well.

We will lose our temper.

We will say things we regret.

Our parental agendas will get in the way of what's best for our kids.

Isn't that awesome? We're all on this journey of imperfection together.

Now, repeat aloud after me and admit to yourself:

Parenting is hard. I am not God. I am not perfect. I will make mistakes. I don't need to get it right all the time. I just need to be safe.

In fact, choosing to be an imperfect parent is choosing to be a safe parent.

Research shows that emotionally safe parents, if they can emotion coach their kids just 40 percent of the time, are doing well. (Emotion coaching is a technique we'll learn in chapter 7). So feel free to mess up. Why? Because research shows that "repair" is one of the greatest parenting strategies you have as a parent.[13]

What does the Bible say about this repair strategy researchers talk about? It calls it forgiveness. And it tells us to practice it—a lot.

By repairing a rupture in our relationship with our kids, we free them from any expectation to be perfect themselves. Not only that, it teaches our kids the appropriate way of handling imperfection when they make a mistake as well.

As Brené Brown writes, "The question isn't so much 'Are you parenting the right way?' as it is: 'Are you the adult that you want your child to grow up to be?'"[14]

Simply using the words "I'm sorry" as they relate to a specific offense with your kids and then changing your behavior toward them speaks more about who you are than anything else you do. Owning your imperfection makes you emotionally safer than trying to be perfect.

Secure parents own their imperfections.

Did You Know You're a Brain Surgeon?

There's never a more important time to begin parenting from the foundation of a safe relationship than in the first year of life. By one year of age, how a child views relationships the rest of his life is pretty well established. How we parent, relate to, and respond to our children in times of fear and anxiety teaches them *from the day they're born* how relationships work.

My wife, Christi, wrote a blog post shortly after our son, Landon, was born. It was about a game we played with him called the Face Game. Babies love to stare at faces. When Mom and Dad make exaggerated faces, they watch intently and learn to respond with the same emotion. Silly faces make for joy-filled smiles and squeals. Serious faces make for frowns.

Also, babies are born with two innate fears: fear of falling and fear of loud noises. Every other fear in life is learned.

When Landon was about eight months old, I accidently dropped a pot in the kitchen, making an obnoxious ear-piercing noise. Standing in his play gym right next to me, Landon immediately jumped. As his bottom lip started to quiver, he looked directly to his mom. What did she do? She smiled.

Her smile told Landon, "Baby boy, there is nothing to fear."

Landon smiled back. Peace was restored.

Our fun little Face Game with our kids goes far beyond the sweet squeals and giggly memories. The Face Game is literally wiring our children's brain. When Landon and Kennedy look at our faces and reflect our emotions, it changes the way their brain fires and wires.

When our children experience something startling—and potentially scary—their amygdala, the fear center (or bottom part) of their brain, starts firing. They look to us to see how to respond. When we respond with a smile, their brain translates: "Baby, there is nothing to fear." And there is an instant calming as the cerebral cortex tells the nervous system, "You can calm down."

It's called neural integration. But my wife calls it AWE-some.

The Face Game is one strategy for creating a Safe House, an environment that literally wires our children's brains for safe relationships. Before going into the scientific foundation for creating Safe Houses and explaining this point further, I want to point out the fantastic biblical connection my wife made while playing the Face Game with Landon. The spiritual parallels with God the Father, who gave the Israelites this blessing and promise, are pretty remarkable: "The LORD bless you and keep you; *the Lord make his face shine upon you* and be gracious to you; *the Lord turn his face toward you* and give you peace."[15] In the devotional words of my wife,

> When we gaze upon our Heavenly Father's face—he turns his face *toward* us, and gives us peace. True peace. Peace is just one intentional look away. He's waiting. I just have to turn toward it, rather than away from it.
>
> And just because God is AWE-some, he allows us, as parents, to share in a little bit of his joy. We give our babies peace when they gaze at our face. Just as our Heavenly Father does for us. How neat is that?
>
> When things are startling and stressful in my life, instead of reacting with anxiety or panic, what if I gazed into my Father's face? I know I would see his smile. His smile would tell me, "Baby girl, there is nothing to fear."

The Bible says, "Unless the LORD builds the house, those who build it labor in vain."[16] The peaceful home is a home where we as parents are turning to God in our own fears. As we do, no matter how stressful life or parenting gets, we communicate to our kids that God himself is safe, and in him, there is nothing to fear. Because perfect love drives out fear.[17]

THE FOUNDATION OF A SAFE HOUSE

As you're probably picking up already, a Safe House is not just a place, it's a relationship. You are the Safe House. To your children, you are home. Before we look more specifically at how that works, let's summarize what we've learned so far:

1. Our story matters.
2. How well we know our story creates the setting (or the posture) from which we parent.

3. At the heart of our children's story is our ability to understand our own story.
4. Our children's story is largely written by the quality of the relationship we have with them.
5. We are the Safe House, the one place our kids experience emotional safety with the person who matters most.
6. A Safe House is where our kids experience the love, attention, affection, and connection they need when they're scared, stressed, hurting, or otherwise overwhelmed (love minus fear).

Here are those six points in one sentence: The foundation of a Safe House is a secure parent.

As we cover the Safe House model of parenting throughout this book, we'll learn about the four walls necessary to writing a beautiful story for our children and simultaneously building their brains. But without a foundation, the walls will either crumble or be built out of balance.

> A Safe House is not just a place, it's a relationship. You are the Safe House. To your children, you are home.

AM I SAFE?

Every family needs to surround themselves with a supporting cast when writing their story. I'm a huge advocate for finding adopted grandparents who can help support you as a family if you're living away from your own parents. In Branson, Missouri, we have an amazing community of friends and extended family who love and care for us and our children like their own. One set of grandparents—Bobbette and Parrish—watch our kiddos every Friday night so Christi and I can have a date night together. There was one particular night, when Landon was about twenty months old, I'll never forget.

As we got out of our car in their driveway, I heard gunshots coming from below the house. Living in Branson, I didn't give it second thought. Probably just someone target shooting, I assumed. As I carried Landon into the house, he joined the chorus of shots fired through the Ozarks that afternoon. "Boom, boom!" he said animatedly.

Here's where the story gets a little smelly. Landon had a dirty diaper. For whatever reason, his car seat always seemed to function as a laxative, so wherever we were going, a diaper change was imminent. For etiquette's sake, it's not good to leave your kid with somebody else with a number two lingering there. So I laid him down and changed his diaper while Christi briefed Bobbette on the dinner we packed for him.

When I finished, I went into the kitchen to wash my hands. After putting the towel down, I turned around, took about four steps, and *Crack!*

Everyone was paralyzed in the moment.

Nobody knew what happened.

Christi looked down at her feet and saw drywall on the floor.

"Everybody get down," I yelled. "Go get Landon."

As I crawled my way through the house, I noticed bullet holes at head level through the hallway about five feet from where I was standing. I followed the path of the bullet into their bedroom and found a 9mm slug lying on the floor.

I don't know what it's like to live in a war zone, but that was close enough for me.

We're still not sure what happened that night, but the shooter fled, so Christi and I left our son and went out on our date. Before you judge us, that neighborhood quickly became the safest in all of Missouri that night with more police patrolling than anyone is comfortable with. Besides, I needed to debrief my traumatized wife.

When we drop our kids off in the care of others, we expect to be leaving them in *a safe place for taking refuge.* Our kids need a place of refuge free from the dangers and fears of the world.

What they don't need are bullets of fear, shame, blame, or punishment coming at them from inside those four walls. That's why a secure parent is the foundation for a Safe House.

For the rest of the book, we'll consider this the parental definition of a Safe House: *a parent whose security in her own story makes her an emotionally safe place for her kids to take refuge.* Don't let the feminine pronoun confuse you. Dads are equally as responsible to make sense of their own story.

The very heart of safe parent-child relationships is the ability to understand the narrative of our lives. Helping our children form a safe understanding of relationships is critical for their ability to thrive and navigate the dangers of the world around them.

At its core, the purpose of a Safe House is to drive out anxiety and fear from our homes. As parents, we thrive when we turn to God and give our anxiety and fears over to him through prayer. When this happens, we draw our energy from "the peace of God, which surpasses all understanding, [and] will guard [our] *hearts* and [our] *minds* in Christ Jesus."[18] The same is true with our children.

Our kids thrive when they turn to us, in their fear and anxiety, to answer the internal question they're all asking even from the first day they enter the world as an infant: *Is what I'm experiencing safe or dangerous?* This question is asked in a number of different ways: *Am I important to you? Am I needed? Am I wanted? Am I worthy of your love? Will I survive?*[19] Each of these questions can be summed up in one primary question our kids are asking (nonverbally) from the moment they're born:

Am I safe?

When our kids turn to us as their parents to have this question answered, our response will either (in a more finite way, of course) guard their hearts and minds by showing them they are safe, or our response will tell their hearts and minds the world around them is a dangerous place. Do you see how important our job is as parents? The way we relate to our children actually wires their brains for how they believe, act, and feel the way they do about relationships for a lifetime. Said another way, as parents we play the role of a relational brain surgeon for our kids from the day they enter the world.

AM I SECURE?

Our children's brains are wired for relationships that provide an emotional safe haven when they are stressed (that is, hungry, angry, tired, injured, lost, alone, ill, feeling threatened, and so on). I'm going to explain the different functions a parent plays as a relational brain surgeon through a simple illustration. It may be simple, but each function highlighted is extremely important for kids to feel emotionally safe in the home—and each is the foundation they need to thrive later in life. Notice the *italicized words* in the illustration below.

One Saturday morning I was leaving to serve as host at a marriage conference. Christi and I were sitting on the edge of our bed together, discussing the day's plans once I was finished. While we were talking, Landon, who was about fifteen months old at the time, felt *safe* enough to be *exploring* in our bathroom. As I turned my head, I saw him come running into our bedroom as proud as punch, carrying high above him, with both arms, a book he had just received as a gift. But as he crossed into our bedroom, he tripped and fell, face first, into the bed frame, unable to catch himself since his arms were in the air. As Christi went to get him, he reached for her and wailed in pain (he was *signaling* to her through his crying and *seeking close proximity to her* by reaching). Tears flowed, his nose swelled, and his mom handed him to me as she examined his face. I've never felt him so limp in my arms. He rested his head on my shoulder, and it was a dead weight. After we realized nothing was broken, I held him until he was able to calm down, repeatedly telling him he was going to be just fine, that I understood he was in pain, and serving as a *safe haven* to give him the comfort and relief he was looking for.

> A child's ability to gain self-confidence is fundamentally relational and based on the safe relationship she has with loving parents, particularly when she's in stressful situations.

Though he never verbalized it, he needed to know, that no matter what happened, broken bones or not, there was nothing to fear—he was emotionally safe. As soon as he felt better, he used me as a *secure base* to explore the house all over again.

Whether five months old, five years old, or fifteen years old, when our kids are feeling scared, anxious, or stressed, and we consistently respond in a safe and secure way, our children come to believe we're *available* and *capable of loving them*. This gives our child a safe foundation to explore. And the ability to freely explore builds her self-confidence. The reason emotional safety is linked to so many areas where kids thrive later in life is because a child's ability to gain self-confidence is fundamentally relational and based on the safe relationship she has with loving parents, particularly when she's in stressful situations.[20]

So maybe we don't need to invest in a private preschool education, worry as much about our child's success on the football field, or ensure our child receives a trophy for every attempt. Our *safe relationship* instills the self-confidence a child needs to thrive.

The issue is our ability as parents to connect why we act the way we do toward our kids, especially when they're in emotionally charged situations—when our infants are wailing, our toddlers are throwing temper tantrums, our kids are talking back to us, or our teenagers are flying off the handle. It's in these moments that we best support our kids by being stable. When a child is instead met with emotional bullets or conflicting messages from a parent in stressful situations—either casting blame, punishing the child in a threatening moment, making the child feel embarrassed by the way they're behaving, or being inconsistently available—it renders an environment unsafe, and therefore makes a child hesitant to explore, leaving the message that relationships are dangerous and not worth turning to in difficult times.

The more we ridicule, minimize, or force our kids to stuff their feelings, the less beautiful their stories become.

These emotionally charged moments and our ability to meet the needs of our infant and child in those moments create a psychological bond where our children use us as a Safe House, a "stronger and wiser" safe haven to turn to in times of anxious need.[21] It's our ability to be our kids' go-to person when they need closeness, to be safe when they are in distress, to be a secure base for them to explore once again that is the foundation for how their brain is wired to relate—or not.

You really are the foundation of a Safe House.

THE MOST IMPORTANT QUESTIONS

As we look at how our children's brains become wired for relationships, it's important to note that they're not always using us as a safe haven. Therefore, not *all* interactions they have with us, as parents, are brain-surgery moments.[22] Playing with Landon at the park while he *explores* the slide with the security of having me nearby, for example, is very different from his exiting the slide unable to find me. Bursting into tears or yelling for Mama or Dada is his way of *signaling* and *seeking proximity* to us in a fearful situation. Our ability to be there for him in those emotionally overwhelming moments wires his brain for connection and tells it whether future relationships will be safe or dangerous.

Remember when I talked about the Face Game earlier? We have what are called mirror neurons in our brains. As parents, our response to our child in threatening or stressful situations where our children are scared (like dropping a pan on the floor, getting lost in a department store, when they're caught in the wrong, or when they fall down and hurt themselves) is imprinted into these mirror neurons so that later in life our children are likely to automatically respond to their own emotions and behaviors in a way that mirrors the way we responded to them.[23]

When I was in graduate school, I had a strange encounter with a guy who later became a very close friend. But one of my first impressions of him caught me off guard. As I walked down a hallway full of graduate assistants, I saw him in a cubicle facing inward toward the corner. As I nonchalantly came up from behind him, I went to put my hand on his shoulder to say hello. As soon as he saw my hand from the corner of his eye, he immediately stood up, turned around with his fists clenched, and was ready to fight.

I stepped back and said, "Dude, what are you doing?"

As our friendship grew, I learned that his dad was physically abusive when he was a child.

The answer to his *Am I safe?* question wired his brain to fight as soon as he felt threatened. This is called *implicit memory* and is the type of memory used to tie our shoe or ride a bike. We don't have to think about it to do it. It just happens. You could call this type of memory instinct.

Implicit memory begins at birth and is present throughout our lives. Not only does it tell us how to instinctively tie our shoes; it also tells us instinctively how to engage in relationships and whether or not they're safe. As parents, our interactions with our kids, particularly in the first few years of life, form our children's perceptions about who they are, if they're worthy of love, if others are safe, if their emotions are safe, and if they can intimately connect with others.

Our kids' answer to the question *Am I safe?* is buried in their unconscious, implicit memory. My friend instinctively stood up to fight me without giving it any thought. His immediate reaction was *I am not safe.* His story at the time was not understood as a coherent narrative.

The question *Am I safe?* can be broken down into two questions that form our *core beliefs about how relationships work*:

1. *Am I worthy of love?*
2. *Are others capable of loving me?*

How our kids answer these questions, along with their personality and other factors, sets the stage for how well they enter into and out of relationships throughout their lives. When children perceive that the answer to these two fundamental questions is yes, they feel safe. A sign that their parent was consistently safe and nonthreatening when they felt threatened early in life, they're now willing to try new things because they're convinced that failure doesn't bring condemnation or abandonment. They can step into the world in confidence and courage, not afraid of failing. To once again make the biblical connection, remember, "perfect love casts out fear."

When the answer to either question is no, people invest every ounce of energy, like my friend who wanted to fight me, to fend off real or imagined attacks, win desperately needed approval, and avoid any risks of failure or rejection. In other words, fear really does drive how we relate. That's why the core purpose of a Safe House is to drive out fear and anxiety and why it takes a secure parent to do it.

A team of researchers at the Johns Hopkins University School of Medicine set out on a thirty-year study *to find if a single related cause* existed for five major issues: mental illness, hypertension, malignant tumors, coronary heart disease, and suicide. After studying 1,377 students over thirty years, the most prevalent single cause of all five illnesses was not what you may think. Diet? Exercise? Not at all. They found instead that the most significant predictor of these five tragedies was a *lack of closeness to the parents,* especially the father.[24]

Why? When a child grows up in a loving, intimate home, particularly with his father (who, through a wealth of factors, including roughhousing and play, can teach them how to control strong emotion), they are better capable of handling stress (that is, anxiety and fear) in life.

Perfect love drives out fear.

REDEEMING OUR LIFE STORY

You may have gotten to this point and are thinking, *Wow, I'm really messing up my kids.* Or perhaps you're thinking about yourself, *Wow, I'm the one who is really messed up.* If you're thinking your situation is hopeless, you're wrong. Safety can be reestablished.

First, I believe in a God who not only created us for relationship to begin with but by his grace also loves to redeem our stories. And I believe, as supported in the research, that he designed us to immerse ourselves in a community of safe relationships, with people we can safely share our stories with, and in turn experience the love and security we need to step out into the world to love others.

From what I see in the Bible, this is what the church should look like.

For my friend, counseling was a way to help him develop a more coherent narrative about how his childhood experiences were impacting his current relationships and behaviors. Today he is a safe husband and dad to two beautiful children.

I went through the same process connecting my own story with how my parents' divorce was impacting my ability to connect in relationships. Though not all of us need counseling to integrate our life stories, I do believe everybody needs safe people to help us put the puzzle pieces together to form our stories and the meaning behind our relationships. I am forever indebted to the safe, godly mentors along my journey and the emotionally healthy church community I'm a part of.

Surrounding yourself with safe people, be it a counseling relationship, faith community, trusted sages and mentors, or the like, is the beginning of reestablishing safety in your life. And as you do, research shows you literally rewire your brain for connection in the process.

As you connect more with your own story in the safety of community, you will better be able to coauthor a story for your children that sets them up to live, love, and lead well throughout their own lives. As neuroscience researcher Daniel Siegel wrote,

> We are not guaranteed a life without difficulties. . . . At least if we offer security of attachment in our relationships with children from the beginning of life, we'll be providing an important starting place of connection in which the brain and the mind can have a source of resilience from which to start the journey of life.
>
> Overall, attachment research validates the notion that parents matter. . . . We can *"prime"* the brain to lean toward security.[25]

For the security of your kids, your story matters because you matter.

Writing Your Story

1. Write down a rupture you had in relationship with your parents (or one of your parents) in the past. Was it resolved? What was that process like?
2. What connections do you see between the way you act with your kids and the way your parents treated you?
3. Who can walk with you as you take the necessary steps to becoming more secure as a parent?

3

Your Story, Your Kid's Brain, and the Science of Safety

It's really not an exaggeration to say that the kind of relationships
you provide for your children will affect generations to come.

—Daniel J. Siegel and Tina Payne Bryson, *The Whole-Brain Child*

When I first began writing about my parents' divorce sixteen years after that fateful day, I had to look up the date. I remembered the time. But the details of the setting were a little fuzzy until I began writing and talking about my role in the story.

The more I wrote, the more I discovered. The more I talked, the more emotion I felt. Somewhere deep within my subconscious were emotions I was afraid to feel. I was unknowingly convincing myself that feeling these emotions would do no good. I was unable to formulate or verbalize these thoughts at the time, but they prevented me from making sense of how my parents' divorce impacted me:

- *I can't be mad at my parents. They've already been through so much.*
- *If I get mad, it may drive us further apart as a family. It's probably better to just keep the peace.*
- *I better do what I can to make everybody happy. I don't want to hurt anybody's feelings.*

I can remember not wanting anybody to be alone. I didn't want my dad to be alone. I didn't want my sister to be alone. I didn't want my mom to be alone. I *definitely* didn't want to be alone. I also didn't want to disappoint anybody. So I chose the path of least resistance and decided to go back and forth between both parents every other week, my sister with me.

Though it sounds exhausting, my parents lived only five minutes from one another and within the same school district, so it really wasn't too bad of a situation. The fact I made *this* choice, however, said more about my beliefs about relationships than it did about not wanting to ruffle any feathers with my parents. By my early twenties, I carried my beliefs about relationships and how to behave in them with me into dating, employee-employer, and peer relationships.

And more often than not, I felt trapped.

It turned out I was the one who usually gave in when it came to relationship difficulties—because I was the peacemaker. In some cases I felt walked on, but I wouldn't say or do anything about it. I knew I needed boundaries, but I had an underlying fear that if I set them, a girlfriend might leave me, an employer might fire me, or a friend or family member might not like me. If I compromised, I reasoned, peace in these relationships would be restored.

At least for the other party.

Me? I kept dancing.

As I began piecing together my story, I learned there's more to a setting than the date, time, and place. How that day, time, and place are interpreted matter. Take your birthday, for instance. For some, a birthday is filled with great fun, family, presents, memories, and delightful surprises. For others, it's a reminder of how Dad made so many promises he never kept, how belittling Mom was toward us in front of others, or how unworthy of love we really felt.

When I was ten years old, I had no clue what that conversation in my bedroom that morning and my parents' subsequent divorce meant for *me*. Sixteen years later I learned it became the compass that pointed to how I behaved in relationships.

But until I put the pieces of the puzzle together through writing and talking about it with a counselor, mentors, and close friends, it was a fragmented part of many other puzzle pieces in my story.

Your story may be very similar or very different from mine—for better or worse. The worse it was, the more work you'll most likely have at weaving the chapters of your childhood together to make sense of your story. On the contrary, even the most secure and loving homes on earth are still imperfect. We all have a story to write.

How Your Story Matters

So far we've remained pretty simple in our understanding of what it means to raise kids who live, love, and lead well—creating a setting of love where your kids feel safe and you have a Safe House. Seems pretty simple, right? I now want to address the complexity of how this actually works, because the intricacies of how a safe environment wires the brain for healthy relationships are quite extraordinary.

Secure parents create safe environments. Safe environments wire our child's brain for relationships throughout her lifetime, namely, *what to expect from* relationships and *how to behave in* relationships. How our children answer the questions "Am I worthy of love?" and "Are others capable of loving me?" informs how they interpret the setting of their story.

These questions are being answered from the moment our children are born and are based on their experiences with us as parents. The answers they develop to these critical questions wire their brains for connection and tell it whether future relationships will be safe or dangerous. Put another way, how they *experience* the answers to these questions form their core beliefs about relationships from day one (see Figure 3.1 for a description of these core beliefs).

The more we understand the complexity of how a safe environment wires the brain, the easier it will be to know what our child needs from us in her scared, stressed, or unsafe moments. When our children are not feeling safe, they do what they can to regain a feeling of security. When our children are safe, they have a foundational setting from which they are free to explore the world around them and engage others in healthy, satisfying ways.

This is why and how our story matters. Research shows the more a parent coherently understands her own story, the more secure she is, and the more her brain is wired to self-regulate—in other words, display self-control. If you didn't catch that, think of it this way: secure parents are able to control their own thoughts, feelings, attention, and behavior. Had I not pieced my story together, I may have very easily carried my peacemaking tendencies into my parenting, sacrificing boundaries in lieu of my kids liking me.

Let's take it to real life as a parent. What's your initial thought and reaction (that is, how well would you control your own thoughts, feelings, attention, and behavior) to the following scenarios?

- When your three-year-old throws a nasty screaming and yelling fit because you took your phone away from her.
- When you find a letter from your thirteen-year-old daughter saying she hates you.

- When you catch your ten-year-old minimizing (that is, lying) to you about an altercation at school, and you find out later from a school official the details of how he instigated it.
- When you find your sixteen-year-old in his room crying, admitting he's being bullied at school.
- When you discover pornography on your teenager's iPad.

Practically speaking, parents who are secure are more mindful and reflective in their own lives, and therefore they are able to more clearly see their child's mind clearly and *respond, not react,* to their emotional meltdowns (whether it be a temper tantrum in a toddler, deliberate disobedience in a child, or withdrawing or talking back in a teenager).[1] Being aware of what we're feeling toward our child and why we're feeling that way in any of these, or similar situations, is crucial to how safe they feel.

This is why rewriting our own story is critical to raising kids who live, love, and lead well. The more secure we are in our own story, the more sensitive we can be to our children's signals for love, affection, and attention—and respond appropriately to them in safety and love, without our own unresolved stories getting in the way.

Relationship Beliefs	Patterns of Feeling and Relating
Secure Am I worthy of love? Yes Are others capable of loving me? Yes	**The Child:** The child feels confident that her parent will be emotionally available and responsive, especially when faced with fear-provoking situations. Kids with secure ways of relating are also brave when it comes to exploring the world around them. **Exploration and Protection:** A secure parent consistently and sensitively responds to her child's signals of distress with loving comfort and secure protection. These parents are also comfortable with their child's exploration and pursuit of autonomy. **Beliefs About Relationships and Emotions:** Kids with secure ways of relating grow up believing they are worthy of love and that others are capable of loving them. As a result, they come to believe their emotions are valuable and actually say something about what they and others around them need. These kids are comfortable sharing their feelings and believe their parents will help calm them down when overwhelmed or scared.

| **Anxious**

Am I worthy of love?

No

Are others capable of loving me?

Yes | **The Child:** Particularly in fear-provoking situations, the child feels uncertainty about whether his parent will be emotionally available or responsive. The inconsistent availability of the parent leads to anxiety for the child about whether the parent will abandon him. Since the parent may be emotionally unstable and otherwise unavailable, the child develops an uncertain sense of self.

Exploration and Protection: Plagued by a fear of abandonment, the child becomes clingy and unwilling to explore the world around him. Staying close to the parent takes precedence over exploration since roaming too far may result in not being protected, especially when he needs it most.

Beliefs About Relationships and Emotions: Since these styles of relating can change over time and are not consistent in all relationships (that is, a child could be secure with one parent and insecure with another), we wouldn't describe these kids as "anxious kids." Instead, we say they have an "anxious way of relating."[2] These kids develop a dominant negative belief that they are unworthy of love. They tend to internalize any distance from the parent as due to their own flaws and constantly work at maintaining close proximity so as not to be abandoned. They desire closeness but can never seem to have enough.

It's hard loving somebody who has an anxious style of relating, because you feel as though you can never love them enough. It's hard being somebody with this style of relating, because you never feel loved enough. |
| **Avoidant**

Am I worthy of love?

Yes

Are others capable of loving me?

No | **The Child:** Particularly in fear-provoking situations, the child has no confidence her parents will be emotionally available or responsive. The parent tends to misinterpret the child's signaling behaviors (that is, crying, anxiety, anger) as weakness or manipulation, therefore minimizing emotion.

Exploration and Protection: These parents tend to overemphasize exploration and minimize, criticize, punish, or reject emotions and proximity-seeking behaviors of their kids. Because of this, these children learn to stop seeking protection from their parents and instead become defensive and overly self-reliant at the expense of a deeper emotional life and intimate relationships. |

	Beliefs About Relationships and Emotions: Kids with an "avoidant way of relating" tend to grow up with an excessively negative view of others' ability to love them, and therefore they become emotionally self-reliant, viewing emotions and vulnerability as a sign of weakness. They may turn to addictive behaviors or substances to self-soothe in place of intimate relationships. It's hard loving somebody who has an avoidant style of relating, because you feel as though they never let you in. It's hard being somebody with this style of relating, because you never feel as though you can trust others enough to let them in.
Fearful Am I worthy of love? No Are others capable of loving me? No	**The Child:** There's a paradox in these children because the source of their loving comfort (the parent) is also the source of their fear and pain. The fearful way of relating is most often developed in abusive, neglectful, or emotionally chaotic homes. **Exploration and Protection:** The part of the child's brain that tells them they are scared and should get away from what they are scared of simultaneously is triggered with the part of the brain that tells them to move toward the caregiver to be protected from harm. **Beliefs About Relationships and Emotions:** Kids who grow up with a "fearful way of relating" desire closeness but tend to sabotage it when they feel too close. It's difficult loving someone with this way of relating, because you often don't know how they'll behave toward you. It's difficult having this style of relating, because you're never certain anyone can be trusted or safe.

Figure 3.1. Implicit beliefs about relationships and subsequent patterns of feeling and relating.[3] This is a developmental model for understanding patterns of secure or insecure ways of relating. It's important to look at this chart, not in a way of labeling yourself or your child, but only to understand whether any of us could have, more or less, any one of these secure or insecure features of relating. Also, though put into categories, none of these are fixed. The more we engage in personal reflection and discover our own story in the context of newer, safe relationships over time, the more likely we are to move from insecure to secure ways of relating.

THE POWER BEHIND THE EYES

We spend a lot of time and money as parents trying to give our kids the best advantages possible. But the reality is, to raise kids who live, love, and lead well, we need to focus on building what's behind their eyes—their emotional and relational brain.

This is pretty challenging to do because it's the tense moments I just mentioned when growth occurs. As parents, our ability to embrace negative emotion—both our own and our child's—is critical to emotional safety. These moments do not happen all of the time. But when they do, our ability to capitalize on them is crucial to building the brains and stories of our children. Here's how it works: the brain grows in two ways, from the bottom to the top and from the right to the left. Let's start at the bottom, the basement of a Safe House, if you will.[4] The bottom part of our brain is positioned at the back of our head, where the brain and the spinal cord meet. This is the part of the brain, to put it simply, known as the fight or flight response. When we're faced with real or perceived danger, our brains are wired to automatically tell us to either fight against or flee the unsafe situation. Since it's based primarily on instinct and impulse, these *reactions* are considered lower levels of functioning. People who "fly off the handle," generally speaking, are functioning from this part of the brain. This is also where temper tantrums reside.

The top part of the brain, the upstairs of a Safe House, is where we find the higher-level functioning parts of the brain. This is the part of the brain positioned right behind our eyes. We are going to discuss ways of building this part of the brain in children of all ages. For now, we need only understand that this part of the brain includes functions such as problem solving, behavioral control, emotion regulation, social skills, cognitive flexibility, and language processing.

These functions of the brain grow when kids feel safe. Generally speaking, writing great stories for our kids is a matter of helping them build their brain from the bottom to the top—that is, helping them learn how to handle anger, frustration, being upset, and scared on their own while maintaining emotional and behavioral control and problem solving.

The brain also grows from right to left. The right side of the brain is our experiential, emotional brain. This is the part of the brain that experiences and lives in the here and now. The left side of the brain is the analytical, language processing side. The reason it's important to write down our stories in a journal or talk about them to a trusted confidant is because our left brain begins to put language to the events of our right brain—events that took place in our childhood that we never made sense of—and begins to weave them into a coherent story.

Think of your brain as a physical book that houses the words to your story. The middle part of your brain is the binding of that book. This is where the neurons wire together the left and right side of the brain. If there is no binding in the middle of a book, you may have a story of scattered pages, but nothing is connected and it'll be difficult to read. The more bound your story is, the more likely you are to write a great story for your children.

> Essentially, the sign of a healthy brain is when we're able to verbalize what we're feeling and why we're feeling that way in a given situation.

Essentially, the sign of a healthy brain is when we're able to verbalize what we're feeling and why we're feeling that way in a given situation. Did you ever catch yourself acting toward your children in a way you never thought you would? Maybe you're more lenient than you thought you would be. Or maybe you're stricter, only to discover that you're actually parenting in very similar ways to your own parents. The implicit, experiential part of the brain activates this response. The ability to be able to put words to where it actually came from triggers the left side of the brain. The goal then is to be able to put words to those experiences.

This is why sitting down with our kids and asking them about their day—their favorite moments, the not-so-favorite moments, and even how they felt in particular situations—getting them to describe that, and processing those details with them is critical for children to develop the higher-functioning parts of their brain, right behind their eyes.

How the Brain Grows Relationally and Emotionally

One of the tricks of the trade for attachment-based and developmental counselors like myself is assessing the quality of one's relationship with their parents. For instance, I can tell the quality of a person's relationship with somebody else based on their ability, or inability, to recall and tell their story in a narrative form. The more descriptive the details, the better quality the relationship.

What if I asked you, "How was your relationship with your mom?"

You may answer, "I had a good mom. She was there for me."

If I took it a step further and asked you how she was there for you, would you be able to tell me? How much detail would you be able go into about her availability to you in difficult moments or her ability to share in joyful ones? What words would you use to describe her presence or lack thereof? Would you tell me about the time you were sad and feeling rejected because somebody was picking on you at school, and she took you to your favorite ice cream shop to talk about it? Would you tell me how, later that week-end, she allowed you to have a close friend spend the night?

Or would your answer be a bit different? Would you tell me how she told you to just suck it up because all kids are bullied? Or maybe you even confused your mom's presence in this scenario, thinking she was just teaching you how to be tough, not recognizing that she was being emotionally dismissive toward you in the process.

This is how the brain grows from the right to the left. We have an experience, in this case with our mom, and over time we put language to that experience. Generally speaking, the more detail we can recall about specific interactions or events, the more we can label and actually feel the emotions that went with those experiences, the more insight we have into that relationship. And the more insight we have, especially with our parents, the more we can recognize how those experiences are shaping who we are as parents.

Let me take this to our relationship with God. You might say, "God is good all the time. God is good." But if I ask you to describe your relationship with God, what would you tell me? Would your answer go beyond how good he is to you because you'll go to heaven for believing in him? Or would you tell me, as did my grandmother, about the time a loved one faced a terminal illness and how you relentlessly pursued him for healing, comfort, and protection. And even though that family member passed away, would you tell me about how you experienced God's goodness, faithfulness, and peace on the other side, because of the intensity of the relationship during that period? How even though you had to wrestle with your own anger toward him for a brief period for taking her so early, how grateful you were to him for how he used your loved one's life to bring others, and your family, closer to him and one another?

Whether it's with our parents, a spouse, or even God, narrative recall speaks volumes about the quality of our relationships. Writing or rewriting the story is important to wiring together the neurons of the left and right sides of the brain. The more insight we have as parents, the more attuned to and present we'll be in helping our kids write their own story.

THE POWER OF THINKING, FEELING, AND RELATING AT THE SAME TIME

I mentioned earlier one of the ways of helping our children write logical and meaningful life narratives was by processing our kids' day with them, what they did, how they felt, and even helping them solve problems they're having with friends, teachers, or even with us. Another way of understanding, at a deeper brain level, how this works is through a different therapeutic trick. In therapy we say that true change happens when we think, feel, and relate all at the same time. When we do, we engage the left side (thinking), right side (feeling), and the bottom part (the basement full of instinctual negative feelings like fear and anger) of the brain at the same time to build the top part (relating) of the brain.

Consider these examples:

- Sitting in a classroom listening to someone lecture is an informative relationship. We may be thinking, and in some cases relating with the teacher, but most of the time we don't feel anything.

- You may read this book by yourself, and you might even begin thinking about how you were parented because of it. But if all you do is think about it (without writing down your story, or talking to a trusted confidant or even your parents about it), deeper-level change is not as likely to occur.

- When people argue at a family holiday, and somebody storms out the door with no resolve, no change occurs. That's because all that happened was intense feeling—very little thinking and definitely no relating.

I remember counseling a juvenile delinquent who was court appointed to meet with me for twelve hours. After the first few sessions, I didn't feel like we were getting anywhere. One night he left a message, asking if we could move our appointment time from 5:00 to 7:00 p.m. because he wanted to play basketball with friends. Despite the fact that I probably could have done it, I chose not to. I knew he'd be mad at me. When he showed up for his five o'clock appointment, he was withdrawn and anxious to leave. When I asked him what he was feeling, he gave the typical teenage response: "Nothing."

I then asked him to look me in the eye. As he did, I asked him, "What are you feeling?"

With now more passion in his voice, he said, "I told you, nothing."

I told him to look me again in the eye. This time, rather than provoking him further, I told him *what I thought* he was feeling. If I wasn't right, he would tell me. If I was right, I knew we would begin getting somewhere. "You're mad at me, aren't you?" I asked.

With a sarcastic tone he replied, "You think?"

Now we're getting somewhere.

Not only did he tell me what he was feeling, but I got him to tell me *why* he was feeling that way. In doing so, he was feeling anger toward somebody who was safe and secure enough to handle his anger. I was not threatened by it. I just sat with him in it and validated it. As I did, we began to discuss responsibility and then problem solved together for the next time something like this happened. In this moment, he was thinking, feeling, and relating with a safe person all at the same time. We progressed more that day than we had in the previous sessions combined.

I gave him the choice of shooting hoops or playing minigolf for our next session together. Not until he felt emotionally safe could we move to deeper issues about his dad's abandoning him.

Many times, our initial reaction as parents in emotionally difficult times is to either tell our kids what to do or allow them to do whatever they want. In either case, as parents we don't allow them to feel anything negative in relationship with us. Raising kids who live, love, and lead well takes the ability to get kids to think, feel, and relate at the same time (strategies for doing this will be covered in chapters 7 and 8). This, of course, requires that we as parents are secure enough to engage negative emotion.

Secure enough to sit with an angry child and be okay that our child is angry at us.

Secure enough to allow our child to disrespect us without disrespecting him back.

Secure enough to use these tense moments to be safe and teach our children how to handle emotion well.

A Safe House is a home where feelings matter.

WHY RENTAL CAR COMPANIES ARE SMARTER THAN POLITICIANS

I saved the outcome research on how emotional safety is the key to raising kids who love, live, and lead well until now because I wanted to show why and how it matters from both a biblical and a scientific perspective.

The experiences we have with our children from as early as birth, and especially in the first five years of life, are critical to raising a generation of kids in our respective family lineage who are emotionally, socially, and spiritually intelligent. When we're secure as parents, we can more clearly see into the minds of our children in a particular situation, read their signals of communication (that is, cries for help, both literally and figuratively), make sense of what these signals mean for our children, and meet their needs in a loving and timely manner. In doing so, we're building their brain from the bottom to the top and cultivating nearly every higher-level functioning part of their brain (which we'll learn more about in the next chapter as we discuss the four walls of a Safe House).[5]

Here's where car rental companies are a bit smarter than politicians. Research shows that the upstairs part of our brain, the prefrontal cortex, is not fully developed until we hit our midtwenties, which is why car rental companies (who require drivers to be at least twenty-five) may have their policies more accurately figured out than governmental policies on driver's licenses (age sixteen) and drinking (age twenty-one). Renting cars to individuals who function and *respond* more out of the top part of their brain is a little smarter than giving teenagers who still *react* more out of the bottom part of their brains a driver's license or even alcohol.

However, kids who grow up in a safe environment are more likely to develop these higher functioning parts of the brain earlier. That's because over time children who take risks (explore) in the context of a safe environment are more likely to handle stress, fear, and anxiety as they mature. The upstairs part of the brain learns how to take calculated risks that strengthen the resolve of our children. This is why and how our experiences with our kids from early in life shape their ability to live, love, and lead well.

Kids who develop a secure relationship with their parent in a safe environment are more likely to be able to

- experience and label a wide range of emotions, from positive to negative
- balance and regulate those emotions, especially intense ones
- learn how to manage and lessen fear
- develop insight into and understanding of their own thoughts, feelings, and behavior
- be more aware of how others are feeling in a given situation and respond to their felt needs
- empathize with others
- have a deeper understanding of the difference between right and wrong[6]

Now, instead of just reading the following outcomes, you have a clearer picture of why the research for children who develop a safe, secure relationship with a parent is so robust.

Emotional safety is linked to kids who live well, love well, and lead well.

Kids Who Live Well

- They have higher levels of self-esteem, self-worth, and self-competence.[7]
- They are more enthusiastically engaged in challenging tasks.[8]
- They are more likely to achieve an authentic and positive identity.[9]
- They associate with more health-promoting behaviors, such as maintaining a healthy diet or engaging in exercise, and avoiding health-related risks, such as smoking, drinking, and drug abuse.[10]
- They are more likely to find and enter into a long-term romantic relationship with another securely attached partner.[11]
- They are more likely to handle stressful events with higher levels of psychological well-being and lower levels of distress.[12]
- They are more likely to be curious, open to new experiences, new adventures, and new information, and maintain cognitive flexibility (that is, more likely to embrace change).[13]
- In the event of the loss of a loved one, they are more likely to experience grief, anger, and distress without being overwhelmed by those feelings, are more likely to grieve without disruption of normal functioning, are more likely to reflect and talk about the deceased in a coherent way, and are then able to move into healthy relationships.[14]
- They are more likely to maintain faith in God and adherence to religion, particularly if the parent adheres to faith practices.[15]
- They are more flexible and secure in maintaining healthy adolescent friendships.[16]
- They are less likely to experience loneliness.[17]
- They are more likely to maintain friendships across their life span, beginning in preschool, throughout childhood and adolescent, and into their adult years that are based on higher levels of trust, self-disclosure, closeness, empathy, and constructive conflict resolution skills.[18]

Kids Who Love Well

- They are less likely to allow work to interfere with relationships in adulthood.[19]
- They have more satisfying romantic relationships in adulthood.[20]

- They engage in more satisfying and meaningful family rituals (family dinners, birthday celebrations, and so on) as adults with their own family.[21]
- As adults, they are more likely to find a romantic partner for a stable long-term relationship, have a more satisfying sexual relationship with that partner, and are less likely to use sex as a means of feeling loved or accepted.[22]
- In adult romantic relationships, they are more likely to show affection and empathy during conflict, more frequently compromise, less likely to use coercive or destructive communication tactics during conflict, less likely to verbally attack their partner, and show less distress after the conflict.[23]
- As adult children, they are more supportive and affectionate toward their parents[24] and display more care and lower caregiver burden on dependent parents.[25]
- Within dating and married relationships, they are more likely to be supportive of and sensitive to their romantic partners' needs and less likely to be controlling or overinvolved in a caregiving role with him or her.[26]
- They are more likely to hold a genuinely concerned and altruistic motive when caring for a romantic partner, as opposed to a selfish motive.[27]
- They are more compassionate and willing to help strangers in need with a genuinely altruistic motive to help the other person.[28]

Kids Who Lead Well

- They have higher academic skills, attitudes, and achievement.[29]
- They are more likely to commit to a chosen ideology, role, career, or occupation without feeling shame, guilt, or remorse about violating other people's expectations.[30]
- They experience more frequent spontaneous reading in preschool and childhood.[31]
- They are more efficient at problem solving during preschool.[32]
- Safe infants were rated by teachers at age ten and eleven as having superior scholastic attitudes (motivation, persistence, and attention) and skills (oral and writing skills), even after controlling for intelligence and perceived competence.[33]

- Safe kids at age seven show higher predicted levels of superior formal deductive reasoning between ages nine and seventeen (even after controlling for intelligence and attention problems).[34]
- Safe kids at age seven also received higher teacher ratings on attention and participation in class and superior school grades at ages nine, twelve, and fifteen.[35]
- They pursue higher levels of exploring careers that fit their related skills.[36]
- They experience higher levels of career commitment and performance in adulthood.[37]
- They are more likely to take responsibility for setting goals, make the decision to set the goals, maintain emotional and behavioral control in the face of adversity, and follow through with goal completion.[38]

> In a heated moment with your child, ask yourself, "Am I sending my child the message that he's worthy of love, and does he know that I'm capable of and willing to love him?"

The next time you're concerned about what to do in a heated moment with your child, remember the overwhelming evidence of what happens when secure parents create safe environments for their kids. Then ask yourself, "Am I sending my child the message that he's worthy of love, and does he know that I'm capable of and willing to love him?"

HONORING OUR FAMILY STORY

Having grown up with divorced parents, I knew the odds for staying married and also genuinely enjoying my marriage were stacked against me. Psychologically, there are emotional and behavioral patterns passed down to us from the way our parents related that can, without insight or knowledge into them, harm our future family relationships. That's why I'm a firm advocate for premarital counseling and surrounding ourselves with safe people who can walk both the marital and parenting journey with us.

When Christi and I were going through premarital counseling, we did an exercise that was extremely helpful for us. Our counselors asked us to separately come up with three characteristics of our respective families of origin that we wanted to carry into our marriage and three that we did not want to bring into our own family. The exercise not only helped us to think about and recognize the patterns in our families of origin but also enabled us to label and define how we could make the most of how we were raised and honor our families' heritage.

Sharing about my parents' divorce as a defining moment for me is deliberate for three reasons:

1. I want the authenticity of my own journey to reflect the healing and redeeming nature of the process of discovering, finding meaning in, and repairing our own stories.

2. No matter how good your story is, understand that nobody's story is perfect and that, no matter how bad your story is, nobody's story is beyond redemption.

3. Finally, always honor your story and your parents. Though your parents may not have always gotten it right, don't dishonor them. Though they may have caused you harm you certainly didn't deserve, as an adult you must take responsibility for your story. You owe it to your kids, because kids who know how their grandparents met are better able to recover from wrecking their bicycle or handling the unknowns of a national tragedy, like 9/11. Sounds ridiculous, right?

In 2001, researchers at Emory University decided to assess the truth of the following observation: children who knew about their family history were better able to handle stress. They asked four dozen families questions from a scale they created called the Do You Know? scale and then recorded the families' dinner conversations.[39] For example,

- "Do you know how your parents met?"
- "Do you know what went on when you were being born?"
- "Do you know some of the illnesses and injuries that your parents experienced when they were younger?"
- "Do you know some of the lessons that your parents learned from good or bad experiences?"
- "Do you know where some of your grandparents grew up?"

The findings of the study are fascinating. The more a child knows about her family history, the higher her self-esteem, the more likely she is to believe her family functions in a healthy way, the more sense of control she has over her life, and the more likely she is to handle and bounce back from stressful events. The researchers found that knowing your family history actually predicts a child's emotional health and happiness.[40]

What's more, there are three types of stories that form the narratives of every family. There's the *ascending narrative:*

Son, your grandfather was the first man in our family to finish high school and start a business from absolutely nothing. Your father was the first one to complete college and has taken the business even further. Now you . . .

In a broad sense, this first narrative is an overly optimistic outlook that our family will always be getting better, doing better, and living better than the generations before it. These are families who may tend to think they have it all together.

The second narrative is the *descending narrative:*

Honey, in the old days, it was much easier to make a living. We had everything we needed. Since the market turned, we have nothing.

The second narrative is more of a doom-and-gloom story line and can constitute families who may play victim to the world around them or see their family members or situations in a purely negative light.

The third narrative, known as the *oscillating family narrative,* is the healthiest story line a family can have. It's what I'm referring to as I ask you to write your own story and help your children write theirs.

Dear, let me tell you, we've had ups and downs in our family. We built a family business. Your grandfather was a pillar of the community. Your mother was on the board of the hospital. But we also had setbacks. You had an uncle who was once arrested. We had a house burn down. Your father lost a job. But no matter what happened, we always stuck together as a family.[41]

Seeing myself as a part of the story in my parents' divorce was important for how I eventually entered into my own marriage and now parent my children. Going back and discussing my parents' roles and how we all felt and behaved during that time was a unifying and healing part of our family story. It wasn't easy, but it was redeeming.

We're all interwoven in interdependent, intergenerational relationships that take place over time. Making sense of our family history and reframing the meaning of how we fit into those events are critical to raising kids who live, love, and lead well.

The more our kids know about their own history, the more they feel a part of something bigger than themselves.

━━━━ Writing Your Story ━━━━

Describe and write down in as much detail as possible the answers to the following questions:

1. What are two ways your mom was emotionally safe for you?
2. What are two ways your mom was not emotionally safe for you?
3. What are two ways your dad was emotionally safe for you?
4. What are two ways your dad was not emotionally safe for you?
5. What is your plan for resolving unforgiveness toward a parent?
6. To honor your parents, write a thank-you letter to both of your parents for the specific ways they were emotionally available to you.

PART 2

Building a Safe House

4

The Four Walls of a Safe House

When the other person is hurting, confused, troubled, anxious,
alienated, terrified; or when he or she is doubtful of self-worth,
uncertain as to identity, then understanding is called for. . . . In
such situations deep understanding is, I believe, the most precious
gift one can give to another.

—Carl Rogers

Christi and I saved enough money to take a vacation to Italy with some friends a
few summers ago. When we visited the island of Capri, an elderly gentleman
who spoke no English walked up to me and pointed to his camera. Thinking he was
asking to take our picture in exchange for money, I looked him in the eye, shook my
head, and boldly declined.

But as we stepped away to gaze at the beautiful ocean and rock cliffs around us, I
noticed a distinct heaviness in my spirit, a heaviness more breathtaking than the land-
scape itself.

As I looked for the man I had just rejected, I noticed him standing by himself,
simply gazing around—alone.

I realized he was asking me to take a picture of *him*.

I felt terrible.

Stepping away from my wife and friends, I walked back over to this frail, seemingly
lonely man and signaled to him that I would take his picture. What happened next
grabbed my attention—and heart—even more. He reached down, unzipped the black
fanny pack nestled around his waist, and pulled back out the camera, a battery-operated
film version from the 1990s. After making sure the film was wound to the next picture,
he handed it to me with anticipation.

As excited as this man could get, he pointed to a random building in the distance.
After making his way slowly to the foreground of where he had just pointed, he turned

around, gestured for how he wanted me to hold the camera, and then looked at me with puppy-dog eyes, offering up what could barely be labeled a smile.

Click. I took the shot. I then walked toward him and handed his camera back, along with a friendly smile.

Not once did we utter a single word to one another. Yet I'll never forget the impression he made on my life. I loosely followed him around the island for a while that day, dragging behind me a heavy heart. He had no wife. No kids. No companions. He was alone. On a beautiful island. And nothing on him but an old-school film camera and a fanny pack.

I walked away that day realizing there was innocence in that old-school camera and fanny pack one rarely experiences in the commotion of everyday living. The exchange of the camera from his hand to mine was about more than a picture; it was a portrait of purity—the purity of untarnished human connection. I wanted to adopt this man as my grandfather, buy him a digital camera, and teach him how to use it.

I wonder often about that man. What his story is. Where he is from. Why, with all of the beauty around him, he wanted a picture in front of a somewhat feeble building.

I'm glad I went back to take his picture that day. Though I'm not sure it was true of this particular moment, I know that by showing hospitality to strangers, some have shown hospitality to angels without knowing it.[1]

If he was an angel, he did his job. I learned that the motivation of another is oftentimes more innocent than I initially fear.

OLD-SCHOOL CAMERAS, FANNY PACKS, AND OUR KIDS

Unable to speak the same language, I initially did not understand what this stranger was asking of me. All I could think about was how he was undoubtedly trying to lure me into giving him money. Built on a foundation of fear, I erected a wall of protection so large I nearly missed the opportunity to serve him. When we live in fear, our relational encounters become one-sidedly about us; when we live in love, these encounters become about the other person.

I'm glad—somewhere in my wall of protection that day—there was a window of understanding large enough for me to climb through. It changed my perspective, leaving me longing to know more deeply about the soul of this one individual.

My hope is for every parent in our generation to not parent out of fear but out of love, intentionally taking time to know deeply and to nurture lovingly the souls of our children.

Because kids who feel understood are kids who learn to understand; kids who understand are kids who love.

To help our children build the higher-level functions of their brain—skills like empathy, insight, and cognitive flexibility—requires that we understand them. Just as I thought the fanny pack and camera was a scheme to take my money, we cannot assume our children's misbehaviors or tantrums are a ploy to manipulate us or seek attention (though sometimes they are). Nor can we believe that it's a lack of motivation for wanting to behave appropriately. Instead, getting down at our child's eye level (sometimes literally) and peering through the window of understanding into his developmental level, a specific situation, and his unique way of dealing with difficult or stressful situations helps us to see what skills our child is lacking and how we can figuratively, even though we cannot understand each other's language in the moment, step in as parents, embrace the innocence of what's given to us in the situation, and take his picture—a mental snapshot of his feelings and motives.

> Kids who feel understood are kids who learn to understand; kids who understand are kids who love.

Choosing to seek the deeper understanding and meaning behind our child's behavior takes us beyond how she's behaving to a picture of *why* she's behaving that way. And the more we understand why, the more our kids feel understood and the more equipped we are to know how much grace to apply in a given situation, what limits to set, and how to set them. In doing so, we can effectively build the brains of our children in a way that serves each child individually and uniquely based on their developmental level, temperament, and skill level.

Not only will we then be coauthors of beautiful stories for our children but artists with an eye for drawing out the innocence behind our kids' behaviors.

THE FRAMEWORK OF UNDERSTANDING

In this chapter the four walls of a Safe House—exploration, protection, grace, and truth—will be introduced. But before we get to the walls, let's start with the framework. After all, the walls of a house require both a foundation and a framework. The strength of the framework is dependent on the security of the foundation: in our case, a secure parent. To be sure the four walls of a Safe House are not flimsy and unstable requires us to first build a framework of understanding.

The framework of a house also leaves open spaces for windows. From a structural perspective, the more precise and solid the framework, the more exact the window will fit. Some frameworks are built specifically for huge bay windows. Others create space for smaller windows of various shapes and dimensions, down to the size of the peephole in the front door. The irony about the peephole is that we can see out, but we cannot look in—an interesting metaphor for the size and type of window we're leaving in the framework of our own story.

Is your story riddled with such pain and lack of understanding that your framework of understanding is closed off, with no room for windows, protected from anybody looking in at you? A clean, spotless window clearly reveals what's on both sides. That's why knowing our own story first is critical to visibly peering through the windows of understanding into the thoughts, feelings, and behaviors of our own children.

Parenting from a posture of love and emotional safety means living out the Golden Rule with our children: "In everything, therefore, treat people the same way you want them to treat you."[2] Though applied a bit differently from the

> In order to be understood, we must first understand.

context of building a Safe House, it's from this framework that we will build all four walls. Now, let's rephrase the Golden Rule as it applies to parenting from an emotionally safe posture. Simply replace the word *treat* with the word *understand:* In everything, therefore, understand your children in the same way you want them to understand you.

In other words, in order to be understood, we must first understand.

A child who feels understood by Mom or Dad is a child who is safely allowed to feel. Her negative emotions are not punished, dismissed, or minimized but instead are validated and explored.

I received a call from a dad whose middle school daughter got really upset at him for not allowing her to go to a football game one Friday night. In the exchange, she lashed out, "I hate you." Imagine how you would respond to this.

A parent who punishes negative feelings may react by saying something like, "What do you mean you hate me? Do you realize all that I do for you? I'm taking your phone until you apologize. Now go to your room!"

A parent who dismisses the negative emotion may respond by saying something like, "Don't be mad at me."

A parent who minimizes the anger may react by saying something like, "You're making a big deal over a football game? Really? There's no reason to be so upset."

When kids do not feel heard or understood or are punished for their negative feelings, they learn to bury these emotions, becoming anxious about even sharing them with their parents.

Parents who instead build big windows of understanding are parents who empathize with their kids, even when they misbehave. It's not that we're condoning the behavior; it's that we empathize with the feelings behind it. Children who feel understood and are allowed to express their feelings and wishes are kids who have access to their parents' feelings as well. The more a child feels understood, the more open she is to understanding why we're protecting her (the wall of protection) or setting limits (the wall of truth).

An emotionally healthy father, in the scenario above, instead of dismissing, punishing, or minimizing the negative emotion, will figuratively, or perhaps literally, posture himself on one knee, arms wide open, and respond, "I understand you're really angry at me. What is it about the football game that matters so much to you?"

I'm glad the father in this case responded in a similar manner. What he came to find out was that his daughter had been rejected by a group of friends for the first few months of the school year. She would see pictures on Facebook and Instagram of her friends getting together without her and sit alone on the weekends longing to be or feel included. This football game was the first time she had been invited to be a part of the group all year.

The father, after understanding the emotion behind his daughter's anger, was able to address her disrespectful behavior toward him. For his daughter, understanding her intense feeling and motivation was the most precious gift he could have given her that night.

When we consistently prioritize our children's behavior over winning their heart, we risk erecting a relational brick wall between us that carries into the teenage years and even into adulthood. On the other hand, when we prioritize our child's heart, we not only send them the message they are loved unconditionally in spite of their behavior but spotless windows of understanding enable us to influence our children's behavior more than we can imagine.

I cannot emphasize it enough: without the framework of understanding, establishing and maintaining the four walls of a Safe House (exploration, protection, grace, and truth) will be truly difficult. Raising kids who live, love, and lead well requires a parent who learns how to maintain a symmetrical roof on the house, where all four walls are level and at the same height. If any of the four walls are uneven, it could very well be a reflection of the insecurity of its foundation (in this case the parent's own story) or a weakness in the framework (a lack of understanding).

Make no mistake, this doesn't mean there won't be times our child needs more grace from us in a particular situation than truth or we have to protect her more than she's allowed to explore. Instead, raising kids who live, love, and lead well requires a parent who learns how to balance the walls of grace, truth, exploration, and protection in her relationship with each of her kids. Maintaining all four walls equally over time creates emotional safety.

I use the phrase *learns how to balance . . . grace, truth, exploration, and protection* because, as parents, that's exactly what we're doing: learning. We're students of our children. Understanding them begins by studying them, each child, uniquely and individually for who they are: their strengths and weaknesses, temperament, developmental level, and motivations. The more we study our child, the more we know our child; the more we know our child, the more we can understand our child; and the more we understand our child, the more we know exactly how to balance the walls of grace, truth, exploration, and protection with each child we raise.

The reason posture matters more than technique is because not every technique will work with every child in every situation. An overreliance on parenting techniques will leave us constantly bouncing from one technique to another, because what works on one child may not work with another, and what works with one child once may not work with him again.

On the contrary, emotional safety (a balance of grace, truth, exploration, and protection) should be employed with every child in every situation every day. Techniques come and go, but our posture as a parent will always remain, even after we're dead and gone.

Sitting beside my dad in his hospital bed after complications from his heart pump surgery nearly took his life, I was reminded why we drove twenty-one hours to be with him. It wasn't because of the techniques he used to parent me; it was because of the incredible memories I had from the posture in which he loved me, a mental representation that became the basis from which I now parent. I've learned, too, that the eternal value of this posture outweighs any other riches we gain on earth. Look at what the Bible says about the value of understanding:

> Blessed is the one who . . . gets understanding,
> for the gain from her is better than gain from silver
> and her profit better than gold.
> She is more precious than jewels,
> and nothing you desire can compare with her.[3]

Simply put, a man or woman of understanding is extremely wealthy. I have worked with many millionaires with kids and teenagers in turmoil, and the message I consistently hear is, "Josh, I would give anything just to help or have a relationship with my child." These parents realize, at the end of life, the legacy we leave is found not in material possessions but in the relational values we leave to the next generation.

Life really is all about our relationships, especially with our kids.

UNDERSTANDING OUR CHILD'S TEMPERAMENT

I remember when bedtime became a chore in the Straub household. Think delay tactics, manipulation, and even playing lovey-dovey to get his way. Yes, our two-year-old is a master manipulator.

And let me tell you, he's good!

In the first few weeks Christi and I found ourselves reading books to him a little later, playing trains a little longer, and "redding up" his toys for him (if you're a fellow Pennsylvania native) or cleaning them up (if you're anybody else), all in the name of "helping" Landon.

Those were the good nights. The troubling part about bedtime is, not only did it get longer, but we found ourselves using the same doggone tactics he used on us: manipulating, begging, pleading, and, yes, whining just to get him into bed. I found myself making promises I knew I wouldn't keep.

How can such a little immature body have the power to turn a mature man into a whiny brat?

Let me tell you, it happens. We're human. You will not be emotionally safe all of the time. Kids will put your character to the test. More than anything I have ever

experienced, having two kids two years old and younger revealed how flawed my character was. The more or less coherent our own story is will determine how much we have
to learn, or perhaps unlearn, as we practice understanding and being emotionally present with each of our kids.

In addition, how we're balancing each of the four walls may look different with one
child than it does with another. For instance, your affectionate but bold three-year-old
may need little to no support from you to walk into his classroom on Sunday morning
at church. On the other hand, your five-year-old may be very slow to warm—for example, to people or new environments—and need more care from you as you help her
transition into kindergarten.

Balancing the four walls of a Safe House requires understanding each child's individual differences, beginning with their temperament. If you're like Christi and me, you
probably already discuss and perhaps even worry about your child's temperament. But
the reason you notice is because you're doing what every parent does: comparing him to
other children his age. It's a sickness, I know. Again, we're only human.

Landon, for instance, was much slower to warm at two years than his friends were.
However, I can remember having to check myself wishing Landon would be braver in
his interactions. Thankfully, since then, we've come to appreciate his apprehension and
learned to offer him the support he needs without coddling him.

Understanding temperament is important because, unlike the executive functions
we're helping to cultivate in our children's brain, temperament is biologically driven and
is therefore what makes our children uniquely who they are. Understanding how our
own temperament fits with our children's can also be significant in how safe we are with
them in certain situations. A driven Type-A parent who loves routine and being on time
could easily be overwhelmed and frustrated with her laid-back Type-B child. Being safe
is appreciating these differences without overwhelming our children or giving in to
them either. A safe parent learns how to balance support and challenge with each child.

To get a general feeling for your children's temperaments, take a look at the list
below and see how each of your children might differ from you:

- *Activity Level.* This describes your child's inclination as it relates to motor
  activity. Is your infant active, busy, and squirmy on one end or quiet and
  attentive on the other? As your child becomes a toddler, notice whether
  she prefers gross motor skills—like running—or fine motor skills—like
  playing with blocks or putting puzzles together.

- *Adaptability to New Situations.* How well can your child adjust to unexpected changes? For example, changes in schedule, routine, a new house, a new school, a different teacher, staying with grandparents overnight, and so on.

- *Approach or Withdrawal.* Does your child tend to eagerly approach new foods, new situations, new people, and new places or is he slow to warm, with a tendency to withdraw from these new stimuli?

- *Distractibility.* Is your child easily sidetracked when working on a necessary task (like nursing as an infant or doing homework as a child)?

- *Intensity of Reaction.* How strongly does your child react, either positively or negatively? Some children get unbelievably excited, dancing around and jumping up and down, at the sound of good news. Others are more restrained in showing their affections. If you have an infant like ours were, they may scream as if somebody is torturing them during a standard diaper change or they may simply whimper at the displeasure of the cold wipes.

- *Sensitivity.* Think senses on this one—how your child responds to textures, sounds, tastes, smells, or temperature. Do certain sounds, clothing textures, or odors provoke a strong response in your children? Or are these senses not really a big deal? Kennedy, for instance, doesn't like being cold and lets us know it. Landon spits out pasta and hands it to us because of the texture on his palate. Lovely, right? Consider how easily your child becomes overstimulated or overwhelmed by sensory information. Lecturing your child or talking too much may overwhelm him, causing him to act out even more. Not being aware of his sensitivity to auditory overload could mean you confuse his behavior of withdrawing or shutting down for willful defiance.

- *Regularity.* Does your child prefer predictability in her biological routines (that is, sleep-wake cycles, eating times and even amounts, and bowel movements)?

- *Persistence.* During difficult activities, how long will your child tolerate frustration and stick with a task? Is she persistent or easy to give in?

- *Mood.* Does your child laugh a lot and approach life with a lighthearted demeanor or is he more serious, quiet, and introspective? How content or discontent is your child? Is he easygoing or irritable?[4]

Understanding our children's individual differences helps us learn what works as we balance the four walls of a Safe House. Consider each of the nine areas above and think through how well your children do in various situations.

As you compare your children to others around them (because I know you do), remember that your children are uniquely created to be who they are. Don't disparage your child for being quiet in social settings or not eating cottage cheese because of the texture. If you shoved cottage cheese in my mouth, I'd throw a tantrum, too. Instead, become a student of your children and learn their individual differences so *you* can adjust how you interact with them in building your four walls.

THE FOUR WALLS

Exploration. Protection. Grace. Truth. These four walls, when balanced over time, create the emotional safety our children need to live, love, and lead well.

First, picture in your mind's eye walking out the front door of your house. Taking that first step outside symbolizes the freedom we have to explore the world around us. This wall represents the first parenting trait of an emotionally safe home: the wall of EXPLORATION. From the time our children begin to crawl, they move away from dependence toward increased independence over time. Emotionally safe parents allow their children the freedom to safely and age-appropriately explore the world around them to test their independence. For instance, the more access we give our toddlers to explore within the safety of our homes, the more confidence we build in them from an early age to safely and securely explore outside of our homes later in life.

On the other hand, we cannot allow our kids the freedom to explore wherever they want and whenever they want to. They have to learn, just as we do as adults, about the consequences when we explore too far. Allowing our kids to play in the street could mean they get hit by a car. Allowing them to eat whatever they want and whenever they want to could lead to an upset stomach now or obesity later. Allowing them free reign to play video games with no protection could lead to lack of sleep and poor grades now and relational incompetence later.

For kids to be emotionally safe, they need to be protected. That's why sitting directly across from the wall of exploration is the wall of PROTECTION. Secure parents are okay with allowing their kids to explore, but they also know when and how to protect them. If the wall of exploration is too high, we may run the risk of overindulging our children. If the wall of protection is too high, we may be overprotecting them. An emotionally safe parent understands how to balance both uniquely with each child.

The walls that sit between exploration and protection and across from one another are the walls of grace and truth. Though these are biblical terms, there are no better words to describe them. The wall of GRACE represents unconditional love of our children. To be true grace it cannot be earned but instead freely given. Grace is loving our children even when they are unlovable. Grace is supporting our children even, and especially, in their worst moments. Grace is understanding the feelings and motives behind our children's behavior. Grace is forgiving our kids when they wrong us. Grace is choosing not to disrespect our kids even when they disrespect us. Grace is helping our kids whenever they need us. The wall of grace is where our kids learn empathy. Critical to their development is our ability to understand and embrace their negative emotion, without judgment, even if it's directed at us.

The wall opposite of grace is truth. I use the word *truth* because it covers much more than just discipline or setting limits, though both fall along this wall. A child who lives in truth does the right thing. The wall of TRUTH takes into account the consequences of our actions, both good and bad. Truth is teaching our children about the values of hard work and responsibility. Truth is helping our children learn the value of discernment when making decisions. Truth is training our children to live with integrity. Truth is walking alongside our children as they learn how to respond to the bumps and bruises of life, like not making the football team. Truth is helping your 135-pound uncoordinated son realize he'll never play in the NFL.

Again, the balance of both walls is extremely important. Parents who have a huge wall of grace and no wall of truth are permissive parents who may simply want to be their child's BFF. If this is you, I respectfully but boldly urge you to go find friends your own age. You're not doing your kids any favors. They will likely grow up with feelings of entitlement and disrespect for authority. Many of the outcomes I've mentioned earlier are a result of a generation of kids who were coddled around a huge wall of grace and a wobbly or nonexistent wall of truth.

On the other hand, a gigantic wall of truth with no grace is an authoritarian parent with little to no understanding of their child's feelings or needs, who sacrifices relationship in the name of following rules. Many parenting techniques and philosophies are built on this wall, trying to get kids to behave appropriately using behavioral charts, stickers, and even physical exercises. If you want obedient children in the short term, these techniques may work. But what they don't do is build the higher-level functioning parts of the brain necessary for long-term success. Grace and understanding must always come before advice giving, problem solving, and discipline.

As John Gottman explained, "My child isn't giving me a hard time. My child is having a hard time."[5] Understanding the difference matters.

How Oreo Cookies Predict Whether Our Kids Will Live, Love, and Lead Well

Other individual differences we need to *learn* about in our children are the strengths and weaknesses of their executive skills. We can assess these by—yes—an Oreo cookie.

In one of the most fascinating studies on human behavior to date, Walter Mischel and his colleagues individually offered preschool children their choice of a marshmallow, an Oreo, or a pretzel stick. The kids were told they could eat their chosen treat right then, or if they waited fifteen minutes, they could receive two treats. For example, the kids had to contemplate whether to eat an Oreo now or wait a short while and have two Oreos.

Could *you* do it?

After following these children for the next twenty years, the child's decision that day to simply eat an Oreo or wait and have two of them proved to have profound implications. The children who chose to delay gratification turned out to get better grades in school and had higher SAT scores when they became teenagers. Even as they matured into adults, they proved to be physically healthier, professionally more competent, and better able to stay committed in romantic relationships.[6]

Another study took children with the same IQ at age five and broke them into two groups: kids who were parented using emotion coaching (see chapter 7) and kids whose parents did not employ emotion coaching. The researchers compared the two groups again at age eight and found that the kids whose parents emotion coached them had higher academic success and scored higher on achievement tests, even when they controlled for IQ.[7]

These studies once again reveal why and how our parenting posture matters. It's not that emotionally safe kids are necessarily smarter; it's that they have the ability to access more of their inherited IQ. In addition to capitalizing intellectually, emotionally safe kids gain social and relational advantages because the emotionally safe environment is more conducive to building the higher-level functions of our kids' brain, such as emotion regulation and self-control.

When our kids can hold off on the impulse to *feel better* in the moment, it opens the door to living, loving, and leading better in the long run. Put off playing with friends to study for a test, you get better grades. Hold off on that cookie, you eat fewer calories. Put off the temptation of the adulterer, and you stay happily married.

Figure 4.1 provides a description of each of the higher-level functions of the brain we're building in our kids as we balance the walls of exploration, protection, grace, and truth. The next few chapters provide specific exercises for building these executive skills.

Middle Prefrontal Cortex[8]	Prefrontal Cortex[9]
Body Regulation: The ability to keep the organs and autonomic nervous system (heart rate, respiration, and so on) regulated and balanced.	**Problem Solving:** A child's capacity to—especially when feeling upset, frustrated, or angry—state a problem, find a range of solutions to the problem, choose one of those solutions, monitor how it is working, and apply an alternative solution if the first one did not work.
Attuned Communication: The ability to recognize our own and others' internal emotions, motivations, and bodily states such that we can interact with compassion and respect.	**Cognitive Flexibility:** The ability of a child to shift from the rules and expectations of one situation to the rules and expectations of another. Children who are inflexible tend to see situations in black/white, always/never, you win/I lose categories. The more inflexible we are, the faster our emotions go from zero to one hundred.
Emotional Balance: The ability to experience enough emotional excitement that it drives us to live with meaning and purpose. Yet not too much emotion that our lives are dramatic and not too little emotion that we live in apathy or exhaustion.	**Language Processing Skills:** A child's ability to label what she's feeling and concisely communicate those feelings and needs to others, then to organize and consider how she'll respond to the reaction of others, while remaining teachable and hospitable if she's confronted about her behavior.
Fear Modulation: The ability to reduce fear.	**Emotion Regulation:** A child's ability to handle strong emotion—like anger, frustration, being upset—while she solves problems and accomplishes goals.
Flexibility of Response: The ability to respond rather than react in situations. Taking a moment to ponder all available options.	**Social Intelligence:** A child's ability to understand the impact of her own and others' emotions on thinking and behaving. Children with social intelligence can effectively think, feel, and relate with another person in a problem-solving situation at the same time.

Insight: To know thyself. The ability to be aware of who you are in a way that connects your memories from the past to your current lived-in present and envisioned future.	**Working Memory:** A child's capacity to presently hold a potential action in mind while at the same time processing the effects of past behavior and the potential effects of future behavior before taking action.
Empathy: The ability to step into the shoes of another, to see from another's perspective, and to experience what another may feel.	**Focus of Attention:** A child's ability to maintain attention, avoid distractions, and choose to change attention, if necessary, for the purpose of solving a problem or accomplishing a goal.
Morality: The ability to think, reason, and act with the greater social and personal good in mind.	**Behavioral (or Self) Control:** A child's ability to maintain balance of and regulate thoughts, feelings, attention, and behaviors for optimum living and relating.

Figure 4.1. Higher-level brain functions developed in a Safe House.

As you read through the skills in the chart, begin to develop an understanding of where your children have the most strength and weakness. As you do, you may begin to find that their tantrums or meltdowns have more to do with skill deficits than with willful disobedience. The more we know *why* our kids are acting the way they do, the better able we'll be at knowing when and how to respond.

SIMPLICITY ON THE OTHER SIDE OF COMPLEXITY

Our end goal as parents is simple: to raise kids who live, love, and lead well. And both research and the Bible confirm the means to the end is also simple: be emotionally safe. What's left are two questions that add a bit of complexity: How do we become emotionally safe? How does emotional safety produce such successful kids?

> Simply put, an emotionally safe home breeds secure children, and secure children develop the brain functions necessary for successful living.

We've already answered the first question. Becoming emotionally safe is a reflection of how secure we are as parents, and how secure we are as parents is a reflection of our own story. Some of us were raised in secure homes and therefore have the relational DNA to raise kids in an emotionally safe environment from the start. Others of us may have broken stories that need to be put into a more coherent narrative to help us understand why we think, feel, and act the way we do toward our children. As neuroscience researcher Daniel Siegel wrote, "A coherent narrative in a parent is the most robust predictor of a child's attachment to that parent."[10]

The second question—How does emotional safety produce such successful kids?—is the focus of the next few chapters. First, research shows that kids who grow up in an emotionally safe home develop secure attachments. Second, eight of the nine functions of the middle prefrontal cortex of the brain, right behind the eyes, are outcomes of being securely attached. These functions, in addition to those of the prefrontal cortex, are the basis for what kids need to live, love, and lead well. Simply put, an emotionally safe home breeds secure children, and secure children develop the brain functions necessary for successful living.

PRAISING THE STRUGGLE

Our son Landon loves wooden puzzles on which he can match the shapes of animals with their corresponding picture. If you're a new parent, you will have no less than ten of these puzzles by your child's first birthday. They are a gift-giving favorite. However, most children are not developmentally able to put these puzzles together by twelve months of age. One of my favorite activities with one-year-old Landon was watching him progress at learning how to match the animals with the puzzle pieces. At first, he was frustrated when the shapes did not line up. Instead of working to make them fit he would simply throw them across the room and scream.

Ah, the joys of parenting a toddler.

Christi and I decided to work with him to help him learn how to handle the frustration, not by throwing the pieces and informing the neighbors of his displeasure, but by trying a new piece and then coming back to the one he was struggling with later on. Sometimes this worked. But at other times, *I* wanted to throw the pieces across the room and inform our neighbors of my displeasure. But our perseverance—and parental self-control—paid off. A few months later, Landon was mastering every puzzle he had.

Was it exhausting for us? Yes. Did we just want to do it for him? We actually did more often than not early on. However, we knew in order for Landon to learn how to complete the puzzles without losing his cool, we had to balance our support for him while allowing him to experience the challenge. True growth—whether it's with our athletic ability, muscle mass, musical talent, or frustration tolerance—is a matter of being pushed outside our comfort zone, yet not too far that we feel like failures. Our kids need us to support them, but they also need us to push them. No matter our child's age, we must view each of our children on a continuum of support and challenge, knowing when and how much support to offer, yet allowing our kids to experience the challenge without being overwhelmed. I call this *praising the struggle*.

Research shows that we too often praise our children over global behaviors. Seeing our daughter Kennedy run through the backyard as a toddler gets me excited as her dad. But proceeding to tell her she's the fastest runner on the planet at her age is actually setting her up for failure. Too often we praise the easy traits in our kids—how smart, fast, athletic, or talented they are. But when they go to do it again, they tend to shy away from it because they fear they won't be as good the next time around. On the other hand, stepping into the struggle and giving them support along the way takes away the power of making them feel as though they need to be smarter, faster, and better every time they do something and instead sets them up for future success. Praising the struggles in our kids actually builds their brain and gives them the confidence they need to attempt difficult tasks and take risks.[11]

Maintaining this balance of support and challenge over time is important. Support your kids without challenging them, and they're likely to be living in your basement and still on your health insurance when they're twenty-six years old. Challenge them and offer no support, and you may have a twenty-six-year-old who is doing well on his own but probably doesn't talk to you.

On the one hand, knowing when and how to push our kids and, on the other, offering them support can be done by clearly understanding the four walls of a Safe House. Doing so also takes into consideration each child's age, developmental level, temperament, and skill level, all of which we'll discuss further throughout the next four chapters as we learn to balance the four walls of an emotionally safe home.

══ Coauthoring Your Child's Story ══

1. Using the example of the dad and the daughter who wanted to go to the football game, which parenting posture would be your tendency?
2. What are some ways you can begin to better seek the motivation of your kids' actions?
3. Go back and read each of the temperaments. Write down your child's unique temperaments.

4. Reread the executive skills. Which skills do each of your children most need to build?

5. How did doing these exercises and reading this chapter help you see your child differently? How will it change the way you respond to them in their most stressful moments?

Explore and Protect

A shaky child on a bicycle for the first time needs both support
and freedom. The realization that this is what the child will
always need can hit hard.

—Sloan Wilson

don't give my bicycle enough credit for who I am today. My first bicycle was my gateway to freedom. I explored places all six-year-olds should be allowed to go. I traveled as far as *my imagination*—and backyard—would take me.

In my inaugural BMX freestyle race, I landed my first major trick in front of a huge audience. The nervy feeling I had coming down out of midair from the one-foot jump off the sidewalk quickly turned to feelings of exhilaration as both wheels landed safely on the pavement. I imagined my parents were anxious but proud.

Landing these tricks made me famous at an early age and allowed me to travel. I biked beaches, mountains, and beautiful countryside. If I wanted to go on an adventure, my imagination took me there.

There was beauty in the freedom I had on my bicycle . . . until the day I realized how limited I was. *If I could just go beyond my backyard,* I thought, *I could do new tricks and actually explore new places. Real places.*

So I did.

Since we lived in town, there was an alley that ran behind our house and was an entryway to the garage at the bottom of our property. Across the alley from our garage was a two-foot drop from the road into a neighbor's yard. Our sloped backyard from the house to the alley created the perfect hill to pick up speed, race past the garage, zoom through the alley, and jump my bike into the yard below.

I'll never forget the day I tried it and nearly died. Though rarely traveled, cars *did* actually use that alley. With the garage situated where it was, it was nearly impossible to see an oncoming car before my tire hit the roadway. At six years old, I didn't think about that. I just went for it.

I can only recall two details after that: (1) staring directly into the grill of the car as we both came to a screeching halt and (2) the frantic feeling of not wanting my parents to find out what I had done. To this day, I think the latter remains true.

The squealing tires, deafening horn, and terrified knot in my stomach were lessons enough for me that day. Though not able to verbalize it until years later, I learned I was freer to explore within the confines of my backyard than outside of it.

The invisible walls of protection my parents put in place were there to set me free—to become a BMX champion, to bike around the world, and imagine. Not until I tried to explore beyond those walls did I become unsafe.

Perhaps these are the reasons we overprotect our kids. We don't want them to learn the hard way. Especially not *that* hard.

So we close off the backyard altogether—their creativity, imagination, ability to wander, to explore, to discover who they are.

Or maybe we think it best for our kids to learn the hard way, like I did that day. So we give them free reign beyond the backyard, allowing them to find their own way, at times terrified, staring into the grill of life, but with no one to tell, nobody safe to protect them.

As we discuss the walls of a Safe House over the next two chapters, keep in mind the four parent types I will describe are *tendencies* each of us, more or less, parent from (Helicopter Parent, BFF Parent, Religious Parent, and Boss Parent). Though more fully explained in chapter 6 in light of all four walls, each tendency will be briefly introduced in this chapter as it relates to protection and exploration. As you look at the grid, take the Safe House Parenting Assessment at the end of this chapter to get a general picture of your parenting tendency.

Keep in mind a Safe House Parent, the fifth and healthiest of the parent types, builds and levels all four walls over time. That is our goal.

THE EXPLORATION-PROTECTION CONTINUUM

Finding Nemo is a family favorite. As a father of two, I can readily identify with Marlin's heartfelt promise to Nemo: "Daddy's got you. I promise, I will never let anything happen to you."

I've often thought about the responsibility of being a parent in those early, quiet nights of rocking Landon to sleep shortly after he was born. How 100 percent dependent this little boy was on us for everything. As he became a toddler I wanted to protect his innocence. I still do. I don't want other kids taking his toys, pushing him, or excluding him from play. I don't want him feeling rejected, alone, or embarrassed.

For many of us, those first moments of becoming a parent are riddled with a strange mix of love, excitement, and, yes, fear. Our minds begin playing the movie that seems to never quit—the clips of everything that could go wrong. From upset tummies to double ear infections, from being bullied to teenage heartbreak, from skinned knees to a face-to-face meeting with the grill of a car, we want to protect our children from every hard and painful experience we had growing up.

But as heroic as it sounds, it's impossible. I love Dory's challenge to Marlin's parenting approach: "Hmm. That's a funny thing to promise. . . . You can't never let anything happen to him. Then nothing would ever happen to him. Not much fun for little Harpo."

We cannot rob our children from the proficiency of painful moments. The more we embrace the undesirable emotions of human experience, the more we appreciate and fully participate in the desirable ones. To allow our children to feel—to genuinely experience emotion at its absolute best, at its absolute worst, and at every level in between—is to raise children sensitive and responsive to the world around them.

> Overprotected children are robbed of the opportunity to develop healthy individuality and self-confidence.

We must let our children live.

As we reflect on our parenting tendencies, we need to consider how well we balance the walls of exploration and protection. Simply put, *exploration* is giving our child age-appropriate freedom to discover and interact with her world. In contrast, *protection* is ensuring her safety by stepping in to intervene when necessary and being a consistent, loving presence for her to come back to as home base. Striking a balance on the exploration-protection continuum is critically important to a child's emotional, psychological, and spiritual development.

How well we do this is largely dependent on our own reconciled story.

Many of us tend to err on the side of overparenting. Piling bricks on the wall of protection, we, like Marlin, are determined that nothing negative will happen to our kids (perhaps because something damaging or traumatic *did* happen to us growing up). We may find ourselves running to the rescue of our toddler every time she trips over a toy, being too helpful to our kids with homework (that is, giving them the answers), or going to bat with the parent of our child's friend rather than letting the youngsters work out their disagreement.

Overprotected children are robbed of the opportunity to develop healthy individuality and self-confidence because they are given few opportunities to tackle challenges and problem solve. Overprotecting can actually hurt kids in the long run because we offer them little to no challenge.[1]

Some of us swing to the opposite extreme of giving our kids too much freedom—known as laissez-faire parenting. The French word means "to let people do as they please." Parenting from this posture often means neglecting the wall of protection altogether and running the risk of overwhelming our children with life's challenges too early for their emotional and age-appropriate development.

For instance, whenever we look to our children for affirmation and equate their happiness with our perceived success as a parent, we're likely to neglect the wall of protection. We may want to be our child's best friend. We want them to fully enjoy their childhood, to live free and uninhibited. It sounds good in theory but not in reality.

> A Safe House isn't about parenting perfectly. It's about knowing your own story so you can move from parenting reactively to parenting proactively.

Without healthy and age-appropriate boundaries, our children may be exposed to any number of damaging influences, not the least of which is an addiction to technology, pornography, or drugs. Worse yet, we miss critical opportunities to actively shape their brain and emotional development. In the pursuit of letting them learn on their own, we abdicate our responsibility to emotionally mold the man or woman they are becoming.

As you're reading these words, you may wonder, *What if I already messed up?*

Remember, a Safe House isn't about parenting perfectly. It's about knowing your own story so you can move from parenting reactively to parenting proactively.

Also, it's about knowing and tuning in with your child in the moment. If only it were as simple as putting the bricks of these two walls in place and moving on. The reality is that in each situation, our child's needs may be quite different. Knowing our own story and subsequent parenting tendencies opens our eyes to the uniqueness of our children and how much protection and exploration they need for their age, tempera-ment, and developmental level.

> How can I be emotionally safe for her right now, offering unconditional support, while empowering her to make age-appropriate decisions and experience the consequences for herself?

When a child feels loved and supported un-conditionally, he develops confidence and curios-ity to explore the captivating world around him. But in the exploring, there are dangers he will inevitably encounter. And that's when it's critical for our child to know that as his parent, we will be there. Not with words of criticism, shame, or embarrassment, but with a loving presence that helps him calm down and assists him in learning to problem solve through the dangers.

No matter what moment we find ourselves in, whether our infant isn't sleeping at night, our toddler just ate ashes out of the fireplace, our middle schooler is asking to go on a date, or our high schooler is failing precalculus, there's one question we can come back to:

How can I be emotionally safe for her right now, offering unconditional support, while empowering her to make age-appropriate decisions and experience the consequences for herself?

THREE WAYS WE PARENT FROM FEAR

When we build or demolish one wall of a Safe House at the expense of another, more likely it stems from a breach in our own story. To be emotionally present with our child is to be aware of our own fears.

Driven by punishment and performance, fear exiles love, as we've talked about be-fore. It complicates emotional security and connection, resulting in a not-so-safe house. So what are the primary ways we parent out of fear?

Bullying. In an attempt to get our child's attention and redirect his behavior, it can be all too easy to use criticism, shame, blame, ridicule, and other forms of verbal attack. We may justify it as toughening him up for the real world or say, "That's how my parents raised me, and I turned out okay," but the reality is that we are wounding our child's heart. Underneath our anger, fear is often at the root. Though you may never physically touch your child in anger, the damage of verbal and emotional abuse leaves bruises that can last a lifetime. As parents we're supposed to be the source of comfort and safety for our children. When we're also the source of pain, our children grow up in a constant state of anxiety, never knowing whether they'll be loved or ridiculed. There is nothing more detrimental to brain growth than living in a continuously anxious state with no safe person to turn to.

Perfectionism. Comparing ourselves to other parents' Instagramming their gluten-free gourmet meals, picture-perfect kids, and awesome vacations can leave us feeling like a lower-class parent. Besides, who posts pictures of morning meltdowns and spilled milk? As we highlight the opposite, we communicate to our kids that they are not allowed to be imperfect, flawed human beings who make mistakes. They become primarily concerned with doing right as opposed to engaging in the messy process of exploration, learning, and growth. Trying to keep up with the Joneses is not only exhausting; it can be incredibly harmful to raising kids who live, love, and lead well.

Parental Agendas. Here's another way to pile more bricks on the wall of protection. We each carry a unique set of worries and fears with us as we parent our kids. We worry they'll flunk out of school, never get married, or end up working an entry-level position the rest of their lives. We obsess over the fact they're too forgetful or too bossy or that they won't turn out smart enough. We want them to follow in our footsteps as a high school quarterback or basketball star. We not-so-subtly let them know they *will* be carrying on the family business or following the family's line of work. These parental agendas render us unsafe for our kids when the preoccupation with our agenda overwhelms our ability to be present with *their* emotions, passions, and dreams.

In order for our children's brain to grow and flourish, we must be proactive about creating a culture of love without fear within our home.

Take a few minutes to reflect on and write down your response to these questions:

- How does fear reveal itself in how I parent? Is it through criticism and anger? Perfectionism? Something else?
- What parental agendas am I putting on my child?
- What am I most afraid of happening to her?

Write down and label your insecurities—and no, you're not crazy for feeling this way. You're just human, like me.

The Lopsided House of Overprotection

We really mean well. We really want our kids to succeed. But sometimes our best efforts can be misguided, ineffective, and even counterproductive.

Parents with the tendency to overprotect intercept life's dangers and challenges in one of two ways: rescuing their kids from consequences by coddling them (Helicopter Parent) or shaming them when they encounter these dangers (Religious Parent). Our tendency to overprotect in these ways makes us emotionally unsafe, either rescuing our kids from feeling negative emotions (Helicopter Parent) or punishing our kids for them (Religious Parent). Keep in mind, as I refer to the Religious Parent, I'm referring to any belief system where a parent religiously instills rules, even unrealistic ones, to "protect" their kids. If the child doesn't comply, he is shamed.

The Helicopter Parent sits in the backyard with the child to ensure he never comes face-to-face with the grill of a car or attempts BMX-style stunts at all.

The Religious Parent overprotects by shaming the child for not obeying the rules. Rather than using the very encounter of the grill of a car itself as a lesson, this parent ignores the child's feelings or further shames him about the incident and instead punishes him, taking the bike away for a month.

Overprotective parents, particularly Helicopter Parents, are pros at responding to their child's needs; however, they often expect too little from their kids (all support, no challenge). They are hyperengaged but often coddled:

> These parents are highly responsive to the perceived needs and issues of their
> children, and don't give their children the chance to solve their own problems.
> These parents "rush to school at the whim of a phone call from their child
> to deliver items such as forgotten lunches, forgotten assignments, forgotten
> uniforms" and "demand [that teachers give] better grades on the final semester
> reports or threaten withdrawal from school."[2]

Such behaviors may create happier kids in the moment, but it neglects brain growth in the long run. When we overprotect children from natural life consequences (Helicopter Parent), they expect life to be easy and miss important opportunities to learn from their failures. When we punish or shame children for failing and subsequently set more boundaries (Religious Parent), they learn *they are* failures. Either way, if our wall of protection is too high, our kids are likely to become powerless and helpless, unable to assert themselves, say no, problem solve, or survive failure. Children who grow up in a home with a larger-than-life wall of protection are "destined to an anxious adulthood, lacking the emotional resources they will need to cope with inevitable setback and failure."[3]

When we parent from this posture, our kids often feel squelched and choked. Though we are attempting to love them as best we know how, our kids (progressively and subtly) hear the anxiety-producing message: You can't do it on your own. Left to yourself, you'll mess it up.

Instead, we need to teach them that, as John Townsend teaches in one of his *Solutions* series, "The hard way is the right way." It is our responsibility as parents to help children build self-confidence, determination, and resiliency so they can tackle and overcome failures, not believe they are one. The only way for kids to develop these skills is to face hardship, know we will be there to support and cheer them on (support), but not rescue them from or punish them because of life's natural consequences (challenge).

FROM OVERPROTECTION TO HEALTHY EXPLORATION

We can only loosen our grip on overprotecting when we understand God's heart and design for our child. "Train up a child in the way he should go; even when he is old he will not depart from it."[4] Notice the verse emphasizes the way *each child* should go, not the way *we* want them to go.

As parents, we can easily become consumed with who we *don't* want our kids to become that we neglect who they *are*. Without realizing it, we shame and pressure our kids to become who we want them to be. Yet shame should never be used as a motivator for guiding our kids.

It's a subtle disposition that's very easy to fall into.

Seeking to know our child's heart is a matter of taking time to affirm her strengths and listen to her dreams.

My friend Frank is a fantastic example of this. His daughter, Juliana, a high school freshman, confided in him how much she hated school and was dreading going back after the Thanksgiving break. Rather than lecture her about the importance of education, Frank applied Proverbs 22:6 to begin identifying and building up Juliana's strengths.

Frank reflected how much of a people person his daughter is. "Honey, instead of focusing on what you hate about school, how about you begin focusing on what you love? I know you love making people laugh and bringing joy to others. You do it better than anybody I know. How might school be different if you make it your goal to bring joy to as many people as you can?"

Frank later told me, "I'd rather my daughter learn how to live out of her strengths and be in the pocket, not in a box. If I had to choose, I'd rather her bring home straight Cs from school but know she's living from her strength of bringing joy to others."

As a parent, can we say the same? How might your parental agendas be getting in the way of your kids exploring who they are?

Parental agendas and perfectionism are the biggest killers of healthy exploration. And I'm not just talking about school here—they begin at birth. As one researcher pointed out, "If your baby feels free to explore his environment, he will become more adept at showing you what he wants. When you put excessive limits on his experimentation, you will almost certainly run up against his wish to assert himself."[5]

When Landon started crawling, Christi and I quickly learned the importance (both for our sanity and Landon's survival) of babyproofing several rooms in our home by removing fragile objects, eliminating electrical hazards, and covering sharp corners. In these spaces, all bets are off—Landon could explore as much as he liked. By creating a safe space for him, we encouraged him to explore and discover his world rather than sitting and waiting to be entertained.

Research shows that, in general, kids' worlds today are far more structured than they've ever been.[6] And yet unstructured, child-directed play is gold for brain development:

> A baby who has lots of opportunity to poke into things doesn't feel more than
> momentarily aggrieved when some things are forbidden to him. Nor does he
> stop loving you when you remove dangerous objects from his grasp and tell
> him "No!" By providing a safe environment for your child you encourage him
> to show you, through his gestures and behaviors, how much he enjoys exploring
> his world.[7]

In addition to giving your kids safe spaces to explore, take at least twenty to thirty minutes each day to explore with them and celebrate what you discover together. This unstructured play is called Floor Time—uninterrupted, child-led play with one goal in mind: to peel back all our adultness and be led by our child.[8] If she wants to color, color with her. If she wants to play dolls, doctor, or go to the moon, go there with her. Resist the urge to criticize, redirect, or tell your child how or what to play. Hold back your desire to correct or teach. Instead, learn to just be present with your child and see the world through her eyes.

As we encourage our child to take the lead as we play, we're teaching her self-confidence and independence. We're raising kids who are more than robots, who know themselves and are able to verbalize what they want. (Chapter 8 outlines age-specific activities for Floor Time that target brain building.[9])

This kind of parent-child interaction is powerful and connecting. In contrast with much of the way we spend our time, it enables us to get to know our child's personality and gifts. One parent noted: "You learn almost nothing about your children from driving them to and picking them up from enrichment classes. You learn even less from sitting with your iPad in a quiet corner of an indoor playground you've taken your children to. . . . Children would far prefer spending time with their favourite people [parents] doing their favourite thing [namely, play]."[10]

The beauty of a Safe House is that as we take time to be present with our child and let him rule in his world of play, we "should then feel perfectly free to set limits in other areas of his life. Because he is increasingly focused on the exciting outside world and wants to do so many things, your child can sometimes overstimulate himself. He may become overwrought and disorganized, and will need your help in calming himself down."[11]

As our child grows older, the principles of Floor Time extend into various life activities. Encourage your child to explore by making breakfast, doing yard work, or trying out a new hobby. But catch yourself. Don't shame and correct her if she doesn't do it the way *you* would as an adult. Though she may not verbalize it, your little girl longs to say, "Hey, Mom, it hurts my feelings when you make fun of the way I cook eggs."

Your little boy's beaming smile at having mowed the lawn for the first time can quickly be squelched by your well-intended criticism. Most likely, he'll shut down emotionally and say nothing, but his heart is crying out, "Hey, Dad, I feel inadequate when you tell me what I mowed wasn't good enough."

My mom, as I grew older, became really good at building self-confidence. Some of my favorite memories are when she would take off work and we'd go fishing—just the two of us—taking the boat around deserted islands and exploring for treasures washed ashore. As I grew into my teen years, she and my stepdad began to entrust me with more responsibility, refurbishing a boat together and even using a chainsaw to cut firewood.

What's the balance between unrealistically expecting our kids to be perfect and letting them off too easy? If effort is there as a toddler, and your child messes up, give him an A for effort and help him do it the next time. The older our children get, however, the more we must consider their quality of work. We cannot reward expected behavior every time, or our kids will be expecting an A simply for submitting a paper in college or a raise just for going to work on time. Again, our goal is to equip them to function competently in the real world, moving them from complete dependence as an infant to full independence as an adult.

One of the areas we tend to overprotect is by shielding our kids from consequences. How do we allow for healthy exploration in this area? If your son comes home from school and refuses to do his homework that night, don't do it for him. Allow him to experience the consequence. But don't punish him either. Allow your disappointment in him to be discipline enough. The more positive and fun environment we create with our kids, the easier it is to discipline them through the rupture in the relationship.[12]

Here are some practical ways to build the wall of exploration in your day-to-day life:

- Let your kids experience natural consequences. Allow discipline to be the felt distance of the relationship that you have with your kids and keep it as natural as possible. Don't jump quickly to rescue them. Be present with your kids when they're overwhelmed and teach them to problem solve in the midst of feeling strong emotions.
- Resist the pressure to always entertain your kids. Research shows that kids with less structured play (that is, free play, drawing, reading, playing outside) and who have time alone to explore are better at setting and achieving goals.[13] Unstructured play helps build the executive functions of the brain more so than structured, adult supervised play. Instead, spend twenty to thirty minutes each day entering your child's world of play with no agenda.
- Don't do for your children what they can do for themselves. As soon as our kids understood how to do something, we always asked them to do it (getting a diaper, brushing their teeth, throwing away trash, putting on their own clothes, and so on).

Figure 5.1. The differentiating walls of protection and exploration and the messages our kids receive based on these parenting tendencies.

THE LOPSIDED HOUSE OF OVER-EXPLORATION

What could possibly be wrong with exploration? Some of us, particularly those who came from overprotective homes, have decided to dynamite the wall of protection altogether and instead allow uninhibited exploration. We may sincerely call it love, but in reality our behavior is sincerely ignorant.

The world is not a safe place, but our kids don't grasp that at two, three, or five years old. Appropriate boundaries and rules provide safety, structure, and guidance as kids learn to develop discernment about who is and isn't safe. Without the wall of protection, our child will live at the whim of her emotions and surroundings. The end result is chaos at best and, quite possibly, situations of serious danger at worst.

A high wall of exploration, to the neglect of protection, presents itself with two parenting tendencies: the BFF and the Boss.

First, in laissez-faire parenting, the BFF Parent hesitates to tell the child no or redirect her at all. We may argue that doing so would squelch her personality, creativity, or uniqueness. So we comply with our child's demands, even when they are unreasonable or downright unhealthy. While this might result in a happier trip to the grocery store or a stress-free weekend, we're teaching our children that the world revolves around them.

Second, we may allow our children to spend time with whomever they want and perhaps whenever they want, failing to protect who influences them. The laissez-faire parent of a teenager may even provide alcohol on the weekend because, as one parent described to me, "At least I know where my child is when he's drinking." Never mind the other lives he's putting in danger.

Technology is another factor to be aware of. No wise parent would place a full-service bar in a kids' bedroom. Yet we will put a full-service search engine on a device in our kids' bedrooms with unprotected Internet access, and in less than a half a second they can have access to the most grotesque images anyone can imagine.

One pediatrician commented, "I guarantee you that if you have a 14-year-old boy and he has an Internet connection in his bedroom, he is looking at pornography."[14]

In spite of our well-meaning desire to be best friends with our child and give them the freedom to "be themselves," without appropriate structure—allowing them to eat, brush their teeth, and go to bed whenever they want to—we are not preparing them to function in a world with rules, expectations, and consequences. Initially, children may enjoy the freedoms parents provide. Over time, however, children become exposed to dangers earlier than they should for their age (that is, allowing a toddler to play unsupervised with older children, a child hanging out at the park after school on his own, a middle schooler allowed to play adult-rated video games), with outcomes neither the parent nor the child realizes are actually harmful.

When something bad happens, however, the BFF Parent, in a seeming contradiction, overprotects her child from experiencing the negative emotion of life's realities. Instead of using the moments to build her child's brain, the BFF Parent is quick to blame the world for the child's problems. If he punches another kindergarten peer in the face during playtime and is reprimanded by the school, it's not his behavior that's in question; it's the other child's actions and the way the teacher handled it. If she gets pregnant at sixteen, it's not because Mom allowed her boyfriend to begin sleeping over when she was fifteen; it's because the condom broke.

The BFF Parent, in returning to the biking illustration I used to open the chapter, allows the child to bike wherever he wants to through town because the backyard might limit his creativity or who he is to become. When he meets the grill of the car in the alley, this parent is writing down every detail the child can remember about the car to hunt down the man or woman who dared drive on that alley while her son was riding his bike.

Despite giving kids excessive freedom—and perhaps even toys, clothes, or material possessions—to keep them happy or "find themselves," many laissez-faire parents actually tend to be emotionally absent, or eventually agitated. Inconsistent or no rules can easily lead to a parent who walks on eggshells around a child who believes the world revolves around him.

In fact, research shows parents who allow high exploration to the neglect of protection raise kids more likely to be impulsive, disobedient, rebellious, demanding, and dependent on adults. When they become teenagers they show poor self-control, poor school performance, and a high rate of drug use.[15]

On the other extreme, some parents neglect the wall of protection by parenting from the motto "They just have to learn the hard way" (the Boss). These parents have rules but an unrealistic expectation that their kids will obey them, and therefore they offer little to no emotional support when they fail. Often these parents expect their children to follow limits or do tasks that are not age-appropriate for their development. If they do not adhere to the rule or perform the task to the liking of the parent (often the first time or with little preparation), they are shamed or ridiculed. Failing becomes synonymous with being a failure. These parents sincerely believe they're preparing their children for life's challenges, yet the kids hear the shaming message: You have to do it on your own because you need to learn the hard way. You're not adequate until you figure it out.

The Boss Parent allows his child to ride bikes, perhaps even bigger than he can handle for his age. But when he meets the grill of the car he hears, "What were you thinking? You know the rules. Follow them. Do you need me to teach you again how to ride a bike? You're lucky you didn't get hit."

As our children grow, they will learn all too soon about injustice and the existence of evil. They will have to navigate, hopefully with our help, the pain of being betrayed by a friend, the disappointment of not making the team, the emotional injury of a breakup. We can't protect them from these realities of life, but we can be *with them* in these moments.

FROM OVER-EXPLORATION TO HEALTHY PROTECTION

Moving our children from full dependence to increased independence over time is a function of offering our support through the challenges our kids face. Like working out in the weight room, our muscles need to be challenged for them to grow. But if we challenge them too much, the muscles, without the support to fully recover, become overwhelmed and ultimately fail us. The balance of support and challenge is as critical to our kids' brain growth as is our muscle growth.

> The goal of parenting isn't protecting children from stress. *It's to prepare them to handle stress* by giving them confidence and security based on consistent love. Children don't grow healthy and strong if they aren't allowed to experiment and explore the world they live in, which necessarily involves successes and failures. *Times of threat, however, are the most crucial moments in the relationship.* It is then that the child cries for help and realizes whether the parents are there to respond.[16]

Moving away from over-exploration is a matter of remaining consistent in offering protection to our children, both in setting limits and being emotionally present when our kids explore too far. The younger our children are, the more protective limits we need to set physically in our home—removing hazards, not allowing our children to run into the street, feeding them well, and so on. Over time, protective limits move from physical dangers to relational ones—knowing who your kids' friends are, setting appropriate curfews, dealing with authority figures, and navigating the dating scene.

Balancing the walls of exploration and protection is a nuanced process. Parenting well necessitates we take time to discern what our child needs in the moment—freedom, protection, or both. Sometimes this is a messy process of trying something and readjusting.

In every parenting situation, we must keep our long-term goal in mind: not ultimately to raise *kids* (unless you want them living with you for the rest of your life), but to raise adults who are equipped to live, love, and lead well long after we're gone.

Here are some practical ways you can build the wall of protection in your day-to-day life:

- *Be involved and talk to your kids about their lives.* Knowing what's going on with our kids, who their friends are, where they're hanging out, or what their interests are equips us to provide appropriate protection when needed. That said, knowing who our kids' friends are is absolutely necessary. Friends can radically alter who our kids become. "Bad company corrupts good character."[17] Or put another way, you are who you spend your time with.

- *Give up your need to be your child's best friend.* You're the parent. In order to protect our children, we have to do some things they won't like at times. Use the problem-solving strategies in chapter 9 to help your children understand why you're protecting them the way you are.

- *Put technology boundaries in place.* I'm not an advocate of sleepovers primarily for this reason. Addiction to pornography begins with those first few unsupervised visits to a website. To protect the eyes, mind, and soul of our children (and ours too), we must unapologetically set limits on and protect our kids' use of technology. Use technology to strengthen, not run from, family relationships.

BRICK BY BRICK, ENJOY THE CONSTRUCTION

Parenting is hard enough without trying to be perfect or force our kids into a mold of who we want them to be. Even without these internal insecurities, we have external pressures that can exhaust us to the point of feeling like we're missing the moments.

The beauty of a Safe House is that it helps us simplify our lives. When we move from techniques to a new way of being with our child, we're free to be present and make memories with our kids. In addition to the already mentioned strategies throughout the chapter, I want to add practical, easy, and refreshing ways to incorporate exploration and protection into your Safe House.

Besides, brick by brick, we're constructing a beautiful soul.

Create More Fun and Laughter
Roughhouse. Play in the dirt. Dance and sing. My way of dealing with perfectionism is to be okay with getting sweaty, sticky, and dirty. If Landon comes to me, even after he's

had a bath and is ready for bed, and says, "Wrestle bed, Dad, wrestle bed," you can believe we're going to get sweaty. Sometimes I may have to bathe him again. Or maybe he wants to scale the wall in the backyard. I hate seeing him fall and get skinned knees. But more than hating the sight of his blood, I hate missing any moments of exploring with my kids.

> The beauty of a Safe House is that it helps us simplify our lives. When we move from techniques to a new way of being with our child, we're free to be present and make memories with our kids.

Spend a Minimum of Twenty Minutes of Command-Free Playtime per Day with Your Children

That means they're guiding and leading the play. You're not saying, "Well, let's do this, Johnny." Just dive in. If they want you to be a nurse, be a nurse. If they want you to jump on the bed, jump on the bed. For extra fun, play the part of the monkey. Join your children. Enter their world. It builds the brain and the hearts of our kids and connects us with them even more.

If Your Kids Ask You to Do Something, Before Saying No, Ask Yourself "Why Not?"

If you can't come up with a legitimate answer, let the memory unfold and enjoy the moment with them. Our children hear the word *no* from us more than any other word. *No* keeps them safe, but *no* can also squelch the healthy sense of exploration we're trying to nurture and develop. Put away your perfectionism and parental agenda and explore.[18]

Say No to Technology at Meals

Instead, talk about the day. Ask questions. Whether you're at a restaurant, a formal sit-down dinner, or breakfast at home, and even if people are up and down, try to eliminate technology at any table. We did this in our home and it has been more freeing than we imagined. Instead of checking your phone, tell stories of your family history. Talk to your kids about how their grandparents met one another or about the day they were born. Teach your kids lessons about what you've enjoyed and experienced in life. Ask them questions about their day and their feelings. Use feeling words as you tell stories and talk about your day as well.

These are just a few of the endless ways you can balance exploration and protection as you build your Safe House. Spend a few minutes this week talking with your spouse about ways you can actively begin building these walls together.

We can't just physically protect our kids. The outcomes we most desire happen when we protect their hearts and souls.

Talk to your child when she's a toddler, and she'll talk to you when she's a teenager.

Validate her feelings when she's scared, and she'll comfort others when she's strong.

Win your child's heart, and you'll influence her behavior.

Influence her behavior, and you become the acclaimed coauthor of a beautifully written narrative that will inspire generations to come.

━━━━ Coauthoring Your Child's Story ━━━━

1. Take the Safe House Parenting Assessment that starts on the next page. What is your parenting tendency? How strong is it? Do you agree or disagree with this tendency? Why or why not?
2. How does fear reveal itself in how you parent? Through criticism and anger? perfectionism? something else?
3. What parental agendas are you putting on your child?
4. What are you most afraid of happening to her? Write down and label your insecurities.

Safe House Parenting Assessment

I bet you're already trying to figure out your parenting tendency. Here's an opportunity to find out. For each of the following questions, circle the answer (0=Rarely True; 1=Sometimes True; 2=True Most of the Time) that *best* describes your parenting approach. Not all items are age-specific, so answer each question based on how you parent or how you believe you would, given the situation.

1. I do my best to help my child feel extra special, especially when she's treated unfairly. She deserves accolades.

   0 (Rarely True)   1 (Sometimes True)   2 (True Most of the Time)

2. I have set very clear rules for our house. No matter the circumstance, I expect my child to consistently obey and respect me without question or negotiation.

   0 (Rarely True)   1 (Sometimes True)   2 (True Most of the Time)

3. I have a hard time telling my child no, because I want him to be happy and I could never do anything to squelch his creativity or personality.

   0 (Rarely True)   1 (Sometimes True)   2 (True Most of the Time)

4. I try to toughen up my child for the real world by not coddling him. The school of hard knocks is the best preparation for adulthood.

   0 (Rarely True)   1 (Sometimes True)   2 (True Most of the Time)

5. My child knows I love and accept her unconditionally, regardless of her behavior.

   0 (Rarely True)   1 (Sometimes True)   2 (True Most of the Time)

6. I have a hard time letting my child experience natural consequences and often find myself jumping to rescue him.

   0 (Rarely True)   1 (Sometimes True)   2 (True Most of the Time)

7. I think my child's fear of making Mom or Dad mad is a powerful motivator for good behavior.

   0 (Rarely True)   1 (Sometimes True)   2 (True Most of the Time)

8. I'm not big on rules; relationship is way more important in my mind. I want to be my child's best friend and help him find his own way.

   0 (Rarely True)   1 (Sometimes True)   2 (True Most of the Time)

9. I expect my child to learn and value the truths of life the first time around. I have little patience for revisiting a lesson we've already gone over once.

       0 (Rarely True)   1 (Sometimes True)   2 (True Most of the Time)

10. I dialogue with my child to understand his point of view and consider the intent behind his behavior. I involve my child in finding a solution whenever I can.

        0 (Rarely True)   1 (Sometimes True)   2 (True Most of the Time)

11. I am a very involved parent and feel a lot of pressure to entertain my child and make sure she is happy and having a good time.

        0 (Rarely True)   1 (Sometimes True)   2 (True Most of the Time)

12. I do not tolerate bad attitudes. My child knows better than to be grumpy, sad, or upset.

        0 (Rarely True)   1 (Sometimes True)   2 (True Most of the Time)

13. My child is amazing and wonderful, and I trust her to make the right decisions for herself with little to no boundaries or rules to consider.

        0 (Rarely True)   1 (Sometimes True)   2 (True Most of the Time)

14. It is critical that my child learns to be independent and figure things out on his own from an early age, rather than relying on me or anyone else.

        0 (Rarely True)   1 (Sometimes True)   2 (True Most of the Time)

15. I affirm and accept my child's emotions (including difficult feelings like sadness and anger) but also set clear boundaries for her behavior (that is, no hitting, no name calling, curfew, limits on technology, and so on).

        0 (Rarely True)   1 (Sometimes True)   2 (True Most of the Time)

16. I'm afraid of giving my child too much freedom to play alone or out of my sight. He needs me there to take care of him and make sure he is safe.

        0 (Rarely True)   1 (Sometimes True)   2 (True Most of the Time)

17. I am confident my child cannot be trusted to make good decisions for herself.

        0 (Rarely True)   1 (Sometimes True)   2 (True Most of the Time)

18. I tend to overindulge and give in to my child's demands (buying what he wants at the store, letting him stay up until whenever he would like) to show him how much I love him.

    0 (Rarely True)   1 (Sometimes True)   2 (True Most of the Time)

19. I have found shame, guilt, and threats to be effective ways to get my child back in line when she misbehaves or makes a mistake.

    0 (Rarely True)   1 (Sometimes True)   2 (True Most of the Time)

20. I allow my child to explore and experience the natural consequences of his behavior as much as possible without rescuing him.

    0 (Rarely True)   1 (Sometimes True)   2 (True Most of the Time)

21. When my child makes a mistake or disobeys, it is most likely explainable by some outside factor. Rarely is she to blame.

    0 (Rarely True)   1 (Sometimes True)   2 (True Most of the Time)

22. I take very seriously my responsibility to protect my child, even if he hates me for it and complains I never let him have fun.

    0 (Rarely True)   1 (Sometimes True)   2 (True Most of the Time)

23. I allow my child to freely explore who she is, what she likes, what kind of people she enjoys most being with, and so on, with little to no supervision. If she gets into trouble, I'll rescue her.

    0 (Rarely True)   1 (Sometimes True)   2 (True Most of the Time)

24. I often don't have too much patience for my child's emotions, telling him to get over it and move on.

    0 (Rarely True)   1 (Sometimes True)   2 (True Most of the Time)

25. I take time each day to play with and listen to my child. I do my best to know who her friends are, what her passions are, what bothers her, and so on.

    0 (Rarely True)   1 (Sometimes True)   2 (True Most of the Time)

26. I quickly take up a fight (with teachers, coaches, other parents, and so on) to prove my child is in the right or to protect him.

    0 (Rarely True)   1 (Sometimes True)   2 (True Most of the Time)

27. I am horrified by the evil I see in this world and see the main goal of parenting as protecting my child from its corruption.

    0 (Rarely True)   1 (Sometimes True)   2 (True Most of the Time)

28. I tend to keep the peace at home by overlooking and smoothing over my child's poor behavior.

    0 (Rarely True)   1 (Sometimes True)   2 (True Most of the Time)

29. I tend to be very critical of my child's failures and mistakes, and I make sure she *knows* it.

    0 (Rarely True)   1 (Sometimes True)   2 (True Most of the Time)

30. I try to calm myself down before responding to my child's misbehavior.

    0 (Rarely True)   1 (Sometimes True)   2 (True Most of the Time)

To identify your parenting tendencies, add the scores (0, 1, or 2) given to each item and follow the directions below.

Helicopter Parent
Add your scores for 1, 6, 11, 16, 21, and 26 and enter the total here:

Religious Parent
Add your scores for 2, 7, 12, 17, 22, and 27 and enter the total here:

BFF Parent
Add your scores for 3, 8, 13, 18, 23, and 28 and enter the total here:

Boss Parent
Add your scores for 4, 9, 14, 19, 24, and 29 and enter the total here:

Safe House Parent
Add your scores for 5, 10, 15, 20, 25, and 30 and enter the total here:

Note: Scores will range from 0 to 12 for each category. Compare your score with the list below:

    0–3: Not likely your parenting tendency

    4–7: Some parenting tendency

    8–12: Highly likely to be your primary parenting tendency

Grace and Truth

Grace lets a child know she is loved. Truth guides her on what to
do and become.

—Henry Cloud and John Townsend, *Raising Great Kids*

These two remaining walls of a Safe House, grace and truth, are defined by parenting
experts in a number of different ways: love and limits, relationship and rules, connection and correction. Like my mentors Henry Cloud and John Townsend, I choose to
use the terms *grace* and *truth* because, across the research and as I've noted from the
Bible, grace and truth go deeper than loving our children and setting limits.

For instance, the wall of truth may be using give, save, and spend jars with your
kids. When they do extra work around the house, they receive a payment. We teach our
kids to put into the give jar the first 10 percent they receive, guide them on a proper
amount to save, and have them place the remaining money in the spend jar to do whatever they want with it.

This goes beyond setting limits on behavior. They can choose to do the extra work.
They can choose to do with the money what they want. In doing so, we're teaching our
kids the truths of money management, hard work, giving back, saving money, and enjoying what's left over as a reward for their labor. That's how the real world works. Helping our children learn these realities helps wire their brains to become independent,
responsible adults.

As you read about these two walls, you'll begin to see how they intersect with the
walls of protection and exploration. Simply put, when our kids' exploration leads to
danger or challenge, they're likely to, in their anxiety and distress, turn to us for protection and support.

Sometimes they may recognize the danger (that is, being picked on at school, yelled
at by a coach, stung by a bee, wetting the bed) and simply turn to us to receive grace.

Other times they may not recognize the danger or misbehavior (that is, name calling, lying, posting inappropriate content online, not sharing) and will need a balance of both grace and truth.

Figure 6.1 outlines the parenting tendencies and corresponding messages our kids receive, introduced in the last chapter. Keep in mind, these are tendencies we have, more or less, and need to be aware of. A Safe House Parent knows her own story well, recognizes her tendencies, and balances all four walls over time. We'll expand on this grid throughout this chapter, implementing the walls of grace and truth.

Striking a balance on the grace-truth continuum is vitally important to raising emotionally healthy kids. As Cloud and Townsend wrote: "Grace establishes and maintains the quality of the relationship, and truth adds direction for the growth and structure of a child's [success]."[1]

Practically speaking, grace is unmerited favor and unconditional acceptance. Grace

Figure 6.1. The differentiating walls of protection and exploration and the messages our kids receive based on these parenting tendencies.

is communicating to our child that we love her, not for her good behavior but for who she is. Grace is bursting with pride, not because of her accomplishments but because she's ours. Grace is reassuring her of our love even when she is unlovable.

In the pursuit of keeping our children happy, many of us tend to err on the side of too much grace. Like Mrs. George in the movie *Mean Girls,* too much grace to the neglect of truth is common of the BFF Parent. Speaking to her daughter Regina, Mrs. George says sincerely: "I just want you to know, if you ever need anything, don't be shy, OK? There are NO rules in the house. I'm not like a 'regular' mom, I'm a 'cool' mom." Our tendency to overextend grace is often rooted in a desire for our kids to like us. After all, no parent wants to hear the words "I hate you" when we tell our thirteen-year-old she can't go on a date.

When we parent from this posture, our kids hear an overinflated message about who they are: *You are amazing. You are the center of the universe.* Though our intent may be to love them, letting our children walk blindly into damaging and harmful situations while we give them space to figure it out on their own is not true love. Sacrifice, selflessness, and emotion regulation are taught not by consistently overlooking misbehavior (BFF Parent) or rescuing our children from opportunities to learn from hardship (Helicopter Parent) but by gently coaching and redirecting them through the challenges.

Another way we tend to build a higher wall of grace is habitually giving in to our child's every request and whim, not because we're a pushover per se but simply because we're stressed or overworked. So rather than deal with the whining and pushback that often comes with telling our kids no, we choose grace to the neglect of truth.

Just opposite, the wall of truth lets our child know where we stand. Truth anchors our parenting so we are not tossed to and fro at the whim of our child's every wish or with every new parenting trend. Truth is setting limits. Truth is disciplining willful defiance. Truth is enforcing age-appropriate consequences so our children learn the connection between their decisions and their outcomes. Truth is being emotionally present in stressful moments. Truth is doing the right thing. Truth is hard work and responsibility. Truth is discernment when making decisions. Truth is living with integrity.

In a world that tells our kids "If it feels good do it" and "Create your own reality," truth is an incredible legacy to instill. By parenting from the posture of truth, we prepare our children to come to know the One who is Truth and who will guide their hearts and lives long after we're gone.

However, in pursuit of teaching our kids the hard way, some of us swing to the opposite extreme of truth with little to no grace. Think Captain von Trapp in *The Sound of Music*. "The first rule of this household is discipline," he informs Maria. When a thunderstorm scares the children, the captain harshly demands, "Did I or did I not say that bedtime is to be strictly observed in this household?" In his passion to enforce the rules, the captain neglects the terrified emotions of the kids.

What they need in the moment is reassurance, not discipline.

With good intent, we, too, can don the captain's hat. Perhaps in reaction to today's pop culture that fosters disrespect for authority, we want our children to know their place in our family. We expect perfection from our child. We use harsh discipline to enforce compliance with the rules. We demand an orderly home. We may publicly praise our kids' good behavior but neglect their emotional needs, never connecting with their hearts.

An all-truth wall with no grace is strictly performance-based. Whereas all-grace children develop an inflated view of self, all-truth children internalize the message: "You're not good enough. You're only as good as your last dance. Love and acceptance are conditional on your behavior." This ultimately puts our kids on a pathway toward perfectionism, anxiety, and depression.

Truth without grace isn't truth.

THE LOPSIDED HOUSE OF GRACE

I love the television show *Parenthood*. No other drama captures every essence and emotion of parenting the way this show does. In one particular episode, Jasmine, in a dispute about discipline, tells Crosby, the father of her child, "You're not his friend, you're his father."

It sounds so noble, so loving. Bulldoze the wall of truth, and let's all just be friends! Maybe you've said the same thing, particularly if you grew up with parents who were strict, absent, or abusive and want to parent your kids differently.

Our desire to be a warm, loving presence for our kids is God-given; yet if taken to an extreme, it can result in a Crazy House, not a Safe House. Consider Mrs. George (again from *Mean Girls*). When she stumbles in on Regina and her boyfriend making out in bed, she asks, "Can I get you guys anything? Some snacks? A condom? Let me know!"

As with the classic BFF Parent (no wall of protection or truth), rather than protecting her daughter to help Regina resist peer pressure and make wise choices, this mom does just the opposite. She leads her daughter into temptation, presenting her with life challenges before she's developmentally ready.

Oftentimes we can unknowingly do the same. Perhaps not this severely, but in a more subtle way, as in the cultural trend of the Disneyland Parent, a term coined by sociologist Susan Stewart to describe parents who don't have physical custody of their kids and compensate by making visitation all about fun.[2] As I've worked with countless parents and as a father myself, I'm convinced we're all, more or less, susceptible to Disneyland parenting; that is, consistently showering our kids with lots of grace, gifts, and fun. Taken to an extreme, however, the BFF Parent destroys the wall of truth and "avoid[s] providing guidance and discipline, make[s] no demands for maturity, and impose[s] few controls on their child's behavior."[3]

> Loving our children in grace is loving them for who they are, but loving them in truth is loving them enough to not leave them that way.

While the wall of grace may seem to rid our home of fear in the moment, grace without truth is not based on true love. Loving our children means *always acting for their best interest,* which may or may not be the same as their happiness and comfort in the moment. Loving our children in grace is loving them for who they are, but loving them in truth is loving them enough to not leave them that way.

Building the walls of grace and truth together, we echo the way God our Father parents us as his children:

> Have you forgotten how good parents treat children, and that God regards you as *his* children?
>
> > My dear child, don't shrug off God's discipline,
> > but don't be crushed by it either.
> > It's the child he loves that he disciplines;
> > the child he embraces, he also corrects.
>
> God is educating you; that's why you must never drop out. He's treating you as dear children. This trouble you're in isn't punishment; it's *training,* the normal experience of children. Only irresponsible parents leave children to fend for themselves. Would you prefer an irresponsible God? We respect our own

parents for training and not spoiling us, so why not embrace God's training so we can truly *live*?[4]

Look at the apostle Paul's words, calling all-grace, no-truth parents "irresponsible." Why? Because when we make parenting decisions that are easiest for us in the moment—or to keep our kids happy—we neglect our responsibility to actively shape our children to become emotionally and spiritually mature adults.

In addition to the BFF parent, the Helicopter Parent also leads from a posture of all grace, robbing the child from the truths of natural consequences altogether. Whereas the BFF parent exposes the child to life's challenges too early by not protecting them, the Helicopter Parent overprotects his children by rescuing them. In both cases the outcomes are rarely good: entitled, disrespectful kids who lack self-control and possess little motivation. That's because the all-grace parent outwardly overestimates how good her child is and yet, in a seeming contradiction, intervenes when trouble comes to prevent him from handling the realities of life either because she doesn't believe her son can handle it on his own (Helicopter Parent) or because it's the world's fault, not the child's (BFF Parent).

If we're completely honest with ourselves, we can all identify times where we piled on grace while ignoring truth. At times, truth offends, truth causes conflict, and truth divides. But without truth, our house will be wobbly indeed.

BUILDING A WALL OF TRUTH

Without truth, we neglect the executive functions of the brain and inhibit our child's ability to problem solve when they hit difficult times.

Children cannot raise themselves. That is why God created families and Safe Houses to provide structure and support throughout the developmental years. Depending on their age, the manifestation of truth and grace may change, but both walls must be present in order to build a Safe House.

For a toddler, this might look like saying: "I know you want to get down and play. It's hard to wait. But first, you need to eat your dinner."

For an elementary school child, we might respond: "I understand you're angry at me because you want a new toy, but it's not okay to yell and scream. How can I help you calm down?"

For a teenager, we might set the limit, "I respect your need to hang out with your friends, and I'm asking you to respect the curfew we agreed on."

Sure, setting limits will likely displease our children. I don't know a single person on the planet who hasn't gotten angry, sad, or disappointed when a limit was imposed on them at some point. In the short term, we may have *more* conflict in our home. And that's okay. Our job is to be present with our children, accept her feelings, and help her navigate her way through the frustration.

> The wall of truth is not about punishing our child into submission. Truth is helping our child see beyond the moment; namely, how limits protect us, not rob us of fun.

The wall of truth is not about punishing our child into submission. Truth lovingly guides and redirects a child to help her mature and learn how to regulate her emotions. Truth is helping our child see beyond the moment; namely, how limits protect us, not rob us of fun.

The true mark of a Safe House Parent is giving our child the freedom to feel while supporting her in making wise decisions even when she is upset. If, as the all-grace parent is prone to do, we rescue our children from consequences and fail to impose limits, we run the risk of raising kids who, according to research, are "impulsive, disobedient, rebellious, demanding and dependent on adults."[5]

Yes, feelings are messy. But I'd rather my children learn that the mess is well worth it. The more I can teach them to handle it on their own under our roof, the more they'll be able to handle it like an adult one day under their own.

Building a wall of truth is being present with our child in the midst of intense emotion and not giving in. For those of us more prone to grace than truth, we must stay our course, be *consistent* with the limits we set, allow our children to grieve, and then move on.

As we model boundaries in a loving manner, our children begin to *internalize* this experience and develop self-discipline, problem solving, and the ability to emotionally regulate. In other words, they begin to set limits for themselves.

Going back to the above examples, the toddler learns that the sooner she eats her dinner, the sooner she can get down and play.

The elementary school child learns that even though she can't get a new toy today, she can save her allowance to buy it next week.

The teenager learns that by coming home on time for curfew, she builds trust with her parents, which enables more flexibility in the future.

Balancing the walls of grace and truth builds critical competencies in our children that change their life trajectory. As Cloud and Townsend noted, "Grace and truth become the 'voices' inside that encourage them through the day, help them feel a sense of hope, love, and forgiveness, and correct them when they do wrong and no one is looking over their shoulders. These qualities cause them to feel appropriate anxiety about the need to get jobs done, or the need not to violate conscience and standards, and they become the fuel to move them along that path."[6]

Here are some practical ways to begin building a wall of truth in your day-to-day life:

- *Set age-appropriate limits while staying connected with your child's heart.*
  Your three-year-old should not be allowed to dictate what she eats for
  dinner, and your nine-year-old doesn't need to stay up until whenever she
  feels tired. However, rather than adopt the cold, harsh stance of Captain
  von Trapp, take time to listen to and understand your child's perspective,
  emotions, and needs as you set limits for their good.

- *Help your children develop self-discipline through delayed gratification.*
  Fight the disease of "I have to have it *now*," and you are equipping your
  kids to avoid spending their adult life trying to keep up with the Joneses.
  If your child asks you for a specific toy, game, or accessory, take time to
  explore with them if this is a wise investment and develop a collaborative
  plan to save money and work toward purchasing it.

- *Teach your kids responsibility and selflessness.* Responsibility is not bailing
  your child out when she doesn't want to do her homework but instead
  helping her develop motivation and, if necessary, experience the negative
  consequences of a poor grade. Selflessness can be practically built into
  your family by serving, giving, and sacrificing to help others. In today's
  me culture, selflessness is not something your kids will pick up from the
  media. They must learn it from us.

THE LOPSIDED HOUSE OF TRUTH

Children should be seen and not heard. Remember that phrase? I can't think of a better way to describe a higher-than-life wall of truth.

Maybe your dad glared at you sternly through his horn-rimmed glasses, or your mom put her hands on her hips and gave you *that* look when you refused to eat your dinner. It's the "shut up and do as I say" posture of parenting that leaves little room for dialogue, questions, second chances—or relationship.

We may not summon our kids with a whistle or require them to wear uniforms, but how easy it is to expect our kids to perfectly follow the rules.

Rules. Rules. Rules.

Despite our good intentions to instill religious truths and limits in our kids and teach them about life's consequences, a higher-than-life wall of truth with no grace sabotages a Safe House. There is little safety in an environment where our kids learn to be hyperattuned to *our* wishes and requests for fear of making us (or worse yet, God) mad. Not only does this result in kids who lack self-confidence, but we can all too easily give our kids a twisted view of who God really is.

Both the Religious Parent and the Boss Parent lead from a posture of all truth, robbing the child from the unconditional love and emotional presence needed in stressful or fearful situations. Whereas the Religious Parent exposes the child to very little challenge by setting legalistic rules and overprotecting them from the corruption of the world, the Boss Parent sets rules but sends the child out on his own into the world with little to no support or emotional protection. In both cases, when the child disobeys or fails, he hears the message: "You're not good enough. I'm ashamed of you. When you act that way, you're not worth my time, my love, or my acceptance."

Using shame or rejection to shut down our child's emotions creates a breeding ground for depression and anxiety. That's because the all-truth parent underestimates the goodness of his child. So he either prevents his child from being exposed to the realities of life by punishing her negative feelings or not meeting his over-the-top rules (Religious Parent) or faulting his child for every failure or challenge she encounters (Boss Parent).

Often with sincere intent, the Boss Parent and the Religious Parent pride themselves in enforcing structure and discipline, but they neglect their children's emotions, longings, and needs. I have worked with many parents who gain a sense of glee over catching their child doing wrong and who misconstrue their own anger as righteous indignation.

Certainly, we can't be our child's best friend, but research shows that a safe, loving, supportive relationship is critical to raising healthy kids. That's why we need a balance of all four walls—exploration, protection, grace, and truth—to build a Safe House.

As Maria pleads with the captain, "The little ones just want to be loved. Oh, please, Captain, love them! Love them all!"

After all, it is through their relationship with us that our children first experience God. When your toddler throws her food on the floor for the umpteenth time or you discover your teenager has snuck out after curfew, your gut reaction may be to drop the hammer, using your authority to punish your child so she'll never forget.

And certainly, consequences are needed. But in these moments, especially if we're prone to all-truth, no-grace, we must remember God's heart for us as his children as described in Psalm 103:

Merciful . . .
    Gracious . . .
        Compassionate . . .
            Slow to anger . . .

Fueled by a fundamental understanding of who our children are and what they need in the moment, God doesn't define us by our mistakes or failures. Understanding our child's true intention makes it easier to connect with him and offer grace even, and especially, when he messes up. We'll look more specifically at how God fathers us in chapter 9.

We must separate our child (grace) from their behavior (truth).

When we dynamite the wall of grace and pile the bricks on the side of truth, we create a home full of fear. As one parenting expert writes about the values we instill, "Overly harsh punishments do not create regret; they only serve to create resentment."[7] That's because truth brought without grace is received as condemnation.[8]

Truth without grace results in anxiety and striving, as our children desperately try to win our approval and acceptance or even give up trying to win. A far cry from God's love, our love becomes fear-based and conditional on whether or not they are following the rules or our directions on how to do something in the moment.

Fear is a powerful motivator. But kids can't thrive and grow in fear—they merely survive. We may teach our kids the *dance* of good behavior, but without engaging their hearts, we're raising kids who will eventually buck the system and rebel, resent us, or both.

Building Up Grace by Understanding
Your Child's Motivation

When I was a teenager, I had a Camaro my parents bought new in 1984 and gave to me when I turned sixteen. Let me tell you, it's never a good thing to give a sixteen-year-old, whose brain isn't fully developed, a Camaro. One of my parents' rules was to not allow anyone else to drive the car.

My girlfriend lived less than a mile from the high school, and her car was in the shop. On a rainy day when I had wrestling practice after school, she asked if she could borrow my car to drive home.

This was in the late 1990s. I didn't have a cell phone. Calling my parents to ask permission wasn't possible. Besides, it was less than a mile. Not a big deal. Nope. Not unless you grew up in a small town where everybody knows you, and a bright white Camaro driving through town is as noticeable and unforgettable as Justin Bieber drag racing a canary yellow Lamborghini down Main Street.

Needless to say, when I got home that night, I was in trouble. Big trouble. (To this day, I don't know how my parents found out.)

Put yourself in my parents' position. Your sixteen-year-old just disobeyed you by allowing somebody else to drive his car. What's your initial response? Pretty fired up, right?

Blatant disobedience. Lack of respect for authority.

How would you respond to your child in this moment?

Now, let's flip the scenario around and look at it through my sixteen-year-old eyes. My underlying motivation wasn't to blatantly disobey my parents. My underlying motivation was to help my girlfriend. Besides, I didn't want her to think I didn't trust her with my car.

For me, *in the moment,* those factors were more important than disobeying my parents. My relationship and reputation with my girlfriend trumped a rule I thought I was barely breaking.

When our kids disobey or fight back on rules we set, *don't immediately assume the worst about them.* Consider the framework of understanding and that the *underlying motivation* of our kids probably has more to do with something else, like their perceived reputation with their friends or fear of losing social status, rather than purposely disobeying us.

Being a teenager is much more complicated in the twenty-first century. Our kids need a reasonable and safe place to land. To learn what it means to be reasonable, let's look at a quote from the first neuroscientist: the apostle Paul. I'm not kidding. Watch how cool this is. Paul wrote:

> Let your *reasonableness* be known to everyone. The Lord is at hand; do not be *anxious* about anything, but in everything by prayer and supplication with thanksgiving let your requests be made known to God. And the peace of God, which surpasses all understanding, will guard *your hearts and your minds* in Christ Jesus.[9]

Let's start with the word *anxious*. When our kids are in or come across trouble, they're anxious. The fight-or-flight response kicks in, perhaps becoming a temper tantrum in a toddler or mouthing off in a teenager. Paul said that when we're anxious, what we don't need is a lecture. That's why further demands and commands on our children in overwhelming moments seem to go in one ear and out the other.

What we need instead is a timeout.

We need prayer.

We need God's presence.

We need to calm our overwhelmed brain.

Think about this. When we're emotionally worked up, it's difficult to think. As a crisis responder, one of the first pieces of advice we provide someone who has just experienced a crisis is to not make any major decisions. Don't sell your home, quit your job, or leave your spouse. When our brain is overwhelmed, we need to allow time to calm down. Not until then can we begin to think straight.

Not until after the peace of God guards our hearts and minds does Paul say to think. First, take your anxiety to God. Then think. The apostle finished the above counsel with the following recommendation:

> Finally . . . whatever is true, whatever is honorable, whatever is just, whatever is pure, whatever is lovely, whatever is commendable, if there is any excellence, if there is anything worthy of praise, *think* about these things.[10]

The Greek word *reasonableness* Paul uses to begin this passage (verse 5) refers to "a disposition or an attitude of seeking the best for another." The word is crucial to maintaining relationship. So as we think about reasonableness in our rule setting, we must seek what's spiritually and relationally best for our kids and teens when they're anxious, distressed, or caught in the act.

Just as "the Lord is at hand" in our anxiety, so, too, should we *be near* for our kids, seeking their best, calming their distressed and overwhelmed brain, then thinking about and setting limits. As Daniel Siegel and Tina Bryson advise, instead of demand and command, we should connect and correct.[11]

As you think about this in regard to setting parental limits, consider how reasonable you're being. First, don't immediately assume the worst about your kids, that they perhaps blatantly disrespected you. Second, be open to considering their underlying motivation. Remember, in order to be understood, we must first understand. When our kids feel understood, it calms their brain. Peace is restored. Then discuss the consequences.

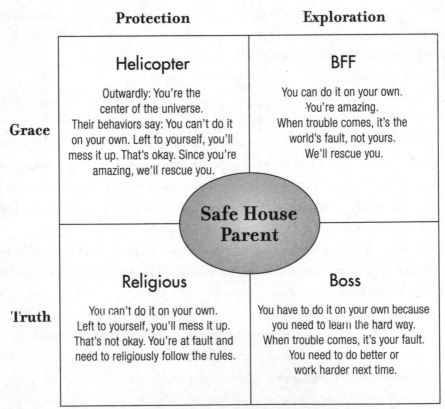

Figure 6.2. The differentiating walls of grace and truth, coupled with the walls of protection and exploration, and the messages our kids receive based on these parenting tendencies.

Here are some practical ways to build the wall of grace in your day-to-day life:

- *Whenever possible, take time to calm down before responding to your child.* Knowing yourself and your triggers is critical. You have a much greater likelihood of becoming the Boss Parent when you're feeling stressed, angry, hungry, lonely, or tired. Sometimes the best course of action in the moment is to create space for you and your kids to calm down before addressing the issue.

- *Dialogue with your child and seek to understand her point of view.* Consider the intent behind your child's behavior, rather than assume the worst. Validate your child's emotions while helping her identify a better course of action for the future.

- *Always communicate your love and full acceptance of your child, regardless of her actions.* By doing so, especially in the midst of your child's biggest failures, you can set her on a path of being able to extend grace to both herself and others as an adult. Never resort to shame, belittlement, embarrassment, or condescension in an attempt to control your child's behavior. These fear-based tactics destroy a Safe House.

THE PATHWAYS OF SAFE HOUSE PARENTING

By now you've probably identified your parenting tendencies according to Figure 6.2. No matter your tendency, take the pressure off yourself. The strategies described in the next two chapters will help you navigate your child's most intense emotional moments and wire their brains to live, love, and lead well.

There are three primary pathways we use to parent our children. Of the three, the Safe House pathway promotes brain growth and emotional maturity. However, there are times we need to employ the other two for the sake of everybody's emotional health, including, and oftentimes especially, our own!

- *The Truth Pathway.* The Truth Pathway is absolutely telling our children what to do. "You'll do this because I'm the parent and I said so," this parent chides. "Case closed." Don't forget, you're the parent. There are times our children simply need to obey with zero negotiation. Particularly in instances of physical danger or potentially harmful situations or if you're pressured for time, this pathway is unquestionably warranted. I love what my mother-in-law did. If any of her kids needed an immediate answer (that is, permission for a sleepover), she would say, "If you need to know now, the answer is no." I use this principle even today as an adult. The point is, don't allow your kids to corner or manipulate you into a making an immediate decision.

- *The Grace Pathway.* The Grace Pathway may very well, on certain days, save your sanity. "Go ahead and do it," this parent quips. There are times we need to temporarily drop our concern. This most often happens when we're worked up ourselves. To maintain the relationship with our child and not say or do something we regret, it's better to resort to this pathway than to ridicule, judge, blame, or criticize our child.

Though there are times we need to instill absolute truth or definitive grace in parenting situations, the pathway that engages our children to think, feel, and relate at the same time and build their brain unites grace and truth:

- *The Safe House Pathway.* "Your concern is wanting to stay out later with your friends. My concern is you have an exam tomorrow. Let's find a way to resolve this together," this parent responds. The most emotionally healthy, academically competent, and relationally stable children have parents who are neither too lenient nor too strict. These parents set reasonable limits for their children, are warm and responsive, and do not use harsh methods of punishment.[12]

A Safe House Parent is collaborative, seeking to problem solve with her children, not always giving in or constantly demanding. We'll discuss more specifically how to problem solve, use safe discipline, and build your child's brain in the next two chapters.

FINDING WISDOM IN SMELLY DIAPERS
AND SLEEPLESS NIGHTS

Shortly after our daughter was born, Christi's parents drove down from Canada to help us adjust to our demanding little girl. Christi's mum is genuinely one of the wisest persons I know. We talked about the practicalities of taking care of screaming, sleepless, and thankless infants. She described to Christi and me what she believes are, generally speaking, the two primary tasks of parents: caregiving and character building. Much of the first two to three years of life are spent primarily in the caregiving role. As our children age, however, we move increasingly away from caregiving to a more character-building role.

Christi and I are wired more as character builders than caregivers. Caregiving drains us. Character building gives us energy. Perhaps you're the opposite.

I was reminded of this as we were about to settle in for another sleepless night. Christi and I had just finished a discussion with her parents about creating a Safe House when her mum read us a passage she used in raising her three children:

> By *wisdom* a house is built,
>   and by *understanding* it is established;
> by *knowledge* the rooms are filled
>   with all precious and pleasant riches.[13]

As I crawled into bed that evening, I couldn't get this verse out of my head. For building character, it made sense. But how was I supposed to apply this verse in the caregiving years?

If a house is built on wisdom, where's the wisdom in smelly diapers and sleepless nights?

After a bit of study, I learned the word *wisdom* in this verse is not a philosophical term but a practical one. The Hebrew word is used frequently throughout the Old Testament to describe the hands-on work of ants, locusts, and even lizards. Though not all that smart, they are wise by how they live.

To build our house on wisdom is to balance all four walls of a Safe House: exploration, protection, grace, and truth. One way to really know if our narrative is becoming more coherent and healing is to measure how much we're growing in wisdom as a parent. Here's a good metric:

> The wisdom from above is first pure, then peaceable, gentle, open to reason, full
> of mercy and good fruits, impartial and sincere. And a harvest of righteousness is
> sown in peace by those who make peace.[14]

These verses are a litmus test for how much *we're* growing in wisdom and how much our past story may be impacting our present behavior as parents. If there are kinks in our own story, we'll know it by the way we're treating our kids.

Consider the first characteristic listed: pure. As you interact with your children—no matter their age or the circumstance—are you doing so with pure motives, applying what you know is best for your kids?

Take a few moments to consider how well you're responding, not reacting, to your anxious, rebellious, and fearful children.

- Am I approaching my kids—their dirty diapers, skinned knees, spilled milk, late curfew, and disrespectful attitude—in a peaceable manner?
- Am I approaching them in a peaceable manner when they are in their worst moments, most fearful, scared, angry moments, even disrespectful moments? Just because our kids disrespect us doesn't mean we should disrespect them back. It's how we model our behavior that matters in terms of whether or not they feel safe.
- Am I gentle in how I talk to, care for, set limits with, discipline, and help my children? Am I growing in gentleness over time?
- Am I open to reason with my children when we don't see eye to eye? (Not in matters that compromise my parental authority.)
- Am I growing in mercy or am I holding my child's past behaviors against him? Consider Psalm 103:9: "[God the Father] will not always chide."
- Am I becoming more kind, patient, faithful, good, peaceful, gentle, loving, self-controlled, and joyful toward my kids and my spouse?
- Am I treating each of our kids individually in our home in the same manner, showing no favoritism?
- Am I becoming less of a hypocrite, living according to the attitudes and behaviors I expect of my spouse and kids?

Using a scale of one to ten, I encourage you to measure yourself according to each of these questions once a month over the next three months. You may even want to give this list to your spouse or children and ask: "Can you help me with this? I want to be a better parent. Next month, we are going to walk through this, and I want you to tell me how I'm doing."

If you don't find yourself improving, it may be a reflection of an unresolved moment in your story. If you need wisdom, the Bible says to simply ask for it. Christi and I pray for wisdom, with our kids present, every night.

As the weeks progressed and we studied Kennedy's behavior, we gradually *understood* her motives and *knew* what she needed. At this point it was tummy pains. The innocence behind the screaming and crying became clearer to us. As we responded by being less short with one another and working more as a team, all the rooms in our house became more pleasant.

===== Coauthoring Your Child's Story =====

1. Do the exercise that closes out this chapter. I encourage you to ask your spouse and children to help rate you.
2. Reconsider your parenting tendency. Do you lean toward the Grace or Truth Pathway in your parenting posture? Describe any connections you see with the relationship you had with your parents and your parenting posture.
3. In what ways do you need to better balance the walls of grace and truth in relationship to your kids?
4. In what ways do you need to better balance the walls of exploration and protection in relationship to your kids?

Safe Discipline

*I think of discipline as the continual everyday process of helping
a child learn self-discipline.*

—Fred Rogers

Living in Branson, Missouri, has its perks. One of those is having a season pass to Silver
Dollar City, an amusement park with great food and activities for the entire family.

On one occasion, Christi and I were entering the gate with Landon when we passed
a woman pushing a stroller on her way out. Staring straight ahead in disgust, and with
a screaming-at-the-top-of-his-lungs young boy out in front of her, she was on a mission
to get that earsplitting child out of the park as fast as she could. She looked miserable.

She also looked familiar.

As we walked passed her, Christi and I looked at each other, and without saying a
word, we both knew what the other was thinking: *Oh, how we understand.*

I wish now I had praised that woman in the moment.

Two days later we were at church, picking up our son from his class after the service,
when a woman standing beside me cautiously looked over and said, "I'm the woman you
saw the other day with the screaming child at the park."

I began to chuckle.

After telling me the story of what had happened leading up to the meltdown, she
said to me, "All I could think about as I passed you leaving that day was, 'Joshua Straub,
don't you judge me!'"

We shared a good laugh about that and the mutual understanding of a common
experience: temper tantrums.

Besides, who am I to judge?

Meltdowns happen pretty often in the Straub household these days. The terrible
twos are upon us as I write. God has an incredible sense of humor that way. Sometimes
watching Landon lay on the floor, kicking and screaming, I think of the temper tan-

trums I throw with God when things don't go my way. Doing so makes it easier to empathize with Landon in the moment. Balancing grace and truth in how we discipline our strong-willed toddler is not easy.

Just the other night I put Landon in timeout. Why is it when a toddler knowingly looks you in the eye and disobeys (in this case throwing his dinner leftovers all over the floor while staring right at me), he has to let out one of those wonderful piercing screams right in your face!

For whatever reason, these moments happen more often than not in public, especially when he's at the grocery store, with just Christi there.

Moms, I know you can relate. And no, I'm not judging you. Instead, I want to praise you.

I praise you because we live in a culture where most people look at you with disgust when your child is throwing a fit, privately thinking you and your child should be acting perfect, according to *their* standards.

I praise you because, in these moments, you're most likely setting limits and choosing not to give in to your demanding child.

I praise you for choosing the harder path of discipline instead of giving in and raising emotionally out-of-control kids who believe they're in charge.

I praise you for teaching your kids self-control rather than raising an entitled, selfish, and impatient teenager or, worse, adult later on.

Discipline isn't easy, but without it, our homes aren't safe.

PUNISHMENT, DISCIPLINE, AND THE KIDS WHO CHANGE THE WORLD

Punishment and discipline are different. Simply put, punishment isn't safe; discipline is. In punishment, we *react* to misbehavior; in discipline, we *respond* to it. The short-term outcome of punishment may be obedience, but the long-term outcome of discipline is self-discipline.

When we punish our kids, shame, guilt, criticism, and contempt become the posture from which we parent. As one parenting expert reflected, "Where did we ever get the crazy idea that in order to make children do better, first we have to make them feel worse? Think of the last time you felt humiliated or treated unfairly. Did you feel like cooperating or doing better?"[1] Remember, punishment focuses purely on behavior and lacks grace for the child. As a consequence, our kids may be well-behaved in the short term, but they lack the skills or the self-worth to make wise decisions in the long run.

Discipline, on the other hand, is postured in both grace and truth. Derived from the Latin root *disciplina,* the word means "to educate and instruct, to teach and to guide." Safe discipline, at its core, is about building skills—developing our child's internal moral compass and equipping her with the self-discipline necessary to make wise choices when we're not around. As H. L. Mencken observed, "Morality is doing right, no matter what you are told. Obedience is doing what you are told, no matter what is right."

> As H. L. Mencken observed: "Morality is doing right, no matter what you are told. Obedience is doing what you are told, no matter what is right."

Though strong-willed children can be exhausting and difficult, if they are guided by loving parents, we can raise a generation of excellent leaders; namely, kids not known for selfish ambition or vain conceit but for humility, kids who genuinely value others as better than themselves.[2] A generation who can influence culture because, content with who they are and knowing they're loved, they live. Their will has not been broken; they've been shaped.

From a biblical perspective, I think this is why the apostle Paul told fathers not to exasperate their kids but to instead "bring them up in the nurture and admonition of the Lord."[3] Whereas exasperation emotionally stirs up our kids, the word *admonition* used in this verse means "counsel" and refers to "placing the mind in a proper place" as to reason with our kids by warning them (admonishing). In real-people language, this verse instructs parents to become counselors to our child, and through our nurturing, calm her brain so that she's able to reason with us and problem solve for the solution that will best honor God.

I love the Message version of this verse: "Fathers, don't exasperate your children by coming down hard on them. Take them by the hand and lead them in the way of the Master."[4] That's discipline: being emotionally safe, taking our children by the hand, and lovingly redirecting them.

While many parenting books are filled with techniques to get our children to behave better, sleep more, cry less, and so forth, my heart is first for *you* as a parent.

Take a moment to consider your own childhood. Were you usually punished or disciplined? Did your parents ever take time to help you calm down? Or did you often feel exasperated and stirred up?

How have these experiences shaped the way you approach your kids?

I encourage you to talk with your spouse or a friend and to listen to their story too. There's nothing more powerful for our own emotional and spiritual health than sharing honestly with a safe friend.

As we reflect on our own story, we must consider how much and to what degree it influences how safe we are for our kids as we discipline them.

FROM EXASPERATING TO EMOTION COACHING

My nephew Jayden turned five in January. Between Christmas and his birthday, the boy was showered with more toys than he knew what to do with. This year the train of overabundance dropped him off in a town called Defiance.

My sister, who is an amazing mom, summoned Jayden for bed. When he didn't respond, she went into another room and found him playing a new game on his Leap-Pad. "Jayden, it's time to turn it off and get ready for bed. Let's go," she said.

In what became a struggle of wills, my sister retrieved the LeapPad and told Jayden to get his pajamas. That's when he kicked her in the leg.

"It took everything in me to not lose my cool," my sister said as she recounted the story to me. "But I'm glad I didn't."

Choosing to bypass a consequence in the moment for the sake of getting him in bed (Grace Pathway), she helped him get his pajamas on.

"That's when he said to me, 'Mom, I don't love you right now.'"

My sister, remaining calm, responded, "You don't have to love me right now, but you do have to listen to me. And I want you to know that even though I don't like how you're acting, I still love you."

After getting his pajamas on, they walked to the kitchen to get his medicine.

"We have a magnet on our refrigerator of a heart," she said. "The heart is split down the middle and breaks in two, but for the moment the heart was on the refrigerator in one piece. Jayden took the heart off the refrigerator and said, 'Mommy, when I love you again I'll put this magnet back together.'"

Bent on getting him to bed, there was nothing else left but prayers. Well, except maybe one thing.

"Mommy, can we read the Bible book Uncle Josh and Aunt Christi got me for Christmas?"

"This is when I realized how glad I was that I hadn't lost my cool on him earlier," my sister said. "When we got done reading, Jayden said, 'Let's pray.'"

My sister prayed first. Then, in his childlike prayers, and I believe through my sister maintaining her cool, Jayden found remorse: "Dear God, thank you for making Pappy better and bringing him home from the hospital and for my Mommy putting new games on my LeapPad. Amen."

> Though we cannot expect our children to act like mature adults, we should model, by our behavior, the kind of adult we want them to one day become.

That's when he gave her a hug, kissed her goodnight, and said, "I love you, Mommy."

"Oh, you love me again?" my sister asked.

"Yeah, and I'll put the heart back tomorrow. Then I'll love you even more."

Our kids teach us a lot, including how little patience we often have. Though we cannot expect our children to act like mature adults, we should model, by our behavior, the kind of adult we want them to one day become. Using the Grace Pathway kept my sister calm and later opened my nephew up for problem solving on how to better handle the situation next time (Safe House Pathway).

When our kids detrain in Defiance, we're the ones often left exasperated. On the one hand, we desperately want to hold ourselves together and avoid the don'ts of discipline (that is, don't yell, don't spank in anger), but on the other hand, we want to exert our authority in the heat of any struggle of wills. Hence the greatest challenge of being a parent: letting your kids know they're loved while teaching them they're not in charge.

That's where emotion coaching comes in. Rather than trying really hard *not* to exasperate our kids—and ourselves—Safe House discipline is proactive, teaching our kids how to understand, accept, and regulate their emotions so they can make age-appropriate decisions. In a Safe House, we primarily do this in the following three ways:

1. *Opening the Door:* Empathizing with our child's feelings.
2. *Moving to Another Room:* Addressing the child's behavior and our concerns.
3. *Building the Fence:* Problem solving together for the best solution.

OPENING THE DOOR: THE GATEWAY TO DISCIPLINE

There are two ways we can respond to our child's misbehaviors: (1) opening the door to our child or (2) closing the door on their emotions.

Closing the door is when we dismiss our child's emotions. Parents who routinely close the door may think negative emotions (like sadness and anger) are toxic for their child.[5] They may reprimand a child for being upset, even if she doesn't act out. "Go to your room until you can be happy," they may say. "I don't have time for your crabby attitude. Get over it and move on."

In contrast, opening the door is when we see every emotion—especially difficult emotions like sadness and anger—as an opportunity to connect. In essence, we're saying, "Your emotions matter. Tell me more . . ." Opening the door means we respect our child's right to feel, and this is the first step toward coaching her to express emotions like contempt and disappointment in appropriate ways. While many discipline techniques encourage parents to remain emotionally detached, the emotion-coaching principles of Safe House discipline consider both the emotion of the child and the parent. When strong emotions are coupled with an attuned connection, the result is often a magic moment.[6] A moment of thinking, feeling, and relating. A moment of closeness, learning, and growth.[7]

So how do we open the door and move toward emotionally coaching our kids?[8]

First, we recognize what our child is feeling. When we do, she won't have to ramp up her negative emotions to get our attention. Remember, it takes a secure parent to be emotionally available to a child in a high-stress situation. Paying attention to her facial expressions, voice, and gestures can help us get a sense of what she's feeling in the moment.

Second, we use these emotions as an opportunity to connect with and teach our child. In these moments, what our child needs first is help calming down—and we may need time to calm down too. Before we discuss the problem behavior or impose consequences, slowing down to find out what's really going on behind the emotion and behavior helps our child not only feel understood (framework of understanding) but also helps us better discern how we can connect with our child and help him learn to navigate his emotions in a more appropriate way. Again, knowing your child's temperament and what makes him unique can help you here. As a toddler, was he overstimulated by too many people? Was he made fun of by a peer at school? Did he receive a poor grade?

Remember, our children are not born into the world knowing how to calm themselves. By being emotionally present with our child, we can validate what he's feeling, identify the skill deficit (from chapter 4) that resulted in the meltdown or outburst, and help him develop new competencies or learn new ways of calming down. Our kids take their cues from us. If we're yelling and upset, he will be too. If we're calm and under-standing, our brain has a calming effect on his. Remember the Face Game?

Third, we help our child verbally label her emotions. When we label our child's emotions, saying, "I can see you're really [angry, sad, upset] right now," we open the door by validating her internal experience rather than close the door to her feelings. Feeling heard and understood are the building blocks of emotion regulation.

If discipline is about teaching, then there's no moment more powerful than when we label and empathize with the feelings behind our child's defiance. Is she sad? scared? angry? Does she feel alone? misunderstood? Opening the door teaches our child that all feelings are acceptable; moving to another room teaches her all behavior is not.[9]

I use feeling words every night with our kids before tucking them into bed. As we reminisce on the events of the day we shared together, I help them learn and remember

> Opening the door teaches our child that all feelings are acceptable; moving to another room teaches her all behavior is not.

how I felt about certain parts of the day. For example: "I was sad when you didn't pick up your blocks. But I was happy when you apologized to Mommy." Again, model-ing is key.

Fourth, we empathize and show our child we under-stand. In my graduate counseling studies we learned an important distinction that applies to parenting: sympathy is feeling bad *for* somebody; empathy is feeling bad *with* somebody. Feeling bad with our child means understanding why she's feeling a particu-lar way. Since our child is not always able to verbalize it, especially in frustration, looking deeper into what she needs in the moment can help calm her down. Anger is a secondary emotion because it stems from the primary emotion she felt first, like disappointment, sadness, rejection, and so on. Taking the time to uncover the primary emotion is how we win our child's heart.

Opening the door to our child means we can't be afraid to put ourselves in a time-out either. We might say, "It's probably best if we both take a few minutes to calm down and come back to this when we're less overwhelmed." Listen to music. Take a walk. Drink a cup of coffee. Then come back to it. Our kids may need space to calm down too—shooting hoops, riding a bike, swinging in the backyard. Their behavior may war-rant we send them to their room for a brief time (a timeout) until we're both calm enough to reconnect.

Finally, when everyone is calm and our kids feel understood, moving to another room (addressing the child's behavior) and building the fence (problem solving) become easier.

Moving to Another Room: The Literal Strategy for Little Ones

Putting toys away. If you're a young parent, reading those words probably just increased your blood pressure a bit. Last night Landon wanted to have a picnic in our bed. (An imaginative one, mind you. I hate sleeping in crumbs.) But before we got out the plastic sandwiches and singing picnic basket, I told him to first pick up the blocks he had strewn across the living room.

Enter meltdown.

Sitting on the floor in protest—crying, whining, shaking, and tensing his body—he turned beet red. He was as mad as a hornet who just survived a tennis racket.

Sitting in anticipation for what he'd do next, I said, "Landon, I understand you're mad because you want to have a picnic, but we need to pick up the blocks first." Everything inside of me was hoping he wouldn't chuck one across the room. At two years old, he's learning our limits. Other than hesitating to pick up the blocks, until this point he hadn't done anything wrong. He was simply trying to deal with his frustration. That's when he picked up a block, squeezed it with all of his might, and held it over the bucket as if squeezing the juice from an orange. When he dropped it into the bucket, he grunted.

So I joined him.

I, too, picked up a block, squeezed it, turned beet red, grunted, and then dropped it into the bucket. When Landon looked at me, I saw a small smile emerge. Handing me another block, he said, "More, again." Piece by piece we took turns releasing our anger over having to pick up the blocks, not by throwing them, but by putting them away.

Afterward I told him how proud I was of how he handled his anger. The reason I didn't yet move to another room to address the behavior is because Landon is only two years old. He's still learning to control his emotions. Opening the door is not only empathizing with our child's emotion but also recognizing their developmental level for handling it. Joining Landon in how to appropriately express his emotion in that moment opened the door for him to move to the next activity.

But what would have happened had Landon gotten so emotionally out of control that he was paralyzed from putting the blocks away or moving on to the next activity?

For most toddlers, there's one word that will become your best friend: distraction. We literally take them to another room and distract them from their meltdown. Depending on our child's developmental level, they may not yet be able to calm themselves down and simply need to be distracted with another toy, person, or environment. Lecturing them on what they should do, shouldn't do, or the consequence if they don't do is nothing but a bunch of do-do. Okay, that was lame, but I hope you get the point. Our children's brains often become overstimulated in these early years, and trying to reason with them is like the president and Congress coming to an agreement on anything. Ouch!

What if, on the other hand, Landon had thrown a block across the room?

These are frequent moments in the Straub household. The one rule Landon most often disobeys is when we say "Stop." Too often he keeps going. In these cases—and this is very important—we *always* address the misbehavior in the moment. Wait too long, and our kids have no way of connecting the dots. Time, space, and sequencing are still being developed in the early years. In most cases, opening the door to what our little one is feeling means we literally, and in the moment, move him to another room to first connect with him and then address the misbehavior.

There's one caveat to this: is your child developmentally able to discern right from wrong? This is a difficult balance because there is a season where you're trying to determine if your son threw the blocks impulsively, not knowing it was wrong, or out of an act of *willful rebellion*. Keep that term in mind. When you can look at your toddler and know they know a behavior is wrong but do it anyway, that calls for moving to another room and addressing the misbehavior.

The following are a few ways we move our little ones to another room.

Set clear limits on behavior and be consistent. Christi and I run into this situation often with toddlers, finding ourselves reevaluating not so much the limits we set but how both of us are following through on the limits in a consistent way. Consistency is absolutely critical in the early years and can be the key to how soon our children pick up on the boundaries we put in place.

When our child willfully rebels, we gently but firmly confront him and communicate our feelings about his behavior. But we never attack his character. We help him understand the family's values and what is and is not acceptable. For example, we might say, "I understand you're really angry right now, but it's not okay to throw your toys when you're upset."

To take it a step further, John Gottman suggested, "When giving the reason for the limit setting, emphasize the specific positive behaviors that are needed, rather than only stating the negative behaviors that should be stopped. Kids learn how to make better choices by first making bad choices, then assessing the consequences, and in the future, making different choices."[10]

Remind your child of the rules and give age-appropriate consequences. "We do not hit in this family," we say. "I know she was irritating you, but I expect you to use your words to communicate what you're feeling—not your hands. Because you hit your sister, you need to take a break from playing and come help me wash the dishes." Consequences should be age appropriate, fair, and not overly harsh. We can't ground our six-year-old for a month or take away television time for the rest of the year. Consequences should also be as natural as possible. Let a child who doesn't do her homework experience the consequences of a poor grade. Let a child who doesn't eat her dinner experience the consequence of being hungry until the next meal. And so forth.

Use rewards to motivate positive behavior and consequences to extinguish negative behavior. The most basic level of moral development relies solely on motivation from outside reinforcement (toys, activities, snacks, and so on) to encourage obedience. We cannot automatically expect our three-year-old to be internally motivated to do what's right. This will come in time as her brain and emotional system develop. However, we play a key role in that. If Landon throws a block, we're going to his room to calm down and talk about what caused him to throw the block. In as few words as possible, I will help him make the connection: throwing the block means no picnic on the bed. Removing privileges specifically related to the offense and in the moment are effective ways of motivating our toddlers over time.

In the same vein, when we see behavior we want to reinforce (that is, using words not actions to express anger, picking up her toys), we offer encouragement, praise, and possibly a reward. Identify appropriate rewards (cartoon time, staying up later, going to a friend's house) to reinforce positive behavior. Of course, these same items can be used as appropriate consequences for misbehavior.

Whenever possible, call a time-in rather than a timeout. I use these terms interchangeably, but experts are beginning to differentiate the two. A time-in is when we join our child in another room to help him calm down and then discuss the misbehavior together to find a solution. A timeout is isolating our child in another room by herself. Of course, there are times for both, but I encourage time-in more than timeouts. Ask reflective questions: "What do you think it felt like when your sister got hit?" (build empathy). "How do you know when you're getting angry? What could you do differently the next time?" (build emotion regulation). "How can you make it right with your sister?" (build problem solving).

Remember, our kids' brains are wired for relationships. Leaving them alone in their overwhelmed state can add shame and guilt, causing them to focus more on the rupture in the relationship with Mom or Dad than on the behavior itself. On the other hand, if we're too overwhelmed ourselves to be safe with them in the moment, a timeout may be the emotionally safest option.

When appropriate, invite your child to have a mulligan. As a terrible golfer, I love mulligans. If you're not familiar with golf, a mulligan is essentially a do-over, a chance to hit the ball again. Suppose Landon threw his toys down rather than put them away as I asked him to. A timeout would not be helpful here, because Landon was intent on connecting with me and having a picnic together. Isolating him in a room by himself disconnects him from relationship for his behavior.

Instead, here's where time-ins are effective. Take him to another room and invite him into the learning process by giving him a mulligan, a do-over, a fresh start to follow through on picking up his toys. Not only does this teach our child we all make mistakes, but it also builds his confidence to complete tasks he doesn't necessarily want to do or believe he can do. Most important, this approach builds on the connection we have with our child, helping him learn over time that though there are consequences to misbehavior (truth), we still love him unconditionally (grace).

That's how, building these walls over time, we win our child's heart.

Moving to Another Room:
The Figurative Strategy for Older Ones

Starting roughly around age eight, there's a big jump in our child's ability to think rationally. No longer is moral development about rewards and consequences or how behavior impacts only one person. Children begin to learn how everyone is impacted by decisions and are able to start problem solving with less influence from us on directing behavior. Though there will be times we need to use the Truth Pathway or the Grace Pathway in making parenting decisions, the Safe House Pathway engages our child in thinking, feeling, and relating at the same time and builds the executive functions of the brain necessary for living, loving, and leading well.

Collaborating with our older child to problem solve about misbehavior, limits, and consequences engages her in the process as an active participant in making decisions.[11] If our goal is to move our child from dependence to more independence over time, we need to guide (discipline) her in making wise decisions. Moving our older children to another room happens figuratively, of course. Imagine sitting together in a family room or around the dining table, engaging one another in the following discussion after your fifteen-year-old daughter returns home after curfew.

"All of my friends are allowed to stay out past eleven o'clock," she says. "Why can't I? It's not fair!"

Though there is some overlap between opening the door and moving to another room here, consider the following steps to safely collaborating with your child.[12]

Empathy is when we allow our child to express her concern without jumping to conclusions or being judgmental. This doesn't mean we agree with her feelings or beliefs. Empathy means we listen well and see the situation from her perspective. This is where the Golden Rule of a Safe House is so crucial: To be understood, we must first understand.

For example, we might reflect back to her: "You believe you should be allowed to stay out until midnight because your friends do. And you're upset at us because you don't think we trust you for that extra hour."

Avoid judgment, correction, or criticism. Instead, build a bridge to connect with her heart. Try to reflect back what her underlying motivation is. What is she feeling? If you get it right, she will likely say, "Yes, you got it." By this simple action, we significantly de-escalate the anger and potential further conflict because she feels understood.

Assertiveness is when we state our concern without attacking her. "You always," "you never," "I can't believe you would . . ." are not helpful here. Never attack her character. The difficult part about assertiveness is identifying the root of why we as a parent are concerned. This constitutes more than just saying: "This is the rule and that's final. If you want to live here, you have to follow the rules."

Rather than jumping to a solution (Boss Parent), simply not allowing it as a discussion (Religious Parent), allowing her to do whatever she wants (BFF Parent), or going along with her (Helicopter Parent), take time to identify and verbalize your core concern.

We really need to discern whether she has broken trust in the past or not. Is it genuinely because we're concerned for her safety because we can't trust her or is it because we're afraid of further releasing her to become an adult?

Being assertive is saying, "I understand you're upset that you don't think we trust you for that extra hour, but we're concerned about [your failing grade in math, the behaviors of the friends you're spending time with, and so on]." If it has to do with her friends, keep in mind to separate the behavior you don't approve of and the friend's character.

Respect can be difficult but critical to building a Safe House. Respect means we refuse to be mean and nasty even if our child is being mean and nasty to us. Respect also means we refuse to judge her or assume the worst about her. "Judge not, that ye be not judged," said Jesus.[13] Instead, give her the benefit of the doubt. This doesn't mean we're going to be a pushover but that we choose not to use disrespect as a way to punish our child. "Who do you think you are coming to us to ask for an extension on your curfew? As if you could handle yourself being out that long. You should be glad we don't push it back to ten." This only adds fuel to the fire.

Since it's the posture from which we parent that matters most, we must give our child a lending EAR (Empathy, Assertiveness, Respect). Doing so builds a balance of grace and truth—we're not letting her off the hook nor are we criticizing her. These skills create an environment for our child to cognitively and emotionally mature. Responding with empathy, assertiveness, and respect can wire her brain and soften her heart.

BUILDING THE FENCE: PROBLEM SOLVING FOR A SOLUTION

The purpose of opening the door is to calm our child's brain by helping her feel understood. Moving to another room is addressing the misbehavior in a respectful way. Once our daughter is calmed down in the above scenario, we can move to building the fence; namely, problem solving together to find a solution.

Inviting our child to help us make a decision is critical for connection and brain growth. For example, we might say, "You want to stay out later, and I'm concerned about your failing grade in math. What can we do about it?" Encouraging her to find a solution to the problem calms the emotional part of her brain (moving her out of a fight-or-flight reaction) and helps increase activity in the executive and problem-solving part of her brain. Whenever possible, the more situations we invite our child to problem solve together, the more she learns to weigh consequences and make wise decisions in the future.

Collaborate with her. Our child may continue in defiance: "I don't care about my grades . . ." Here, we could choose the Truth Pathway and say, "Too bad, we do. You'll be home at eleven." Or we could use the Grace Pathway: "Fine, do what you want." But a collaborative Safe House response says: "You may not care about your grades, but they're important to us, and we want you to do well. What can we do to come up with a solution that will work for both of us?"[14]

I can't stress enough how challenging it can be to maintain a demeanor of empathy and respect when our child is acting just the opposite. But I have to remember, my daughter is watching me and modeling my behavior. Even our reaction to her defiance teaches her to react or collaborate, which are critical life skills.

Collaboration can and should be used proactively. When we see a problem coming, address it beforehand. For example, "I know you're making plans for this weekend, but you have a test coming up and your grades are not looking good. Let's create a plan to make sure you can have fun this weekend with your friends and still do well on the exam."

Having our child collaborate with us to determine limits and consequences helps her experience the realities and boundaries of life. We can also come back to the drawing board to reevaluate a solution that may not work out for the best. Doing so provides incredible teaching moments for us as parents, but it also unites us with our child in raising her to live, love, and lead well.

There will be many fences built and negotiated around issues from curfew to cell phones to screen time over the course of raising our kids. Whenever possible, *encourage her brain to do the work to come up with her own solutions.* We must be careful not to tell her what she ought to do or problem solve too fast.

"My baseball coach is always singling me out," a twelve-year-old complains. Rather than setting up a meeting with the coach, we can use this as an opportunity to reflect with our son. "Well, what would help you? How could you respond?" Empower him with the belief that he can solve his problems himself. Of course, we're going to help, but let him generate some ideas. We might say, "What do you think you could do differently?" Help him learn that he is part of the solution, not just the problem.

SOME NUTS AND BOLTS OF SAFE DISCIPLINE

To follow are some of my favorite nuts and bolts relating to safe discipline.[15]

Ask "what" questions. In approaching a defiant child, try to use "what" questions, not "why" questions. Just like adults, kids experience "why" questions as criticism, putting them on the defensive: "Why did you just say that? Why can't you calm down? Why can't you be more like your brother?" Instead, try asking "what" questions: "What was going on that got you so upset? What did you need? What were you feeling?" Parenting from this posture allows our child to reflect on her behavior while seeing that we have her best interests at heart. This type of dialogue encourages cognitive flexibility, as our child imagines new and different possibilities for both thoughts and actions.

Use educated guesses when our child says, "I don't know." When we ask our child questions to better understand his problem and goals, he may not know how to answer. Try to help him by making educated guesses about the problem: "It seems like you're really disappointed. If I were in your shoes, I would be pretty angry." He may honestly not know the answer or he may just lack the ability to put his feelings into words. If we guess near the right answer, it might help our child to name the problem. And just like that, we have a moment of emotional connection in the middle of a conflict.

Don't criticize character. The language we use with kids should never be judgmental or evaluative. When Landon spills milk on the table, he doesn't need to hear, "What's wrong with you? I told you that would happen! You're so clumsy!" Instead, describe the behavior. Be a little empathetic. "Uh, oh. The milk spilled." We then give Landon a plan for cleaning it up. Be careful not to yell either. Research shows that yelling only increases stress and anxiety levels in our child, making it harder for him to problem solve.[16] Imagine how you would treat a guest who was over for dinner and spilled the milk. We should treat our kids the same.

Describe behavior and be specific. Labels—both positive and negative—are disabling. "You're a genius!" we might say with good intentions, but this needs to be framed. Instead, describe your child's behavior and then say how you feel about it. For example, "I see you're being kind by sharing your blocks with your sister. I like how you're doing that. That makes me happy."

Process matters. As much as posture, process is everything. Say your son is playing with a friend and gets angry and hits him. Mom pulls him aside and slaps him in the arm and says, "It's not okay to hit." Sound ironic? It happens all of the time. Our kids are more likely to do as we do, not as we say. If we don't want our kids to yell, we can't be yellers. If we don't want our kids to cuss, we can't cuss. If we don't want our kids to hit in anger, we can't hit in anger. They're watching us. Be the person you want your child to be.

Pick your battles. Everybody is born with a sense of dignity. We want our child to develop her self-concept without feeling shamed. We want her to know, I can respect myself because my parents respect me. For example, perhaps your son is playing basketball while Uncle Jake is trying to nap. Uncle Jake asks him to stop shooting the basketball. Your son may bounce it a few more times to show he has power. He then may stop. Pick your battles wisely. We may allow our child to separate her food on her plate. This teaches her that what she wants is important and that her wishes are respected. Children need to know, within reason, they're respected and their needs are important.

When possible, avoid the word "no." Our kids hear "no" more than any other word. When Landon tries to postpone bedtime by saying, "Let's play blocks," I typically respond, "Right now it's time for bed, but tomorrow we can build a tower."

Small successes are okay. Christi and I are both firstborn Type A's. We expect results pronto. We've learned, however, that when it comes to parenting, we need to ease up on our expectations of our kids and praise the small successes. Children, like adults, are works in process, with good days and bad days. Don't expect them to just get it overnight. Remember, consistency is key.

Have fun. Find ways for your kids to shine for you. Do things together that are fun, adventurous, and enjoyable. When kids act out, it's often because there are no positive ways for them to get attention and affection. When our kids ask to do something, instead of automatically saying no, we pause first and ask ourselves, "Why not?" If we can't come up with a good answer, we have fun.

Coming Together for Our Kids

Discipline can be a messy process. No one child is the same, just as no situation is the same as another, which is why safe discipline is as much a learning process and character builder for us as the results are for our kids. By making adjustments along the way, discipline will stretch us. That's why I encourage you not to get sidetracked by critics, especially the ones not in the arena with you.[17]

Whether it's from our friends, people who don't even have children, strangers in public, or, of course, family members, it's easy to sense judgmental stares, whispers, or not-so-subtle hints on how to discipline our children.

Intentional or not, with judgment comes shame.

With shame come questions about how we're parenting our kids.

With questions come inconsistency in how we discipline, insecurity in our techniques, and an ultimate lack of purpose in our parenting approach.

Nothing is as powerful as shame in coming between you and your spouse in how you parent, threatening your emotional presence with your kids, and robbing your home of fun-loving joy. And shame is born in judgment.

Christi and I know this formula firsthand. And since we're as susceptible as anybody to shame, we regularly come together to not only make sure we're consistent in how we parent but to honestly assess where we're messing up (truth), dispel the lies of shame (truth), and encourage each other that we really do have what it takes (grace).

Discipline and consequences can be a huge source of conflict, not just between parents and kids but between you and your spouse. Rather than approach your spouse with an agenda ("This is the way I see it!"), ask instead, "What does our child need? What skills is she lacking that we can help develop through discipline? How can we be a united front?"

This is challenging, especially if you're coparenting, but it's still possible. No matter what your marital status, the end goal is to raise healthy, mature, and moral adults.

So the next time you see a child throwing a temper tantrum in a store, on a plane, or in a restaurant, offer an encouraging word or a helping hand. Just two words can be very powerful: "I understand." Let's be a generation of parents who publicly praise one another's efforts for raising disciplined children and reduce the shame we're likely already feeling with a screaming child.

━━━ Coauthoring Your Child's Story ━━━

1. Describe where you've had the most difficulty as it relates to discipline.
2. What did you learn in this chapter that can help you with that difficulty?
3. In what areas do you and your spouse need to be more consistent when it comes to discipline?

8

Nurturing Our Child's Brain
from Infancy Through Adolescence

Play is the highest expression of human development in childhood,
for it alone is the free expression of what is in a child's soul.

—Friedrich Froebel, founder of kindergartens,
The Education of Man

The other morning I had a moment. Maybe fifteen seconds. But it was a moment I'll remember for a very long time.

Landon is always a bit more cheerful after a restful night's sleep. Thankfully, he had a good night. When I went to get him out of bed bright and early at 6:30, he was already cheerfully asking for Mama. After a quick diaper change and his first sippy cup of milk to start the day, he turned our hallway into a racetrack, sprinting as fast as his toddler legs could to find and officially greet her.

Landon entered our bedroom full of babbles and kisses. Sitting on the bed for no more than a minute, he jumped down, ran to the bottom of our bed, and took a nose-dive into the pillows stacked on the floor. After a few more giggles, he confidently stood up near the bedroom door, raised his hand, and jabbered as if he wanted to show me something. So I followed.

With Muffins, his blue teddy bear who goes everywhere with him, in one hand, and his sippy cup in the other, he led me to the picture window in the dining room.

He wanted to look out the window. The sun was rising over the hill, and it was stunning.

I soaked it in. Not so much the sunrise, but the seventeen-month-old looking out that window, lost in seemingly big-boy thoughts, as if contemplating the full life ahead of him.

Then it happened. As Landon gazed out on the Ozark hilltops, he couldn't have been more excited. I watched as he crinkled his face into an excitable signature smile and pulled Muffins and his sippy cup into a hug, all the while still gazing out the window.

About fifteen seconds later, Landon turned around, looked up at me, smiled from ear to ear, and broke into a small rhythmic stomping on the floor, dancing uncontrollably. His body tried all it could to show the excitement he was feeling in the moment.

I joined him in the dance.

Had anybody walked by our house at that very moment, the height of the windowsill would have blocked Landon from their view. But they would have seen a grown man dancing, shaking, and stomping enthusiastically. Creepy, I know.

But my little boy and I shared a moment, bonding in the only language he had for the excitement he was feeling. One of the most powerful ways to build the brain of a child is to uninhibitedly join him on the dance floor.

Two minutes later, Landon turned from the window, looked up at me, and babbled with joy.

By then I was on the phone. The moment was over. E-mails, text messages, and push notifications don't care about moments, about your relationships, or even care about your kids. They only care that you prioritize them right away.

In spite of what marketing experts purport, one of the most damaging influences on our child's brain is technology.

Before you label me an old-school pessimist, consider first that the chief technology officer of eBay sends his kids to a nine-classroom school where technology is totally absent. So do executives of Google, Apple, Yahoo, and Hewlett-Packard.[1] Bill Gates only allows his daughters on the Internet forty-five minutes a day, including video games. He also didn't permit them to have cell phones until they turned thirteen. Steve Jobs? He didn't give his children iPads.[2]

Feeling convicted? I am.

If the people creating these devices are protecting their children, why aren't we?

As a young parent, I believe we're falling victim to the greatest enemy of healthy brains: busyness.

I have to work. Christi has to work. Watch the kids. Clean dirty bums. Pack lunches. Load dirty dishes. Pick up toys. Do laundry. Get Kennedy to nap (which is a feat not for the faint of heart). Add soccer practice, gymnastics, or whatever your child loves to do.

You all know the drill. Busy means we're exhausted.

So we go the path of least resistance. And though none of us would neglect to feed our kids, sometimes in the busyness of life, we neglect to feed their brains. Rather than spending one-on-one time playing, listening to, or talking with them, we turn to virtual babysitters so we can get stuff done.

I get it. We're as guilty as the next parent. Sometimes we need Mickey Mouse, Daniel Tiger, or family pictures from an iPhone. And I'm okay with that. I'm not *against* screens, but I'm *for* raising emotionally and spiritually healthy children.

> There could be nothing more detrimental and threatening to our society than the next generation of kids addicted to vices—their devices.

In spite of being busy and exhausted, we cannot ignore the way these invasive devices literally change the wiring in our children's brains (and ours too). There could be nothing more detrimental and threatening to our society than the next generation of kids addicted to vices—their devices.

That's why I advocate for screen-balanced families and using technology to give our kids an advantage. If we're not healthy, our kids won't be either.

This chapter is devoted to practical ways of nurturing our children's brains and wiring them for emotional safety from infancy through adolescence.

Our kids need to know we genuinely enjoy dancing with them more than staring at our phone.

Our kids need to learn they can turn to us, not to a screen, when they're feeling stressed, sad, or angry.

Being emotionally safe means feeding their brain like we do their tummies.

As long as you're okay with being the creepy adult who dances in front of the window at seven in the morning.

WHAT SPEAKING A SECOND LANGUAGE
AND FALLING IN LOVE HAVE IN COMMON

Did you know that the brain is the only vital organ not fully developed at birth? As one researcher put it, "The brain is in a remarkably unfinished state."[3] Like raw materials piled at a building site—lumber, drywall, siding, shingles, wiring—the majority of our infant's brain cells are not connected.

Simply put, brain development is the process of connecting brain cells with one another. That's where we come in as a parent. As we create a Safe House, we help lay the foundation for an internal Safe House in our baby's brain.

During the first several years of life, every single experience our child has is like wiring the electrical circuits in a house. When our child experiences any of the five senses, the brain makes a connection. The more an experience is repeated over time, the more the brain becomes wired for that activity.

That's why freely and joyfully dancing matters. Give your kids relational experiences, especially during intense positive or negative emotion, and their brain becomes wired for relationships. Give your kids a screen, and their brain becomes wired for a screen.

Though billions of our child's brain cells have the incredible potential to form complex internal connections, timing matters. While the brain doesn't reach full maturity until age twenty-five, it grows at an amazingly fast rate, as much as 1 percent a day, during the first ninety days after birth. After that, the first few years of life contain key windows of opportunity for learning, because the brain remains very sensitive and pliable.

Here's where I wish my preschool, not my high school, had offered Spanish 101. Language, motor development, and, yes, emotional control and social skills are best learned in the first few years of life. Consider Figure 8.1.

Windows of Opportunity

Researchers believe there are extensive opportunities for a child to learn social skills and emotional control at specific stages in the first ten years of life.[4]

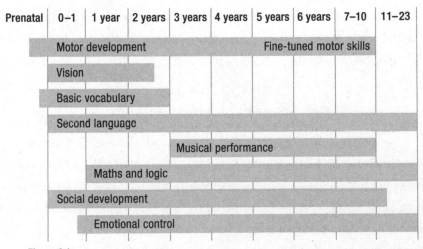

Figure 8.1

As child development expert Stanley Greenspan wrote: "Bright, emotionally healthy, and moral children don't just happen. . . . All the wonderful things you wish for your child do not have to be left to chance, intuition, or genetic endowment. Nor do they require hours of flash cards, educational TV, or special computer-based learning exercises." So what's the key to nurturing our child's budding brain? It's surprisingly simple: fall in love with your child. This is otherwise known as sensitive caregiving.[5]

> Parenting isn't rocket science. It's brain surgery.

In short, the answer is *you*. And not just your physical presence but your emotional presence.

Think about it. When we're in love, we're hyperattuned to the object of our affection. We hang on her every word. Watch her every move. Touch. Talk. Delight in each other's presence. Never miss a moment. Next time you're out, just watch the young couple that can't keep their hands off of each other. All giddy and twitterpated. Adoring one another. Cozying up close.

Parenting isn't rocket science. It's brain surgery.

By being present, engaged, and safe with our child in the day-to-day moments of life as we feed her, change endless diapers, play together, read, sing, and maybe even dance, we are brain surgeons for her brain. Add *that* to your résumé!

And though technology is here to stay, it's not all that it's cracked up to be when it comes to brain development.

You, Mom and Dad, are irreplaceable.

Stop stressing about the latest brain-building apps. Just be present. Relax. Enjoy being together. Woo your child. Be playful. Fully engage.

Fall in love.

THE MOST IMPORTANT QUESTION
A PARENT CAN ASK

As parents, we face emotionally intense moments all of the time with our kids, especially in the early years. No wonder we're exhausted. When you can't figure out what's wrong with your six-month-old who wakes every two hours through the night and screams when you lay him down. When you don't know what to do when your five-year-old kicks you because you took his LeapPad.

On the one hand, you want to stick to the wisdom of the research and be there for them, but on the other hand, since you're barely surviving and feeling like you're losing control of your home, you also want to bring the hammer down. Where's the balance?

That's a question we tackle nearly every day in the Straub household.

Since every child and developmental stage is different, I want to first offer the most important question we as parents can ask ourselves when approaching these volatile and emotionally intense situations. Before we get to age-specific ways of building our child's brain, there are two important ways of answering this question we must first consider.

Whenever I'm faced with a difficult parenting decision, I ask myself, *How can I respond in an emotionally safe way so my child knows she is loved?* Or put another way, *What can I do for my child to feel safest in this situation?*

Let's be honest, we're not going to always get it right. But using this question as a filter can help us be more consistent in making the emotionally safest decision possible. This question helped me in many instances to decide that the Safe House Pathway, in the moment, wasn't going to work because *I* was too worked up. In these situations, you may find it best to resort either to the Truth or Grace Pathway of parenting. There are times I simply need to send Landon to his room to be by himself so I have time to cool off myself, otherwise I may react (punish) rather than respond (discipline) to his misbehavior.

Being emotionally safe, especially in the formative early years, happens in two primary ways: (1) calm and soothing touch, and (2) connecting and talking.

A calm and soothing touch is our baby's first language. In fact, research shows that skin-to-skin contact actually releases powerful neurochemicals in the brain. Scientists call this *attachment*. Cuddling, stroking, and massaging our baby, especially while feeding, facilitates the release of oxytocin, otherwise known as the love drug. Oxytocin helps our little one feel close, safe, and bonded. It actually drives out fear in the brain by downregulating stress and promoting the development of trust. When we lovingly touch our baby, we not only calm her; we also trigger her brain to release opioid endorphins, dubbed pleasure hormones.

Kissing a boo-boo to help our child feel better or giving him a bear hug after a rough day at school isn't just an act. Endorphins released in the brain help our child feel happy and relaxed while reducing physical and emotional pain. Opioids also build an internal sense of safety and security. Perhaps it's no wonder, then, that many adolescents who turn to an external source of opioids by abusing illicit drugs lack close, loving relationships with their parents. When they become stressed by a test, a breakup, or a family conflict, they seek out external drugs to calm and soothe themselves, because they've learned that people aren't safe, loving, or available.

Connecting and talking with our child is also critical to brain development. Through the relationship we have with our child, her brain begins to create expectations for relationships. When we're emotionally attentive to and interactive with our baby (a process called attunement), our child learns that she is safe and worthy of love and attention. On the contrary, if we're harsh, inconsistent, or dismissing, we teach her that the world is unpredictable and dangerous and that people will not be there when she needs them most. Consistent, safe, loving interactions wire our baby's brain *toward* relationships long before she can form words.

> We need to ask ourselves, *What is she feeling right now? How can I respond in an emotionally safe way so my child knows she is loved?*

Attunement is actually most critical when our child is crying, upset, angry, sad, or afraid. Babies are born emotionally helpless; their brains do not have the ability to naturally calm down. By responding to, reassuring, and soothing our child when she is overwhelmed and emotional, we're literally offering our brainpower to co-regulate her emotions. Over time, our child's brain internalizes and maps out how *we* handle her feelings, constructing either a Safe House or a Crazy House.

This is why it's important as we interact with our kids, no matter their age or the situation, that we ask ourselves, *What is she feeling right now? How can I respond in an emotionally safe way so my child knows she is loved?*

Nowhere else has this been a battle in our house than with sleep. I swear we're being tested because of our beliefs about slumber. Both of our babies have been the worst sleepers. As a result, we've tackled every sleeping question you can imagine: Should she sleep in our room or a separate bedroom? Do we let him cry it out or not? Is it best to help her settle in and calm down or just put her in bed? When you're already overly exhausted and living in a fog, it's easy to get caught up trying to find the perfect technique, forgetting that the posture from which we parent matters most.

Though we may have paid a bigger price as parents because of it, we decided we did not want to put our child's emotional well-being, especially in those early, formative years, at risk for the convenience of a few extra hours of sleep. Remember, the first year of life is critical to brain growth and secure attachment. And with an inability to calm and soothe themselves as infants, our children come to trust whether we'll be there for them or not in those emotionally charged moments.

When it comes to brain growth and sleep, here are a few suggestions we have based on way too much personal experience and research.

- While structure is important, be careful not to cling religiously to a sleep schedule at the expense of your child's needs.
- Dads, pull your weight where you can. If you're formula feeding, take turns with your wife, alternating nights. If your wife is breast-feeding, get the baby during times he doesn't need to be fed. If she is pumping, use bottles during the night to take your turn and give your wife some rest.
- Co-sleeping is important, especially in the first four to six months. Co-sleeping means sleeping in the same room with your infant or sleeping in the same bed. Though we did keep our babies in a cradle in our room with us, they were in our bed only when we felt they needed us or when it meant we would get more sleep (the best of both worlds!).
- If your infant is so uncontrollable that she wakes and screams every time you try to transition her, you may try letting her cry for a few minutes, then going in, picking her up, talking to her, caressing her head, holding her hand, or gently patting her back to help her calm down, and then put her back down again. This requires work, but it's safer than leaving your child to cry with no solace.

Taking time to soothe our baby teaches her that she can trust us. The same goes for our toddlers, children, and teenagers. Using calm and soothing touch and connecting and talking with our kids, especially in intense emotional moments, instills a deep sense of safety and security about how relationships work and equips them to also one day love and be present with others.

Does your toddler know she can come to you when she is upset, hurt, or angry? Or do you dismiss her emotions and tell her to get over it? How about your teenager? Are you emotionally connected with him, eager to hear his ideas, dreams, and plans? Or do you find yourself constantly correcting and criticizing him? "Do your homework. Don't eat that. Go to bed. No, you can't go out tonight . . ."

Remember that whenever you're faced with a difficult parenting decision and want to make the best brain-building decision, take a moment to filter it through the most important question you can ask as a parent: *How can I respond in an emotionally safe way so my child knows she is loved?* Or asked another way: *What is she feeling? How can I be emotionally present and do what will best build her brain, and not just do what is most convenient for me?*

JOINING YOUR CHILD IN THE WORLD OF PLAY

There are grandmas. And then there are memaws.

I had a memaw.

As a boy I went to her house often. She personified love. She did anything to help my sister and me mature into respectable adults. We spent many nights at her house cooking, creating, and playing with homemade toys, and romping around in the huge sand piles situated at the block company next to her home. She taught us that to have a little fun was just enough.

Grandparents, you have no idea the influence you can have in shaping your grandchildren. As noted child therapist Gary Landreth noted, "A child's play is his 'work,' and the 'toys' are his words."

If this is true, Memaw was definitely our employer.

Surprisingly, "research has found that the availability of play materials (like toys and games) is one of the most consistent predictors of intelligence."[6] Studies show that when it comes to playthings, inexpensive, simple, and open-ended toys and games facilitate the most brain development, as opposed to newfangled or fancy technological devices that often leave little room for creativity. Boxes, bubbles, blocks, bowls, and baby dolls are all great props for engaging in imaginative play.[7]

Viewing my childhood through the loving environment Memaw created for us, I have a deeper gratitude and appreciation for her simplicity than ever before. Her simple environment was actually a creative factory for our brain growth.

While there are many different ways to play, *unstructured relational settings* seem to present the greatest potential for brain development. When our child plays by herself or with other peers, she begins to develop a healthy sense of self and learns to set and achieve goals independently.[8] However, Floor Time with Mom and Dad is just as critical to brain growth.[9]

As we discussed in chapter 5, Floor Time requires us to set aside parenting agendas, enter our child's world, and let her take the lead in inviting us into her play. No iPhone.

Just our undivided attention for at least a half hour. It's seeing the world through our child's eyes.

Carefree. Curious. Fully engaged.

Try to make this a daily habit. Floor Time should never be used as a reward for good behavior, so don't cancel it if your child misbehaves or has a rough day. And don't sit there like a bump on a log either. Engaging with our child means being an active participant. We're not *watching* her play; we're playing with her.

These kinds of play experiences don't start when your child can toss a ball or put a puzzle together. Floor Time begins at birth. If you have multiple kids, consider creative ways to make the most of your children's varying schedules. I try to have Floor Time with Landon when Kennedy is napping and vice versa. Or, if possible, recruit your spouse, so each child is getting quality time with Mom or Dad each day. If you have school-aged children, you can plan Floor Time with your toddler while your second and sixth graders are in school. You can hang out one-on-one with your teenager once the younger kids are in bed.

NURTURING YOUR CHILD'S BRAIN: AGE-SPECIFIC EXERCISES

Each section below highlights age-specific activities for Floor Time that target brain building.[10]

Brain Builders: Birth to Six Months

During the first few months after birth, our baby's brain is going a mile a minute, taking in and responding to many new sensations: bright lights, our smiling faces, warm soothing touch, and, of course, hunger pangs. As our infant connects with us, we model for her how to be both calm and attentive, especially by the way we respond to her when she is crying or upset. As we care for and play with our baby, the brain-building goal to keep in mind is to try to *engage* her "senses, motor skills, and emotions in a single activity."[11]

Think. Feel. Relate.

When our infant simultaneously looks, listens, moves, and feels at the same time, she takes in information from many sources. Again, this is gold for brain development. For example, while nursing or bottle-feeding, stroke her softly and sing a song or tell her a story.

We can never underestimate the power our face and voice have on our infants' developing brain. We don't need fancy mobiles and electronic toys. Whenever possible, our baby needs us to engage her, which is why it's best to avoid leaving her to passively take in the world when she's awake and ready to interact.

As our baby connects with us, we can begin to challenge her brain to grow by interacting with more of her senses. Talk to her. Make goofy faces. Stick out our tongue. Cuddle with her. With these exercises, we can transform the mundane tasks of the day—bath time, feeding, diaper changes—into opportunities to connect with our little one and fall in love.

Brain Builders: Six to Twelve Months

Our baby is no longer content with being the object of our affection. He wants to communicate. We may catch him spontaneously smiling at us. He may babble, reach his arms toward us, put a finger in our mouth, or scoot himself along the floor, looking our way for affirmation. The brain-building goal during this stage is *two-way communication*. Though our child can't form full words yet, his sounds, gestures, and facial expressions become increasingly purposeful. By picking up on and responding to his attempts to communicate, we're wiring his brain for relationships.

Playing with our little one is a great way to encourage his sense of curiosity and his expressions of needs and emotions. This is also a critical time period to affirm our approval of his newfound sense of independence and exploration, which lays the foundation for his sense of self. The more rooms we babyproof in our home, the more we can follow our child's lead in play.

Responding to our baby's focused attention is a fun way to build his brain too. For example, every time your child pokes at your nose, make the noise of a honking horn. When he giggles, coos, or tries to form a word, echo it back. If he's cooing as he holds a rattle, talk to him about the rattle's color and the sound it makes. Hold out your palm and see if he will offer it to you. Shake it for a moment, and then give it back to him. See how long you can keep the two-way communication going.

Brain Builders: Twelve to Eighteen Months

Our baby's wobbly first steps represent a fundamental shift in her focus. Our little one now possesses the ability to move toward the things she likes and away from the things she wants to avoid. In this process, she's learning to identify and communicate what she wants. She may use her voice, hand gestures, and facial expressions to let us know she wants more food. She may try to squiggle out of our grasp when she doesn't want her diaper changed. (Every parent's worst nemesis.) She may, like Landon, use her body to communicate excitement about the world by dancing.

During this stage of development, her brain is beginning to recognize and decipher patterns, understand cause-and-effect relationships, develop spatial understanding, and problem solve. She learns if she turns the knob to the right, the volume of the music goes up. The brain-building goal to keep in mind during these months is to *help our baby problem solve* without doing the work for her.

Playing interactive social games, such as roughhousing and hide-and-seek, help orient our child to space. Roughhousing incorporates touch, movement, and emotion, and hide-and-seek encourages exploration and problem solving. Imitative games are also fun, as our child often imitates our behavior. She may pick up the phone and pretend to talk on it or put our shoes on and try to walk across the bedroom. Keeping play open-ended is a great way to begin to focus more on talking about, exploring, and labeling our child's emotion. Though it's easy to want to control our child's behavior during play-time, her emotional experience is expanding well beyond happy and sad to include excitement, defiance, humor, closeness, and more.

Brain Builders: Eighteen to Thirty Months

During these months, our child is becoming aware of ideas and symbolic communication. He's learning to use words to communicate what he wants. Rather than crying when he's hungry, he's now learning to use verbal shortcuts, words like nana (banana) and a-sauce (applesauce) to symbolize the food he wants. The brain-building goal to keep in mind here is to *foster his discovery of ideas and connections.*

This is a critical stage to support our little one's exploration by reassuring him of our acceptance, love, and presence. When we do this, our child begins to feel more freedom to play, using us as a portable security blanket to explore in areas we're not present.[12]

When he enters a stage of volatile emotions and tantrums, it's important that we learn to tolerate and accept our child's feelings. By doing so, we collaborate with our child to explore his newfound world of emotions and instill in his brain the ability to accept and use feelings productively.

This is a great stage to once again bring out the kid in us by encouraging creativity and imaginary play. Structured games, like puzzles or educational television programming, don't foster imagination like pretend play does. Dress up together, do puppet shows, have tea parties, cook in a play kitchen, build forts with blankets or boxes. Turn pots and pans into a drum set. Make music with brooms and buckets. Whether we play dolls, race cars, or transform our living room into a construction site, we should be sure to follow our child's lead and never belittle his imagination by saying things like, "That's not a fort; that's just a box." Engaging in back-and-forth conversations about what our child enjoys challenges his continuing development of communication.

Brain Builders: The Preschool Years

Though the toddler and preschool years hold a bad reputation, this is an incredible time for brain development. Our child, who less than a year ago could only point, squeal, and perhaps say the word "no," can now emphatically tell us, "I don't want to take a nap. I'm not tired!" Our child is beginning to build bridges between ideas and feelings and grasp the concept of time. When we ask something of her, she will often ask us for evidence. "Why? When? How come?" The brain-building goal during these critical years is to become "a debating partner, opinion seeker, and collaborator in exploring the world."[13] Notice the term *debating partner.* Here's where we can expect to have regular discussions about bedtime, playtime, bath time, and more as our child tests our limits.

Building the brain at this phase goes beyond giving our child a simple yes or no answer. Though this may seem easier in the short term, when we encourage reflective discussions, our child develops the capacity to consider the what, when, why, and how about a topic or situation. As our child's personality grows, respecting her opinions and helping her reflect on what she wants helps her form abstract thinking. As we go through our day, we can encourage her to make age-appropriate decisions. We might pick her pants and then ask her to pick a shirt that matches. Invite her to make us a meal in her play kitchen or pull out the Play-Doh and mold her creations together. As we expose our child to a range of activities, we can pay attention to what she really enjoys.

Engaging in complex, imaginative, and storytelling play, while challenging our child to incorporate emotional themes, helps her link ideas, feelings, and behaviors together. For example, a dolly who gets hurt and cries can be comforted by our little one. A scary monster can be fought off by our brave son and his mighty little buddy next door. A stuffed animal who gets angry can rejoin the play once he calms down and starts feeling better. Amazingly, it's through play that children learn to appropriately express and manage their emotions.

Brain Builders: Childhood and Adolescence

Challenging our child to explore new activities and interests helps him discover what he loves doing and is genuinely good at. However, we cannot overinflate his sense of self by telling him he is amazing at everything he does. As parents, "speaking the truth in love" to our child can be difficult but necessary to help him succeed.[14] He may not love or be good at basketball. And that's okay. Though he needs us to be there for him when he fails, is afraid, or is unsure of himself, he doesn't need us to overprotect him from these feelings. Instead, these are great opportunities to teach him how to calm himself down and make wise decisions about his life, even if he's overwhelmed with emotion.

Floor Time isn't just for little ones. Our emotional presence with our older children and teens is the greatest brain-building tool we have. Throw the ball. Go on a hike. Play chess together. Have a culinary adventure in the kitchen. Go on adventures. Make memories. Enter their world. The world of play, no matter our kids' age, is a fantastic way to encourage independence, problem solving, and social skills. This type of play, however, is not pushing our child to do what *we* want, but instead helps them to discover who they are.

Being safe for our child's emotions without being defensive helps him learn to own and verbalize his feelings without attacking others; for example, helping him assert, "I'm angry that I can't go to my friend's house," rather than yelling at us. By doing so, we're developing our child's ability to emotionally regulate. Using the strategies from the last chapter, we can help our child reason through his options, weigh consequences, problem solve, and make wise decisions even in the midst of strong emotions. When we engage him to think, feel, and relate all at the same time, we're wiring together critical brain pathways that will enable him to live, love, and lead well.

WHY MISTER ROGERS IS SMARTER THAN BABY EINSTEIN

I remember the Saturday morning I sat Landon in front of the television for a little treat. As would be the norm in our house, this particular day didn't star an animated tomato, cucumber, or even Mickey Mouse. Instead, I introduced him to the nostalgia of my own childhood, my ol' buddy from years ago, Mister Rogers.

As you know by now, I love research. Forget blogs and people's opinions. Show me the data behind why I should or shouldn't do something, and I'll listen. Which is why my son and I left Mickey Park that day and traveled to *Mister Rogers' Neighborhood*.

Research reveals how screens can negatively impact the brains of our developing children, especially kids under the age of seven. The primary finding is what's called the overstimulation hypothesis. That is, when our kids have prolonged exposure to rapid image changes during the critical period of brain development, it preconditions their mind to expect high levels of stimulation, which leads to inattention later in life.

I don't want my children having attention problems because of too much idle screen time. Heaven forbid they can't go to a restaurant as an adult without a phone as a placemat.

If you think this isn't a problem, watch a television episode with your kids and notice how many screen changes happen in a twenty-second span. Many people claim that products like Baby Einstein are an exception and actually make their kids smarter. Research shows, however, there's nothing more to this than great marketing. In fact, when you watch "A Day on the Farm" by Baby Einstein, you'll average about seven scene changes in any twenty-second clip. Send your kid to school a few years later to study farm animals, and school becomes boring because the lessons are too slow.

In the study on television shows I'm referring to here, *Mister Rogers' Neighborhood* was the *only* program to show no differences in later attention compared to kids who watched no television.[15] That's because it was a show designed to expand a child's attention by keeping the child focused on face-to-face interaction with one person. The pacing of screen changes for *Mister Rogers' Neighborhood* is radically different from other children's programs, including *Sesame Street* and Baby Einstein, both of which cater to a child's shorter attention span by increasing screen changes.

So though our child may be mastering his ABCs a bit quicker than the Jones kids next door, what we're sacrificing are the higher-level functions of our child's developing brain—*the ability to problem solve, display behavioral control, regulate emotions, plan, negotiate, and delay gratification*—all critical components for both academic and social success.

Also, 85 percent of the apps purchased for children on tablets are drill-and-practice apps that solicit children to simply repeat an action or recall simple facts. As one study reveals, "These 'consumption' based apps [lead] to lower-level neural development [and their] excessive in-game rewarding [leads] to unrealistic expectations."[16] For more helpful apps, use ones like Beck and Bo (ages three to five), Explain Everything (ages twelve to sixteen), Toca Builders (ages five to twelve), Toontastic (ages five to nine), My Story, and ARTmaker. These apps require input and creativity from your child.

The American Academy of Pediatrics now suggests limiting screen time to a maximum of *two hours a day* apart from homework, for kids ages eight to eighteen.[17] To put this in perspective, children less than five years old average four and a half hours of screen time per day, which is 40 percent of their waking hours.[18] Kids and teens between eight and eighteen spend an average of seven hours and thirty-eight minutes a day on screens, not including homework.[19] For the sake of comparison, parents average two to three hours a day with their kids.[20]

It's not hard to see how technology holds a massive influence over our kids' day-to-day lives and development.

In 1970, the average age of first screen exposure was four years old. Today, it is four months.[21] Research clearly and consistently shows that television is not good for young kids, but at least most kids back in the day were already past their most critical years of brain development before being exposed to a screen for the first time.

If you're like us and need screens sometimes to maintain your sanity, such as providing distraction for trimming your kids' fingernails or getting ready in the mornings, use them wisely and sparingly. Screens used to be in houses only; now we take them with us everywhere we go.

My recommendation is to keep your kids' screen time under age eight to less than one hour a day and for ages eight to eighteen to two hours a day. Invite your kids in the evening to help you cook dinner, do yard work, or even discuss parts of your workday with you. Having them *help you* problem solve some of your difficult situations not only builds their brain but invites them into your inner world.

Pediatrician and researcher Dimitri Christakis summarizes this chapter with the following recommendation: "We need more real-time play; less fast-paced media. Change the beginning and you change the whole story."[22]

OUR BRAIN MATTERS TOO: KEEPING OUR SANITY

After reading this chapter, you may be thinking, *I'm just trying to survive. To make it through another day without losing my sanity. There's no way I can do any of this extra stuff.*

Let me tell you, I'm there. I was tempted more times than I can count to sit Landon in front of the television so I could write this book. And sometimes, I gave in.

Hungry babies, whiny toddlers, needy kids, unruly teenagers—the continual demands of parenting can wear us down.

So what about our brains? Being emotionally engaged or nurturing with our kiddos when we find ourselves frazzled and exhausted is difficult. After all, we are the foundation of our Safe House. We set the emotional tone for our family.

Thus, the old adage "If momma ain't happy, ain't nobody happy" may not be far from the truth. Dads, the same is true for us. If we're anxious, depressed, stressed, or exhausted, our children are likely to pick up on it, causing these emotions to take over the atmosphere of our home.

But we don't have to live like this. In addition to the strategies found in the next chapter, I'd like to share one very important way we can take care of our brain to be the best parent we can be: build your own Safe Life Team.

It's tough, if not impossible, to build a Safe House on your own. Just like a general contractor needs subcontractors, architects, and consultants, we need a life team.

Jesus had one. When he was in agony and deeply distressed, he called on Peter, James, and John to be with him.[23]

When Adam was alone with God in perfect union before sin entered the world, it was "not good" that he was alone.[24]

Being a great parent begins by understanding that we were created in a system built on the foundation of relationships. We're not the source of life to ourselves.

Though some days it's all we have, our most powerful brain fuel, surprisingly, is not coffee. Our ability to parent for the long haul and move from surviving to thriving is largely based on identifying and reaching out to emotionally safe people to get the fuel we need to keep our loving engine going. Otherwise, it's too easy to slip into fear-based parenting. Fear always sabotages brain development.

So what is a Safe Life Team?[25] It's a handful of people in our life (usually three to eight close friends, mentors, and confidants) whom we can turn to and share anything with, without condemnation or judgment.

These are people who love us as we are, but they love us enough to not leave us that way. In order to be safe for our child, we need people in our life who will be safe for us, no matter what. People who embody grace and truth, support, and challenge in their friendship with us.

My wife, Christi, has a group of friends she depends on. She's a mom who deals with a toddler whose screams could peel paint off a wall and a newborn who demands her continual attention. She's a wife, but she also writes and runs a business with me. Trying to balance it all is exhausting. She needs others. So I stay home and watch the kids one night a week while she spends time with her Safe Life Team, other moms with young children. To parent well, she needs it.

So do I. My Safe Life Team is made up of friends and mentors locally and at a distance. My goal is to connect with all of them at least once a month. Some I meet with weekly, others biweekly. They're husbands and fathers who support me, and I support them, with complete transparency, grace, and honesty.

You may be in a season of life trying to keep paint on the walls—nursing infants, wrangling toddlers, or detaining teenagers (before the authorities get them first).

You desperately need safe people to fill your gas tank of love so you can be the best parent you can be at home.

═══ Coauthoring Your Child's Story ═══

1. What limits or boundaries on technology do you need to set in your life? in your marriage? with your kids?
2. Who is on your Safe Life Team? If you don't have one, who could you consider adding to one? What step will you take this week to build one?
3. Based on your child's age, what activities will you begin doing to work on the brain-building goal of your child's developmental level?

PART 3

A Safe Village

The Bible and Safe Parenting

Think about the comfortable feeling you have as you open your
front door. That's but a hint of what we'll feel some day on arriving
at the place our Father has lovingly and personally prepared for us
in heaven. We will finally—and permanently—be "at home" in a
way that defies description.

—Charles Stanley

When I think of what it means to be a parent, I think of shepherds and sheep.
My mother-in-love, Lora Lee, grew up on a farm. Though her parents were
mixed—farmers raising both livestock (primarily hogs) and crops—they decided one
year to raise sheep. Their initial purchase was about eight hundred to a thousand sheep.

Not too long after their purchase, Lora Lee's parents had an engagement out of town
and left the work of the new sheep to her and her three brothers and sister. The five of
them decided that weekend they would work smarter, not harder. So rather than pitch-
forking hay out of the loft every day, they threw out the amount of hay they needed for
the weekend into a heaping pile in a spot, of course, where the sheep couldn't get to it.

As they arrived the next morning to care for the sheep, to their horror, they found
a pile of sheep atop the hay. At the top of the pile was a layer of bloated sheep, eating
themselves to death. In the middle of the pile was a layer of barely alive sheep also eating
themselves to death but being smothered by the sheep on top of them. And at the bottom of the pile was a layer of dead sheep that had been smothered to death by the sheep
on top of them.

Lora Lee said the most frustrating part about that morning was trying to save the
lives of the still-living sheep. When they threw the sheep off the pile, the animals would
get up and shake off the dirt and waddle back into the haystack, dumbly walking back
to their demise.

On another occasion with the sheep, she watched some sheep drop dead because dogs were circling their pen, trying to find a way to get inside. Even though the dogs couldn't get to them, the sheep fell over dead from fear that they would.

Do you realize the Bible uses sheep more than any other animal to describe you and me? No wonder parenting is so difficult. We're nothing but a bunch of panicky worry-warts bent on our own destruction.

Just think about the dogs running around your pen now as a parent. Perhaps you have a screaming, colicky infant who won't sleep at night. A toddler who constantly throws a temper tantrum when it comes to transitions. A special-needs child who is not being treated fairly by other kids or even her teachers. Or a teenager who loves technology.

Let's be honest, being a Safe House Parent is not for the faint of heart.

Think, too, about the other types of dogs running around your parenting pen—your critics—the judgmental attitudes of the peanut gallery (in-laws, parents, friends, people in the grocery store, well-intentioned but misinformed people at church who don't know anything about you but still want to tell you what you *should* do to get your baby to sleep) and the condescending remarks of the so-called experts who think their way is the only and right way to do it.

As fellow parenting sheep on this journey with you, Christi and I get it. We've experienced colicky babies with attitudes and screams that would leave the most cold-hearted in tears. Babies who wouldn't sleep, no matter what we tried (trust me, everyone had an opinion). In addition, Christi, due to a volleyball injury in college, has thrown her back out numerous times, leaving her temporarily (usually for a week at a time) unable to lift our kids as infants and needy toddlers. And all of this is just the tip of the iceberg.

As parents, we all have a lot of dogs running around our pen when it comes to our decision making. Add our already insecure thoughts that we're not enough or don't have what it takes, and the result is a lot of skittish and fearful parents.

No wonder our most favorite time of the day as parents is when the kids are down and it's time for bed.

What's most interesting about scared sheep though, especially without a shepherd, is what we tend to do in our most stressful moments: we waddle back into our haystacks.

I'm not sure what or whom you turn to when you're feeling angry, lonely, tired, or even hungry as a parent, but our natural tendency is to return to the haystack—something that fills us up and makes us feel better about ourselves when we're starving for affirmation, connection, or anything that tells us we're doing okay as parents.

Some of us turn to work instead of our families. Some turn to social media and the false affirmation of likes, comments, and followers. Others turn to perfectionism, ensuring there's not a scratch, bump, or bruise on their overly dressed kids or their reputations. Even more parents are actually making their own kids into the haystack, finding their significance and self-worth in their children or their children's achievements. Others may turn to less socially acceptable haystacks, like alcohol or pornography. Regardless, parenting has split many a marriage and left many innocent children smothered at the bottom of the pile.

> Our haystacks will smother our kids and us every time we mosey back to them. Which is why every one of us needs a shepherd who is safe.

Our haystacks will smother our kids and us every time we mosey back to them. Which is why every one of us needs a shepherd who is safe.

THE EXPERIENCE OF THE FATHER

The image of shepherds and sheep came to me one night when I was putting our firstborn down for bed. I cherished these nighttime moments with both of our kids as the most precious part of my day while they were infants—when I got to hold them in my arms and sit and rock them to sleep as I prayed over them.

I remember a night when Landon was about eight months old. As I sat in the glider, I hugged the stillness and joy of the moment, staring at him sleeping soundly in my arms, a nightlight reflecting on his face. He was a little lamb in need of a shepherd.

That's when I imagined myself lying there. As dependent as Landon is on his mom and dad, I realized I, too, was an infant. I was a lamb lying in the arms of a God I am 100 percent dependent on for everything in my life, and I am in need of a shepherd.

The mystery is astounding. Not only am I a fearful sheep, but now, as a parent, my kids need me to be a secure and loving shepherd. What does that look like? Where do I learn how to do this?

Christi insightfully described the mystery from a Christian perspective in a post she titled "Loving Tiny Humans." Notice the irony.

Family is our first experience of being connected to another in love—it's the most selfless, grounding, strengthening, wings-to-fly kind of love.

But love starts out in a funny way.

We're born into a strange world through a horribly painful process. We emerge from a dark tunnel to find two strangers who take us into their home—and there we find a home set up just for us.

We, tiny humans, demand love, food, and attention—though we do nothing to earn it. We take and take and expect our needs to be met without the slightest thought about what that love costs—until we're about thirty.

Then we have our own tiny human.

We endure a horribly painful process, and push something the size of a watermelon through a dark tunnel the size of a magic marker. We find a tiny human stranger—who looks oddly like E.T. We take them into our home—where we've lovingly created a special home just for them (costing us a small fortune). And we begin to care for our tiny human's needs.

We notice quickly that our tiny human does nothing to thank us and gives us little in return. Instead they cry and scream incessantly. They wake us from our precious few hours of sleep and demand we do something for them. They demand food whenever they want it. They emphatically resist our attempts to help—a standard diaper change and a doctor visit—they don't understand and don't care to. They want to be held and rocked and cuddled—they don't care how tired our arms are, or that we haven't eaten yet today, or that we haven't showered in days. And then, they want to eat, *again*. "Feed me!" they demand—and then they spit up on us.

And *this* is how love begins?

Why would any mentally sound and moderately intelligent person sign up to take care of an ungrateful, helpless, thankless tiny human?

Tiny humans demand a lot and give back very little. It sounds far too sacrificial to me. And yet *this* is what begins a family? Whose idea was this?

Abba, Father. Our Daddy.

Paradigm shift.

He is our Daddy. We are but tiny humans.

He gave us a second birth through a horribly painful process called the Cross. We, tiny humans, emerged from a dark tunnel of sin and utter hopelessness to find a Stranger who took us into his home. He cares for all of our needs, yet we do little to thank him and give him nothing in return.

We, tiny humans, are so consumed by our needs, we cry and scream to get him to *do something* for us. He seems to be sleeping when we want his help, so we cry loudly so he will get *his* schedule straight. We demand blessing, comfort, and favor whenever we want it, though we did nothing to earn it. We emphatically resist when he bothers us—dealing with the consequences of our behavior and spending time in prayer are not what *we* planned for today. We resist his attempts to help us because we don't understand—and we don't care to. We want to be pampered and loved and have the greatest of things, because that's just what we want. We don't care that his arms have been holding us all along, or that our selfishness is hurting others, or that our wants are ultimately making us miserable.

We're in want, again. "Feed me!" we demand—and then we spit on him.

And *this* is how Love begins.

We, tiny humans, demand love, food and attention—though we do nothing to earn it. We take and take and expect our needs to be met without the slightest thought of what that love costs—or how to offer it.

Until we realize *who* Love is.

Love is patient and selfless; Love keeps no record of wrongs; Love is not resentful or irritable; Love is sacrificial. Love signed up to take care of billions of ungrateful, helpless, thankless tiny humans.

Family is our first experience of being connected to another in love—the most selfless, grounding, strengthening, wings-to-fly kind of love.

It is a love that bears all things, believes all things, hopes all things, and endures all things—*even tiny humans.*

What's fascinating is that both Scripture and scientific research reveal that our ability to love others is proportionate to how well we experience the love of others, particularly God.[1] Remember, "We love because [God] first loved us."[2]

In order for my kids to learn they have a safe and loving heavenly Father who is the real hero of the story, they have to see that my love for them emanates from my continual experience of God's love for me. Without that, I only have a finite amount of love to give before I burn out and naturally turn to my sheepish parenting ways.

I remember speaking at a marriage conference in Texas around the time Landon was eighteen months old, the age when he started to miss me when I was away.

And I loved it.

Though the emotions of being away from my son are filled with both the angst of missing him while we're apart and the joy upon our reuniting, Landon is no less of a son to me relationally while I'm away. He's still my son. I'm still his dad.

> We live in a society where many people claim that God loves them, but they don't act like it by the way they treat others or even their kids.

However, when I got home from that Texas trip and walked through the door, our relationship was different.

As I turned the corner I saw a little boy just down the hall, looking right at me. As his eyes locked onto mine, he bent over at the waist and knees, ever so slightly, like a bull ready to charge. As soon as he realized I was standing before him, he put a smile on his face as wide as he could muster and charged at me like Fred Flintstone revving his leg-propelled car. As he got closer, I braced myself and picked up my little boy, threw him into the air, and brought him down into my arms, squeezing him tightly, experiencing the joy of re-union. As I held him in my arms, he reached out and touched my face as if to say, "Dad, it's really you! I've missed you!"

Though my relationship to Landon was relationally no different while I was away, when I got home—experientially—it was different.

We live in a society where many people claim that God loves them, but they don't act like it by the way they treat others or even their kids. I want my children to grow up experiencing the love of God from the way I treat them. But the only way that happens is by locking eyes with the heavenly Father, bending my knees before him, and taking charge, running into his arms, reaching for his face, and knowing the love I give my kids comes from the love he first gives me.

IS GOD AS FATHER REALLY SAFE?

Perhaps your experience of God is nothing like what you've read so far. Maybe you grew up in a legalistic home, full of rules, where you were taught that God's love for you was dependent on whether you followed the rules. Your experience of God's love, therefore, is based on how well—or not—you behave. And since the rules are consistently impossible to follow, God's love seems elusive.

Or maybe you didn't grow up in the church, but you had parents whose love was nonetheless conditional on your behavior, and as an adult your beliefs about God reflect your childhood experience. In fact, you may now be anxious in your relationship with God, frequently questioning whether you're "good enough" to go to heaven or whether God will really be there for you when you need him most. Your pursuit of God may even be based purely on experience, going from one worship service, concert, or conference to another trying to feel close to God. But when the feeling wanes, you're again worried about whether he really loves you.

You also could be reading this with absolutely no question about God's love for you. In fact, if called upon, you could recite every Bible verse related to God's love. But because emotions were dismissed or minimized in the home where you grew up, to truly experience how proud God is of you or to read a description about running into his arms like a little child seems sacrilegious, over the top, or even silly.[3]

Or maybe you don't believe in God. That's okay. I'm excited we're on this journey of raising emotionally safe kids together. My hope is for you to keep reading this chapter to discover what the Bible says about God as a father figure. Even if you don't agree with it or believe it to be true, the research is nonetheless valid.

What I love is how the research on emotional safety and secure attachment supports what the Bible says about God—that he is the safest, most loving Father any of us could ask for. The principles the research shows as essential for creating emotional safety in the home and raising kids who live, love, and lead well are no different from the scriptural commands and proverbs necessary for raising kids to be spiritually mature. Furthermore, every one of the principles is reflective of either the character of God or the character of the parent, which is why I once again repeat the phrase that best summarizes a Safe House: it's the posture from which we parent, not the technique, that matters most.

Even God's commands are a reflection of his character. Just as a parent wouldn't allow his son to have access to anything he wants to look at online or her daughter to text anybody she wants at all hours of the night, God's commands aren't in place so you and I cannot have fun. They're in place because he loves us enough to protect us even when we don't know what we are being protected from.

That's why God's character is a perfect reflection of the four walls of a Safe House:

exploration (free will), protection, grace, and truth. God loves us so much that he gives us free will to *explore* the world around us, including behaving in any way we choose and believing whatever we want to believe. Unconditional love is allowing our children to become who they want to be, not controlling or manipulating them into being someone they're not. Without free will and the ability to *explore,* we'd all be robots manipulated by a remote control in the hands of God.

That said, *exploration* can lead to trouble, whether real or perceived, whether a result of our own actions or those of another. And when we face these dangerous, stressful, or fear-provoking situations, God is always there relationally and emotionally to *protect* us, no matter how ugly our circumstance. He is "our refuge and strength, a very present help in trouble."[4] God's wall of *protection* is equally as high as his wall of *exploration.* He said, "I will never leave you nor forsake you."[5]

When we get into trouble, God is going to respond in one of two (oftentimes both) ways: with "*grace* and *truth.*"[6] Going too far online could expose your son to pornographic images he didn't know existed. Allowing your daughter to text all night with whomever she wants could lead to a lack of sleep and poor grades in school at best or being bullied or abused at worst. There are always natural consequences for our behavior. As the apostle Paul noted: "Do not be deceived: God is not mocked, for whatever one sows, that will he also reap."[7]

God loves us so much that he puts commands in place, not so we cannot have fun, but to *protect* us from the consequences of *exploring* where we should not go. Too often, however, when our willful disobedience demands a consequence, he is there to meet us between the two walls of *grace* (unconditional love and acceptance) and *truth* (limits and discipline).

Before all four of these walls were found to be consistent throughout the research for building a Safe House, they were first and foremost, in their most perfect form, character traits of God as our Father. If the Bible is your lens for how you parent, you can trust that building a Safe House really is a home surrounded by the walls of God's character. As David declared, "Unless the LORD builds the house, those who build it labor in vain."[8]

A NANCY GRACE HEADLINER

There's a story in 1 Kings 3 about two mothers, both with infant sons and living together in the same house, that points us toward a deeper understanding of God's character as a father and the posture from which he parents us. It's a shocker Nancy Grace would salivate over.

One night, while both mothers were asleep with their infants (imagine that, both asleep at the same time), one of the women accidentally rolled over on top of her son, smothering him to death. When she realized what she had done, she switched her son with the other woman's baby, laying him at her breast. Upon waking the next morning, the other mother realized that not only was the child in her arms dead but he wasn't her son.

Just when you think the story couldn't get any more shocking than a deceitful mother, fast-forward to the trial where the two mothers, along with the living son, stand before a judge. After listening to their stories, the judge takes a sword and declares, "Divide the living child in two, and give half to the one and half to the other!"

What?! There's already one dead baby. How can the judge order the other baby to die too?

In an act of godly wisdom, the judge, Solomon, sets both women up to expose their true feelings. Immediately, the real mother of the living baby speaks up, because the Bible says she "felt great *compassion* for her son."[9] Another translation says "her bowels yearned" for him.[10] Have you ever felt literally sick to your stomach because you yearned for or were anxious about someone (perhaps your own kids) in a dire situation?

"No!" she passionately begs, "Please let the baby live. Give him to her."[11]

Exposing her jealousy, the other mother chimes in: "He shall be neither mine nor yours; divide him."[12]

Solomon, seeing the compassion of the woman begging for the child to live, knew that a real mother would rather see her son in the care of another than dead.

"Give the living child to the first woman," he decided, "and by no means put him to death; she is his mother."[13]

The same word used in this story to describe the woman's compassion for her son is the same word used to describe God's compassion for you and me as our Father. David wrote, "As a father shows compassion to his children, so the Lord shows compassion to those who fear him."[14]

Words in a book cannot describe the depth of feeling this compassion entails. It is as deep and visceral an emotion as one can feel for another.

Why does he love us so much? The next verse tells us why: "For he knows our frame; he remembers that we are dust."[15]

The word *frame* here means "weak." That is, he knows how we are formed. He sees us in the womb. He recognizes our dependency. And because he's well acquainted with our condition, his compassion as a father is profoundly beyond comprehension.

SURVIVE AND ADVANCE

As a parent, it doesn't take long to realize how weak we really are. A screaming baby who won't transition to a crib, swing, rocker, or anywhere for that matter to stay asleep. A toddler who pushes other adults out of the way saying no to them as soon as they come into our house. From the time we bring that tiny screaming human home from the hospital, we're plagued with questions of whether our kids will ever learn to sleep, share, or be kind to others—especially before they've exhausted us to death.

My friends Adam and Stephanie are in the same season of life as we are, with our kids being only months apart in age. When Landon was born, Adam was a few months ahead of us in the newborn phase. Because he had played Division I basketball, his advice to me in surviving those first few months was simple. "Think March Madness," he said. "Survive and advance one day at a time." I'm not sure there's a much better word to describe what we're doing as parents some days—surviving. To think about going above and beyond to raise kids who live, love, and lead well seems like a pipe dream.

There was an irony to rocking my kiddos to sleep as infants as I held their weak, dependent little bodies in my arms, begging God each night they would stay asleep. In fact, I felt like the weak, dependent little body looking for help to survive. Today, it's something Christi and I pray for with our kids nearly every night, that God would give us wisdom and strength for our most difficult parenting decisions.

We are too weak on our own.

We are skittish.

We are worriers.

We are sheep.

THE DISCIPLINE OF A SAFE FATHER

As a young dad, I wanted to find out what it meant to shepherd the little lambs God entrusted Christi and me with. But I first had to discover how God shepherds us.

This journey led me to one of the most famous passages that describes God as Father:

The LORD is merciful and gracious,
    slow to anger and abounding in steadfast love.
He will not always chide,
    nor will he keep his anger forever.
He does not deal with us according to our sins,
    nor repay us according to our iniquities.
For as high as the heavens are above the earth,
    so great is his steadfast love toward those who fear him;
as far as the east is from the west,
    so far does he remove our transgressions from us.
As a father shows compassion to his children,
    so the Lord shows compassion to those who fear him.
For he knows our frame;
    he remembers that we are dust.

As for man, his days are like grass;
    he flourishes like a flower of the field;
for the wind passes over it, and it is gone,
    and its place knows it no more.
But the steadfast love of the LORD is from everlasting to everlasting
      on those who fear him,
    and his righteousness to children's children,
to those who keep his covenant
    and remember to do his commandments.[16]

As part of my journey of learning what it meant to be a shepherd as a parent, I read Margaret Feinberg's book *Scouting the Divine*. She writes eloquently about visiting a shepherdess in Oregon to better understand the significance of sheep and the good shepherd referred to throughout Scripture. She discovered a few traits of a good shepherd that point back to this passage and, more important, back to God as a safe and loving Father. Every one of them also highlights the four walls of a Safe House.

First, Feinberg writes that a good shepherd will discipline his sheep. Before I describe this, it's important to address the problem of how often the word *discipline* is misunderstood in our culture today. The root for discipline is *disciple,* meaning "student." Neuroscience researcher Daniel Seigel makes the following important distinction between discipline and punishment: "Whenever we discipline our kids, our overall goal is not to punish or to give a consequence, but to teach. . . . Punishment might shut down a behavior in the short term, but teaching offers skills that last a lifetime."[17]

Keeping this distinction in mind, listen to how God disciplines us according to the passage above:

> The LORD is merciful and gracious,
>> slow to anger and abounding in steadfast love.
> He will not always chide,
>> nor will he keep his anger forever.
> He does not deal with us according to our sins,
>> nor repay us according to our iniquities.[18]

God is "merciful and gracious" (the walls of exploration and grace). He gets angry at our bad choices, but only slowly. As he disciplines (the wall of truth), his anger isn't because of the inconvenience our behavior has on him as much as it is because of what could happen to us down the road if we don't change our ways (the wall of protection).

It's hard to feel safe in the Father's arms when we live in fear that he'll punish us for our sins. Our Father will discipline us, but he won't repay us for our willful disobedience toward him.

As finite, mediocre parents, on the other hand, how often does our parenting go something like this? "I'm angry at you, Parker, because I had great plans for us today and you ruined them. Since you inconvenienced my day, you're going to sit in your room with no television or Internet today." It's too easy to have an axe to grind and punish our kids, especially when they inconvenience us.

As parents, we act this way because we're sheep.

God, our Father, as the Good Shepherd, does not treat us this way. His discipline (the wall of truth) is meant to teach us, as disciples, to change our ways so as to not continue on the road we're on—a means of protecting (the wall of protection) us from what could happen to us if we don't learn now. Will his discipline feel good? Of course not. The most valuable lessons in life are often learned in trial and consequence. He won't rescue us from the natural consequences of our behavior. He loves us too much. Though he disciplines us from a posture of mercy, grace, and steadfast love, he disciplines nonetheless, because he knows the consequences otherwise.

Every good shepherd does.

While visiting the Oregon shepherdess, Feinberg wrote of a particular ram that kept ramming her leg in defiance. Immediately, the ram was put in a timeout away from the other sheep. Whether a shepherdess tames a ram with a timeout, water bottle, or even neutering him if necessary, a sheep must be disciplined. "If I don't discipline him now," the shepherdess said, "he will grow up to be dangerous and of no use to anyone." Feinberg goes on to say that if a ram grows up without a healthy fear of its shepherd and no respect for the other sheep, the most humane act is to slaughter it because it will hurt or kill others if it's not destroyed.[19] There have been moments in my life when I lost the fear of the Shepherd and, thinking I had things under control, *explored* further on my own than I should have. Every time that's happened, I consequently lost respect for other sheep and I hurt people. I paid the consequences and it hurt, but God was always merciful and gracious, safely bringing me back into his arms every time.

A good shepherd, from a posture of mercy, grace, and steadfast love, will discipline his sheep. But he's also quick to teach his lambs the lesson and move on, for he knows if he doesn't, he could "provoke [his] children to anger."[20]

DEFENSELESS

My mother-in-love told me she sometimes saw sheep die because they fell on their back, like a turtle rolling over on its shell, and were unable to get back over.

Do sheep sound dumb to you?

Be careful. Remember, we're described as sheep more than any other animal in the Bible. In *Scouting the Divine,* the Oregon shepherdess pointed out: "From the outside, a lot of sheep's behavior looks dumb. And it's true that they aren't always aware of the consequences of what they're doing. . . . [But] they are not dumb; they're defenseless. There's a big difference."[21]

I remember when Landon first started to crawl. He was all over the house. We had to get on our hands and knees to see what he could possibly get into next. Every now and then, I would see him grab at electrical cords or try to climb onto a chair. Bath time was his favorite part of the day, and his favorite toy in the tub was none other than a cup. He would fill the cup up in the bathtub from the spigot and try to drink from it like a big boy, but he would end up dumping the water all over his face because the weight was too much for him. Once he crawled onto the hearth, opened the grate, and began eating ashes. After calling poison control, we learned ashes weren't much different from burned toast—in case you're looking for an alternative to your daily carcinogen intake.

As our children explore the world around them, would you say they're dumb for doing such things?

I wouldn't say Landon is dumb; I would say he is defenseless and in need of a shepherd.

I've made no secret that Christi and I had some very difficult days with both of our little ones right from the start. As a young dad trying to balance work, lack of sleep, and a wife who was struggling with breast-feeding, sleeping, and chronic back pain, I was barely keeping my head above water. I'll never forget Christi coming to me in tears in those first few weeks and saying, "I just don't feel like we're connecting. I feel alone." She was right. The only thing I was connecting with in those weeks was coffee—lots and lots of coffee. We were barely surviving, hardly connecting. But I realized what Christi needed during those times in order to survive was connection and the assurance that we were on the same team. To me, we were. But my game plan of completing tasks *for* her wasn't the same as her strategy of my connecting *with* her.

I wouldn't say I was dumb. I was defenseless.

Not only did we start to surround ourselves with safe people to help us with the kids and allow us time to reconnect, but we also began fighting for one another to get time to connect with the Shepherd as much as possible during those days. We realized quickly that being good shepherds to our kids meant that, as sheep, we needed to stay closely connected to the flock.

I encourage you to come together with other parents who have kids at similar ages so you can experience together the love of the Father and the character of the Shepherd. Be willing to admit when you're defenseless, and reach out for the support of safe people around you. Especially if you're a single parent, I applaud your sacrifice and am sincerely humbled by your perseverance and hard work day in and day out. The more you experience the Shepherd's love for you, the more you'll see your posture as a parent change, discovering more grace, mercy, and love toward your kids than you ever thought you could have.

Whatever we do as parents, no matter our situation, we cannot isolate ourselves.

Feinberg discovered that a good shepherd counts his sheep because he knows that a sheep left in the field is usually weak. And a lonely, weak sheep is quick to give up. Perhaps that is why a shepherd celebrates so much when he finds and returns that lonely, weak sheep to the fold.

> What do you think? If a man owns a hundred sheep, and one of them wanders away, will he not leave the ninety-nine on the hills and go to look for the one that wandered off? And if he finds it, I tell you the truth, he is happier about that one sheep than about the ninety-nine that did not wander off. *In the same way your Father in heaven* is not willing that any of these little ones should be lost.[22]

When you're feeling exhausted, alone, defenseless, and perhaps hopeless as a parent, don't isolate yourself, lest you return to your haystack. Instead, remember your Father in heaven is relentlessly pursuing you as the Good Shepherd he is:

> He tends his flock like a shepherd:
>   He gathers the lambs in his arms
> and carries them close to his heart;
>   *he gently leads those that have young.*[23]

As I sit with my kids and rock them to sleep, I picture myself, experientially, safe in my Father's arms (the walls of grace and protection), knowing he is gently leading Christi and me as shepherds to watch over the defenseless sheep he's entrusted to our care.

AN ABANDONED SON

In biblical times, pastures were situated in the deserts of the Middle East and therefore were not lush and green as we might imagine from passages like Psalm 23. In order for shepherds to feed their sheep, they had to search for land with sprouts of vegetation. Nomadic on the mountainsides, they would build fences of rock and wood around the sheep to keep them in and predators out. But it was the gate that meant the most. And what did they use to build the gate?

Their own body.

A good shepherd literally lies at the gate, making sure no predators get inside. In one of the most profound passages in all of the Gospels, Jesus calls himself the Good Shepherd to declare his deity: "I tell you the truth, I am the gate for the sheep. . . . I am the good shepherd. The good shepherd lays down his life for the sheep."[24]

And lay down his life he did.

The only passage in all the Bible where Jesus does not address God as Father is when he was hanging on the cross. There, he said, "My God, my God, why have you forsaken me?"[25] The word *forsaken* in this verse means "abandoned." Jesus gave up his relationship with the Father so you, your kids, and your grandkids could have it. He was forgotten by the Father so you and I could be remembered, as Psalm 103:17 declares, "from everlasting to everlasting."[26]

The Father knows our frame. He knows our brokenness. He knows our weakness, especially as parents. He knows we're sheep. Yet his compassion for us is so deep, deeper than anybody could ever feel for us or our kids. That's why he sent the Good Shepherd to lay down his life for us.

In his eyes, we are enough and have what it takes to provide the love and safety our kids need from us as parents. What's beautiful about the Father's Safe House is what it promises us:

> But the steadfast love of the LORD is from everlasting to everlasting
>> on those who fear him,
> and his righteousness to children's children,
> to those who keep his covenant
>> and remember to do his commandments.[27]

This is an amazing promise I pray over our family often. It also highlights all four walls of a Safe House.

God loves us unconditionally (grace). Therefore he wants to *protect* us. His commands (truth) are meant to *protect* us from harm. The more we experience his grace and love, the more we will obey. The more we obey, the more freedom we will experience (exploration).

The trouble in families comes, however, with the last part of the verse. Just as our infants do with us, we're answering the two questions in our relationship with God: *Am*

I worthy of love? Is God capable of loving me? When we don't *experience* the love of the Father or *feel* safe with him, our tendency is to either begin questioning ourselves—wondering whether we are worthy of love, if we are enough, or if we really do have what it takes as a parent—or our tendency is to question whether God is capable of loving us. Either way, imperfect love leads to fear. As unsure and insecure parents, when we're not feeling loved, we tend to run in fear to whatever will restore a feeling of love, safety, acceptance, and confidence. But when we do, we turn away from the walls of truth and protection the Good Shepherd has built for us, oftentimes failing to keep his commandments by running back to our haystacks.

Don't be a frustrated sheep heading toward a haystack. Instead, get to know the voice of the Good Shepherd, your Father in heaven.

He knows you're a lamb in need of his care.

He steadfastly loves you.

He has mercy on you.

He gives you grace.

He is slow to get angry at you.

He will discipline but not punish you.

He will not be angry at you forever.

He will not blame you forever.

Instead, he will keep a Safe House full of steadfast love ready for you and righteousness to your family lineage every time you return to him and follow where he leads.

As you do, remember his posture.

He is teaching you how to be a shepherd.

Coauthoring Your Child's Story

1. Describe your relationship with God.
2. Have you ever thought about God as Father in this way before?
3. What will you do to begin helping your child understand the love of the Father as described in Psalm 103?

10

A Safe Marriage

The family is a haven in a heartless world.

—Christopher Lasch

If you're a single parent, fight the urge to skip this chapter. The reality is your home is likely safer than those who are married but only stay together for the sake of the kids. If you're the latter couple, consider the very real possibility that you're not doing your kids any favors by not seeking wise counsel to rekindle your romance. Our children learn how to treat others, particularly the opposite sex, by watching how we treat our spouse. Simply put, an unsafe marriage creates an unsafe environment for our kids inside the home.

At the same time, know of my grace for your situation. You may be living with a spouse who lacks the insight or motivation for change. That's an incredibly difficult road to walk. If you're a single parent, I'm speechless. Some of you started out as single parents perhaps because you adopted while single. Others found yourselves as single parents against your wishes. I cannot imagine your sacrifice. We struggle nearly every day with our kids, and there are two of us. Christi and I have the utmost respect for you.

No matter the structure of the family unit—whether it's a traditional home, a blended family, single parents, a homosexual union, or any other familial background— all children are precious to our Father in heaven and deserve a Safe House. I come from generations of divorce. But I chose to rewrite my story so I could create for my own children the safest environment possible. Although marriages are the focus of this chapter, the lessons here apply to any parent, regardless of marital status and even for single parents who decide to begin dating again, to give your children the best developmental environment possible. No matter the current condition of your marriage or relationship, your children are watching how you relate.

Make no mistake, research consistently shows a continuous, stable, safe two-parent home as the best environment for children who will live, love, and lead well.[1] In addition, studies clearly reveal that children need both a mother and a father. In fact, and what may come as a shock, these studies show "the quality of contact with the mother was not as strong a predictor of the child's later success or failure with school and friends [as the quality of the child's relationship with the father]." The researchers believe the reason for these surprising findings "is because the father-child relationship evokes such powerful emotions in kids."[2]

CLEAR EYES

I owe a great deal of gratitude and honor to the director of the graduate counseling program I was a part of: Dr. Craig Ellison. Though his quiet monotone lectures made Ben Stein's Clear Eyes commercials seem electrifying, he was one of my favorite professors—a tall, humble, and caring man whose soft voice and gentle spirit doubtlessly made him a genius behind the confidential doors of a counseling office. He had a way of knitting academic knowledge into the fabric of our personal stories.

In my first class with him, he taught us about the current state of marriages and families in our culture. It was an eye-opening portrait into the consequences of divorce, fatherlessness, cohabitation, broken families, and abuse. Statistics and outcome research, by their very nature, are emotionless at best. They leave us apathetic to those who hurt and judgmental at worst. And we find ourselves being accusatory and unsympathetic to the countless Americans living with broken family relations (like the estimated 24.7 million kiddos living without their daddy at home).[3]

To make sure we didn't fall into either camp, Dr. Ellison made it personal. He knew there were no perfect families. I also think he saw through a twenty-two-year-old kid sitting in the front row who was blinded by his own story.

To help us *feel* these statistics, one of our assignments was to put together a genogram of our own family history. A genogram is similar to a family tree, but it goes deeper, including patterns that have been passed down through the generations. These patterns involve job history, personalities, illnesses, education, and religious affiliations.

As I outlined both sides of my family back to my grandparents, I uncovered a pervasive pattern staring me square in the face: divorce. Not only was this a general pattern; I began to see specific personal and relational elements that each marriage embodied on both sides of my family that, one could argue, led to marital conflict. Without putting it on paper though, nobody would recognize it.

But there it was, right in front of me—my eyes were clear.

A Truly Blended Family

My passion for the family is a product of the high value placed on it despite the prevalence of broken marriages. For instance, peek into my grandmother's home every Christmas, and you'll see our entire family celebrating together. Ironically, even my grandfather and step-grandmother attended the same Christmas celebration. I can't describe how often my step-grandmother has helped out my grandmother in times of need. Though it appears senseless on the outside, it's truly a testimony of genuine concern and emotional stability on the inside.

Another such example is the solidarity of my immediate family. When I graduated from my master's degree program, my mother and stepfather and my father and stepmother all attended my graduation in New York. Afterward, we all enjoyed the city one last time—together. When my paternal grandmother was dying, my mother and stepfather were at the house with my dad and sister to console them nearly every day.

We have redefined the term *blended family*. In spite of the multigenerational divorce in my family, there is a genuine care and concern for the well-being of everybody else in the family, on both sides. My parents' ability to regulate emotion and respect the boundaries of others strengthened everybody, even in the midst of adversity.

Though I didn't come out unscathed, I am grateful for the way my parents helped my sister and me navigate the effects of dealing with divorced parents.

A few years after the insights of the genogram had begun to take effect, I met a good friend, a father figure of sorts, after moving to Virginia to begin my doctoral studies. Standing in the counseling department one day, he asked me if I wanted to take my seven-eighths fishing with him and his wife. Confused, I asked him if my seven-eighths was some type of special lure. After an emotional belly laugh at my expense, he said: "No, your wife. I don't know about you, but my wife is my seven-eighths, not my better half."

I then broke the news to him. "Sir, I don't have a wife yet."

"What?!" he answered. "How old 'er you, son?" he replied in a thick southern accent.

"I'm twenty-four."

"Well, we need to get you a seven-eighths," he concluded.

As we walked to our cars together after work that day, I explained to him how I gained insight into my own personal flaws from doing a genogram years earlier and that I was focused on what I needed to do to become a good husband. I told him divorce would not be in my vocabulary.

Just before departing to our own cars, he said something I'll never forget.

"It sounds like it's time for you to start a new Straub family lineage."

"What do you mean?" I asked.

"From what you're telling me, it's time for you to start a new lineage, not one marked by divorce, but one defined by marriages full of joy and the unconditional love of Christ."

So began the journey to a new lineage.

FINDING MY SEVEN-EIGHTHS

I'm understanding more every day what my friend meant by his seven-eighths. For too long I thought I was the seven-eighths. I thought marriage was about finding the person who, for lack of a better phrase, completed me. I believed all I had to do was find the one-eighth whose love could free the insecurities of my heart, make me happy, and help me live a more fulfilling life. I'd then be whole.

What a pile of narcissistic, egotistical gobbledygook. As if I wasn't self-centered enough, Western culture fuels this mindset, getting us to believe its propaganda—another instance of teaching us that our right to *feel better* trumps the hard work of learning to *love better*. When we begin a marriage with this premise, we once again prioritize happiness over sacrifice. And what happens when we're not happy? Due to supposedly irreconcilable differences, we begin looking for another who can more fully complete us. But as my Ozarkian pastor Ted Cunningham eloquently observed, "If you start finding greener grass on the other side, there's most likely a septic leak."

I'm indebted to the countless mentors, counselors, and friends who helped me piece together my own story coherently enough to rewrite a new one. In doing so, I found a woman who truly embodies the seven-eighths of our relationship, somebody who gives of herself and serves our family more than I imagined possible. Yet somebody who is spirited enough to respectfully and maturely put me in my place when I start acting as if I'm the seven-eighths.

You can get a real idea of who Christi is through what she gives me for Father's Day.

For my first Father's Day, Christi had a hardcover book made with pictures of Landon and me together throughout his first year of life. Last year, she topped it.

Here's what she gave me:

- The *sacrifice* of choosing to be a stay-at-home mom while struggling with internal feelings of losing her identity in the process.
- The *decision* a few months ago to lead our business part time while still balancing mommyhood.
- The *frustrations* and *weight* of managing the budgets and finances both for our personal lives and our business.
- Because of this, she *makes* meal plans each week for our family (and does the *cooking* too, lest we eat pizza and cereal every night).
- And because of that, *she does* nearly all of the grocery shopping.
- The *exhaustion* of dealing with the brunt of toddler temper tantrums all day, every day.
- The *opportunity* for me to bathe our son and enjoy fun stuff with him nearly every night.
- All the while *carrying* our next baby (and dealing with the first five months of all-day *sickness, incessant trips* to the bathroom throughout the night, *heartburn, unpredictable hormones,* and all of the other *gifts* pregnancy affords that I don't have to deal with).
- A *date night* roughly three times a month.
- The *privilege* of having *a best friend* who encourages, affirms, and loves me for me.
- But who *loves* me enough to not leave me that way.
- And a wife who *spends* her morning with Jesus before dealing with me or our adorably unpredictable toddler.

Since this list was created, I cannot tell you the further sacrifices Christi has made for our family. The crazy part is that these gifts don't even scratch the surface of all she's given me. I don't know what it feels like to be a mom who

- feels like she's not doing all she can for her kids
- feels, at times, like a failure
- feels inadequate
- feels helpless with a screaming toddler (or a rebellious teenager)

- feels imperfect
- feels overwhelmed
- feels exhausted

"Thank you" seems trite.

To the moms reading this book, thank you for all you do investing in your children.

Whether you realize it or not, those long days, insecure feelings, and exhaustion are universal. They live in every home, every mother, everywhere, including our own. And in spite of your *imperfections, parenting mishaps,* and *questions of self-worth,* it's the unconditional love of your family that makes the world a better place.

To dads, thank you for investing in your kids. Your presence matters more than you'll ever know. I worked with juvenile delinquents for fifteen years, and I never met one who had a loving relationship with his or her dad prior to the delinquency. But when the dads and their kids were reunited, radical changes began to happen.

As parents genuinely invested in building a Safe House for your kids, be sure to begin by honoring your seven-eighths. That seven-eighths is your kids' mommy—or their daddy.

Husbands, begin by writing a list of all your wife does and is for you and your kids, and share it with her. Do so on a romantic evening out together, away from the kids. I think you'll begin to realize quickly she is more than your seven-eighths. It's way too easy to take our wives for granted.

Wives, do the same for your husbands. Honor him by thanking him for when he supports you, leads well, holds your hand, cleans up after dinner, disciplines the kids, roughhouses with them, and gives you a break, even if it's only for a few minutes. Since you're the most important woman in his life, your words have more power than anybody to make him feel like a man.

The Bible says to "outdo one another in showing honor."[4] An emotionally safe home is where honor is frequently practiced. Do one thing each day to show how much you adore your spouse. Leave love notes. Speak highly of your spouse in front of others, especially your kids. Wives, text your husbands, letting them know how proud you are of them. Dads, get up in the middle of the night and tend to the baby. Do one selfless act that will brighten your spouse's day and unify your oneness.

As a coauthor of your kids' narrative, you're already developing two characters for their marriage story: how your kids learn to treat their spouse and the kind of spouse you're showing them they deserve.

How to Change Your Spouse

One of the biggest questions you may be asking right now is, What do I do if my spouse is the problem? I get this question a lot. First, rate your marriage on a scale of one to ten, with one being "absolutely miserable, on the verge of walking out," and ten being "absolutely amazing, can't get much better." To better help you put a number on where you're at, choose one of the following phrases that may best describe your marriage:

- bored
- miserable
- going through the motions
- focused on the kids
- joyful
- adventurous
- good
- administrative

Perhaps you rated your marriage a one because your spouse is either abusive or neglectful of you and your kids. You may even be worried that the behavior of your spouse is hurting your children's emotional well-being and safety. To be forthright, there is absolutely no place for abuse in any relationship. I urge you to seek counsel and guidance from a local counselor on taking the appropriate steps to protect yourself and your children.

No matter where we rate our marriage, emotional safety must remain a constant practice. The more safe we feel with our spouse, the more vulnerable we are and connected we become. The opposite is also true. The less safe we feel, the less vulnerable we are and the less connected we become.

Knowing this, there are five action steps I generally provide to couples that come to me in distress. One of the most common themes, when a person first asks for help, is an explanation of what the other person is or isn't doing in the relationship. These are the steps I give to the one spouse who desires change but doesn't know what to do because the other person isn't willing. If this is you, I'm sorry you're in such a predicament. But let me encourage you that you can change your spouse! Here's how:

1. *It begins by understanding one principle—the only person you can change is you.* You cannot directly change or fix your spouse. But you can change how *you* interact with your spouse, which in turn will indirectly require him to make a decision about how he responds to you. That said, when it's the wife coming for help, I always start by sharing with her this verse:

   > Wives, be subject to your own husbands, so that even if some do not obey the word, they may be won without a word . . . when they see your respectful and pure conduct. Do not let your adorning be external . . . but let your adorning be the hidden person of the heart with the imperishable beauty of a gentle and quiet spirit, which in God's sight is very precious.[5]

   In other words, don't preach to him. It will only push him further away. Don't make him feel any more like a failure than he probably already does. Shame won't change him.

2. *Begin praying each day for your spouse, specifically that God would show you how he sees your spouse.* Don't allow your situation or your spouse's action (or inaction) to make you bitter and resentful. The most effective way of regaining empathy and genuine concern for your spouse is to pray that God shows you a glimpse of who your spouse is in his eyes. Search for the hurt, the loneliness, and the pain she must feel. Pray this prayer multiple times daily, especially when you're frustrated.

3. *Stop blaming.* The single biggest obstacle to couples connecting is blame. This is a hard one, especially if your spouse wrongly blames you. But resist the temptation to become defensive and cast blame in return. Otherwise, the defensive walls will grow stronger, and your spouse won't change.[6]

4. *Seek to understand the motivation behind your spouse's heart and actions.* Rarely, unless your spouse is abusive, will she say something to intentionally hurt you. Instead, hurtful words and actions are usually emotionally charged bad attempts at avoiding more hurt and getting our spouses to connect with us. But these offensive words and actions usually produce the opposite of what we really desire—positive connection and affection.

5. *Finally, apply the Golden Rule of a Safe House in your marriage as well. That is, understand your spouse the way you want to be understood.* In order for your spouse to begin opening up with you about his own hurts and fears, he needs to feel safe and not like he's blowing it as a husband and dad (or, for her, as a wife and mom). The more your spouse feels understood by you, the more he'll begin to open up over time.

If your spouse is unable or unwilling to respond to your safe actions, if you're already in the middle of a divorce, or if your kids are exposed to emotional chaos in the home, research shows that the emotion-coaching strategies discussed throughout this book for raising kids to live, love, and lead well actually provide a buffering effect. In fact, being emotionally present for your kids, helping them deal with their negative feelings about the family turmoil, and walking with them through stressful events has been proven to safeguard kids from the harmful outcomes of divorce and family conflict.[7]

That said, all five of these actions foster one thing: emotional safety. And it's emotional safety that predicts marital satisfaction. The safer you are for your spouse, the more likely your spouse will change.

FIGHTING FOR, NOT WITH, ONE ANOTHER— WHILE RAISING KIDS

Christi and I love sports. We refer to our family as our team. That began immediately in our wedding vows when Christi stated, "You are my teammate." In response, my vow was to "fight hard for, not with, her." And before kids, we were winning together, celebrating often in the locker room of marriage.

Then came our greatest opponent yet. Weighing in at eight pounds one ounce: our sweet, innocent, chubby-cheeked, high-needs firstborn baby—who wouldn't sleep.

For the first few months our kids slept in a cradle in our room with us. One night when Landon was about three months old, I heard him whimper. You know, the more polite cry just before a child starts wailing to be fed. I gently nudged Christi and asked, "Honey, do you want me to get him?"

She said, "What time is it?"

"Almost four o'clock."

Since Christi was breast-feeding, she responded as I had hoped: "No, I'll get him because it's time for him to be fed anyway."

To show my support, I inquired further, "Are you sure, honey? I really can get him." (Though inwardly I was celebrating, *Yes! I can sleep.*)

No more than two minutes later, Landon started wailing. Since Christi was motionless, I started to get out of bed. All of a sudden, she jolted up and frantically asked, "What's wrong? What's going on?"

I calmly replied, "I'm just going to get Landon. It's time for him to be fed."

"How do you know it's time for him to be fed?" she asked.

"Honey, we just had this conversation two minutes ago. Don't you remember?"

"No, I don't remember. We talked about this?"

I swear researchers will one day find the onset of dementia happens from the middle-of-the-night moments with our infants.

These are the deliriously sweet moments we look back on fondly.

There are other moments, however, that began to interrupt our game plan. Not only were we not getting much sleep, but Christi had to deal with multiple infections and other postpartum hurdles with Landon. Then medical complications forced her to quit breast-feeding our daughter. The guilt and shame of feeling like an inadequate mother who couldn't breast-feed, coupled with lack of sleep, created a sensitive young mom—and wife.

To add to it, Christi's back goes out on her multiple times a year. When this happens, it puts more stress on our team as I try my best to pull double duty, both working and taking care of the kids.

I write all of this first to show appreciation for Christi's perseverance and commitment to our family in spite of extenuating circumstances out of her control. Second, I simply write them to say, "We get it." Parenting can put an unreasonable amount of stress on a marriage and expose our greatest weaknesses.

With little sleep and the extenuating pressures of life tearing at us, Christi and I began getting short with one another, casting blame, growing defensive, and fighting— not for one another—but for self-preservation.

I learned quickly that when we're in survival mode, we're most likely to find ourselves with different game plans (at best) or in different locker rooms (at worst) in our marriage. Since then, when we start to fight with one another, we call team meetings (or marriage evaluations) to reevaluate our game plan against the opponents threatening our family unit, beginning with our marriage. I would encourage you to do the same, especially as you begin to discern when and how your spouse starts to change the game plan without telling you, or worse, head for her own locker room. Your empathetic and understanding posture as a spouse matters as much for your marriage as it does your parenting.

How we handle the newborn phase right from the beginning speaks volumes about the trajectory of our marriages—and ultimately whether we'll be on the same team as parents. The sooner we develop the same game plan, the safer our kids will be.

How Fifteen Minutes Changed Our Marriage

Christi has a knack for being painfully honest. I came home one day from work and started telling Christi about my day: who I talked to, what I did, and quite a bit about the projects I had cooking. Visibly irritated and nearly in tears after a hard day of temper tantrums and feeling as though she was slowly losing her identity, Christi looked at me and was, well, painfully honest.

"Why don't you ask about me?" she asked. "I feel like it's always about you. You never ask about what's on my heart."

#self-centered

Not long after this lovely interaction with my wife, I attended an Ultimate Leadership Summit held by my friends and mentors Henry Cloud and John Townsend. In a nutshell, at these meetings you learn about how your own character issues are helping or hindering you from being a great leader. Or in this case, from being a great spouse.

One of my takeaways from the event was how the most effective and balanced leaders are able to engage both sides of their brain in conversation. I realized that when I process my day with Christi, it is usually content-based (that is, what I did, who I talked to, and so on) rather than process-based (that is, what I *felt* about what I did or who I talked to).

Translation: I needed to be more in touch with my feelings, especially with Christi.

I know for guys this may sound mushy, but it's what makes us great husbands, fathers, and leaders. The more in touch I am with my feelings, the more mindful I am to what's going on in Christi's heart.

So I came home from this leadership event with a plan, and it's one I challenge you to follow to foster an emotionally safe marriage.

Christi and I found it's too easy to go into a mindless zone after the kids are down, either drowning our sorrows in our favorite television shows or numbing our brains and feelings on social media. The former we justify by saying we're spending time together; the latter we justify as connecting with others. In reality, we're slowly disengaging from our spouse.

Instead of numbing yourself with a heartless device that cares nothing about your relationships, carve out fifteen minutes of your evening with your spouse and do two things:

1. *Inquire about your spouse's heart.* Ask "What's on your heart today?" "How are you feeling?" But here's the kicker: make it a priority to *not* fix anything! Just sit with your spouse, with no condemnation, and listen to his or her most prevalent feelings from the day. Don't try to fix it; just validate it.

2. *Then share your heart with your spouse.* Use feeling words to describe your day. "I felt sad when . . ." or "I felt angry at . . ." Simply using feeling words engages both sides of the brain and strengthens our bond with others.

Practice this for fifteen minutes even if it's just a few times a week. The investment is worth it, both for you and your kids. When Christi and I are in survival mode and find ourselves becoming insensitive toward one another, these are the steps we use to reunite. Practice them, especially during heated exchanges.

When we practice with our spouse the emotion-coaching skills we learned for connecting with our kids in emotionally charged moments—acknowledging our spouse's feelings, showing empathy, and problem solving together—research shows we experience more marital satisfaction over time and grow a deeper connection that our kids will learn to imitate.[8]

PAYING HOMAGE TO THE KING AND QUEEN

According to the Bible,[9] and outcome research supports this, the foundation of our family is our marriage, not our kids. Our kids will one day leave us. Hopefully, our spouse won't.

If our goal is to genuinely raise our kids to live, love, and lead well, then our desire should be to prepare them from the time they're born to leave us and start their own team. How well they securely attach to their own spouse as an adult is in large part due to how well we train them to live independently on their own while maintaining a healthy interdependence on others, beginning with God, and then with their own spouse. That's why in homes where both Mom and Dad are present, our kids must see that our priority relationship is for their mommy or daddy.

I don't know a kid who doesn't love seeing her dad open the door for her mom. Or rub her feet after a long day. Or hold her hand during a family movie. When our daughters see their dad actively loving Mom, they learn how a husband should one day treat them. Sons learn how they should adore their wives.

I also don't know a child who doesn't love seeing his mom kiss his dad, telling him how proud she is of him. Or massage his neck when he's stressed. Or choose to take the time to date him. When our sons see their mom giving Dad time and respect, they learn how a wife should one day treat them. Daughters learn how to affectionately love and support their husbands.

That's why the greatest gift we can give our kids is to love their mom—or their dad.

Too many spouses today emotionally turn away from one another and instead revolve their lives around the kids. The more kid-centered the home, the more unsafe the marriage. I know kids can be all-consuming, but an inability to pay attention to your spouse's heart will wreak havoc on your children. That's because when our emotional needs for love and companionship aren't being met by our spouse, we tend to place that responsibility onto our kids, either asking more of them emotionally than they're mature enough to give (too high a wall of grace and not enough truth) or giving them anything they want in exchange for their time and affection (too high a wall of exploration and not enough protection).

> The greatest gift we can give our kids is to love their mom—or their dad.

The degree to which we prioritize our kids over our spouse is the degree to which they disrespect and lose trust in the spouse we're not prioritizing. As my friend Claudia Arp told me, "Your kids will wait while you grab a few moments to build your marriage; but your marriage won't wait until your kids grow up."

That's why I now make it a priority to greet Christi as soon as I'm home, before engaging our kids. I want my children to learn that Mom is the queen of the house and that she carries the authority of the queen. Landon is a prince. Kennedy is a princess. But what they're *not* is king and queen of the Straub family home. Any time Landon or Kennedy try to move from their role to that of king or queen, Christi and I quickly remind them of their position and use it as a way to teach them both that one day they will be king and queen of their own household. Our job as parents is to teach them how to become noble kings and queens.

Pay homage to the king and queen of your house by prioritizing your marriage over your kids. Doing so allows your children to experience firsthand an emotionally safe marriage—and there's no safer relationship for a child to *experience* than two parents still madly in love.

THE SECRET TO THE GAME PLAN

I thought my first business trip three weeks after our daughter was born would be a welcomed reprieve. Besides, it was only a two-day trip. But when I went to say goodbye, a feeling of grief overwhelmed me like never before.

Not more than an hour later, I found out why.

While I drove to the airport, I happened to notice the exit we had used to take Landon to swimming lessons that past winter. As I passed it, I reminisced on how much he loved to go down the slide into the pool, float on his back as I sang to him the ABC's, and how difficult it was to get him to blow bubbles in the water.

As I continued to the airport, I grieved those days. They were over now.

I missed my family even more.

In fact, as soon as I got to the airport, I immediately sent Christi the following text:

> Monday 12:20 PM
>
> I know it's more work but I'd much rather be with my family at an airport than by myself any day. Missing you 😭

And it's all true . . .

Airports are a lot more work with infants and preschoolers.

Days are much longer with toddlers.

Nights are even more exhausting with newborns.

And marriages are a bit more tense with screaming kids.

But I'd never trade the long days, exhausting nights, tense moments, and hard work for anything. Ask me in the moment, and I might say otherwise. But stepping back, alone in my car with time to reflect, I realized how much fuller my heart is because of my wife and kids.

I love to speak, travel, and work. But I can genuinely say there's no place I'd rather be than with my family.

As I stood waiting at the airline ticket counter, I glanced out a window and noticed an airplane on the tarmac. But I didn't see a plane. I saw Landon running toward that window, pointing with excitement, saying "Da-da pwwaane!"

> The safer our marriage, the more in the moment we can be.

As I came back to reality, I realized in that moment the gift God gave to get us through the long nights, colicky babies, talking-back toddlers, and chaotic homes. A gift that's often undervalued. A gift we're generally ungrateful for. Yet a gift so strong it's the glue that keeps our family's hearts connected—memories.

Why do memories seem so elusive? Why do we not see them as a gift?

- Maybe it's because when I called Christi on FaceTime during that trip Kennedy (our three-week-old) was crying (okay, wailing) in the background and Landon (our two-year-old) was whining to hold the phone.
- Maybe it's because Christi was awake nearly every hour that night while I rested peacefully in my hotel room bed.
- Maybe it's because you have a hungry, angry, tired, or bored little one at home, and you're not sure how to handle it anymore.
- Maybe you're simply trying to survive the teenage years with as few blemishes on your parenting record—or your teen's—as possible.

These scenarios have tendencies to divide the affections of husband and wife more than unite us. One of the greatest tragedies of a disconnected marriage involves the memories we lose, not just with one another but with our children. I think Tim Keller described it best:

> Marriage has the power to set the course of your life as a whole. If your marriage is strong, even if all the circumstances in your life around you are filled with trouble and weakness, it won't matter. You will be able to move out into the world in strength.[10]

As the memory-makers of our family, we need the energy to not only plan family time together but the concentration to exist in the moment, to be participants in the memories unfolding before us, whether they happen at Disney World, in our backyards, or in the moments of reconnection after our kids disobey us. The safer our marriage, the more in the moment we can be.

The secret to a connected family is making memories. But it begins with the husband and wife stepping out of their locker room together, in strength, ready to record the game film. Christi and I found three ways to make this happen:

1. *Get away together.* Christi and I are indebted to the supporting cast we have in our story—our parents and even our kids' adopted Branson grandparents. With them, Christi and I are able to get a date night once a week, just the two of us. Even if you cannot do this once a week, try to do so every other week. Some of our favorite memories together are just dropping the kids off, then coming home, putting on pj's, ordering food in, and watching a movie. Sometimes we do game nights at a local coffee shop. Whatever the date, it doesn't have to be extravagant; it just has to be together.

   Don't be afraid to step out of your comfort zone. Create memories together by doing things your spouse loves to do. Even when it's an effort or an activity you don't enjoy, put their desire above your own. It is not about the actual event, it is about the bond that grows out of it.

   If you struggle at finding time to be creative with your dates, or you live in the middle of nowhere with limited options, Ted Cunningham and I created ten date night ideas around certain themes like play, laugh, dream, curiosity, and adventure. Not only do they provide creative date night ideas, but they also have fifty-two questions for each date night to help trigger conversation.[11]

   In addition, find time once a year, at a minimum, to go off together for a weekend without the kids, just the two of you. And make it extra special.

2. *Get away alone.* This one is critical. It's why I didn't realize how much the simple drive to swimming lessons with Christi and Landon meant to me until I was alone in my car.

   - Christi has a girls' night with life-giving friends once a week; husbands stay home and watch the kids.
   - If one or both of us miss our quiet times, we find our fuses with each other much shorter than usual. So we tenaciously do what we can to allow the other time needed alone with God.
   - Husbands, here's where you can bless your wives. Give her a day off from the kids. A spa day every now and again. A pedicure. My wife simply likes to go to a coffee shop and read for a few hours.

No matter the means, you need to get away from the mundane every so often to appreciate the moments.

3. *Experience the joy of the moment.* The mundane can be a tough place to live. But it's in the mundane that I've seen my son kiss his baby sister any time he hears her crying. It's also in the mundane at 4:30 a.m. that my baby daughter and I have had our sweetest moments together—cooing, smiling, and praying.

These are also the everyday, ordinary moments that simply make you smile and appreciate the affection you have for your spouse. Christi has this little dance she does that's absolutely adorable to me. On days she breaks into that dance, I simply smile, walk over to her when she's finished, and embrace the moment.

I think a lot of us miss joy because we are waiting for something extraordinary to happen. One study[12] looked at widows and widowers. Without exception, every participant mentioned the mundane moments they remembered most about their spouse.

If I could just walk back downstairs every morning and see my husband reading the newspaper at the kitchen table, drinking his cup of coffee.

My wife used to send me crazy text messages throughout the day. I would do anything to get one of those text messages again.

Even when you're frustrated, stressed, and tired, embrace the small moments. Write them down later. And try to fight the urge to pull out your phone. This is a tough one for all of us, but the moment you do, you move from being a participant in the memory to an observer.

Many of my best memories are captured in my heart and mind, not on my phone.

As I drove by that exit again on my way home, I remembered playing with Landon in the pool and how he struggled to blow bubbles in the water. Then I smiled. Because the night before I left, he was in the bathtub, Christi and I were looking on, and he plunged his face into the water and blew bubbles.

It won't be long until he's swimming faster than we can.

Moments *we* don't want to miss. Moments that keep us all connected.

━━━ Coauthoring Your Child's Story ━━━

1. From your perspective, what are your kids learning about love and romance based on your marriage? What are they learning about how to treat the opposite sex?

2. In the spirit of Hebrews 13:4, write down ways you can begin honoring marriage in front of your kids. What applications from this chapter do you most look forward to doing?

Establishing Faith

The ultimate test of a moral society is the kind of world that
it leaves to its children.

—Dietrich Bonhoeffer

Tablets are heavy. I learned just how heavy after leaving our iPad on a plane. As Christi and I came to the agonizing discovery while we unpacked our bags the next day, a feeling of vulnerability resonated inside of me. So many thoughts raced through my mind.

Who has it?

Have they seen our family pictures?

Did they get access to our home address?

What about our financial apps?

While Christi looked around the house, I started changing passwords. It wasn't the iPad I was concerned about; it was the feeling of being violated, knowing that perhaps a stranger was voyeuristically looking at all of our personal information.

My heart felt exposed.

Imagine the private information you have stored on your tablet. What if it fell into the hands of another? What would the information on it say about you? The music you listen to. The pictures you take. The places you frequent. Who your kids are. Perhaps even how much money you make and spend each month. Electronic tablets are heavier than we think, not because of the weight of their frame but because of the weight of their content. What's stored or written inside matters.

Do you remember the days we would write our personal feelings and details down on paper, perhaps in a diary?

Christi still keeps a journal on a paper tablet. In fact, her life is chronicled in dozens of journals she's kept through the years. On the day of our wedding, those tablets were given to me in a box, as a gift, a sign that she was giving me her entire life story.

Her heart exposed.

Those journals record a deep commentary into the heart of Christi's spiritual journey prior to becoming the woman I married. Tablets that matter.

Believe it or not, Moses had the same experience with his tablet. Exodus records the time Moses met with God on Mount Sinai, where God gave to him "two tablets of the testimony, tablets of stone, written with the finger of God."[1]

Can you imagine God giving you a handwritten testimony of a conversation he had with you on a stone tablet? Talk about heavy.

If I received a hand-signed tablet from God, I would probably buy a fireproof safe or take out an insurance policy on it.

Moses needed one.

Having just led the Israelites out of slavery from Egypt, Moses walks down the mountain, tablets in hand. When he gets to the bottom, he finds the people he'd sacrificed his life to rescue now worshiping an idol. Their hearts had turned away from him and, more important, the God he served. He was so angry by their misplaced affections that he slammed the tablets onto the ground, shattering them to pieces.

His heart exposed.

As I consider the evolution of the tablet, from stones to paper to the electronic devices that own us today, I can't help but notice the weight of it, no matter its form. That's because over time more and more data is being written on our tablet, deep commentary that exposes who we really are. Perhaps that's why the Bible refers to our heart as a tablet:

Let not steadfast love and faithfulness forsake you; . . .
     write them on the tablet of your heart.[2]

Keep my commandments and live; . . .
     write them on the tablet of your heart.[3]

As parents, Christi and I think and pray about the evolution of the tablets in our home quite often. Nobody has more control over what's written on the tablet of my heart than me. We also realize the powerful truth that nobody else has more influence over what's written on the tablet of our children's hearts than we do, which is a responsibility we don't take lightly. We understand what Jesus meant when he said, "Where your treasure is, there your heart will be also."[4]

Establishing faith in our kids begins by understanding the power of such a responsibility. When we settle for our kids' happiness and grades to become the measuring stick of success, they learn *their* happiness and achievement matter more than caring for and loving others.

Yet we're told to write something different, something much deeper on the tablet of our kids' hearts: steadfast love and God's commandments.

This can be a very humbling, and if we're not careful, shaming conversation to have as parents. But we need to have it if our desire is to establish faith in our children. Not doing so could actually render our home unsafe for our kids. Remember, our children more often do what we do, not what we tell them to do.

Not as a matter of condemnation but as a matter of self-reflection, ask yourself, *Who is writing the most messages on the tablet of my kids' hearts?* Think about the music they listen to. The movies they watch. The people they spend time with. The websites they visit. Where they spend their time. What are the messages being written on their tablets? Who and what are influencing their hearts the most?

The older our kids get, the more we see their heart exposed by their words, actions, and friends.[5]

Talk about heavy.

The content of the tablet matters.

THE SPIRITUAL FOUNDATION OF A SAFE HOUSE

Just as the foundation of a Safe House is an emotionally secure parent, the surest way to establish faith in our kids is to construct our homes on the foundation of a spiritually secure parent. Both research and the Bible show this to be true.[6]

One particular experiment found that children who developed an emotionally secure attachment to their parent were more likely to rely on God as a safe haven and secure base, particularly when they were in distress.[7]

Studies also reveal a positive relationship between a parent's level of spiritual involvement (praying, reading the Bible, attending worship service, adhering to the Sabbath, and so on) and their teenager's intimacy with God. In one study, students emulated their parents' spirituality and relied on God more in homes where spiritual disciplines were routine, whereas students who avoided God viewed their parents as hypocritical and having less of a personal relationship with God.[8]

Another study found similar results. Those who had a more avoidant attachment to their parents were more likely to be agnostic or atheist. Secure respondents not only had the highest level of faith commitment but also were likely to identify that faith as based on a relationship with God and Jesus.[9]

I love how the Bible describes our spiritual foundation. Look at the words of Jesus:

Why are you so polite with me, always saying "Yes, sir," and "That's right, sir,"
but never doing a thing I tell you? These words I speak to you are not mere
additions to your life, homeowner improvements to your standard of living.
They are foundation words, words to build a life on.

　　If you work the words into your life, you are like a smart carpenter who dug
deep and laid the foundation of his house on bedrock. When the river burst its
banks and crashed against the house, nothing could shake it; it was built to last.
But if you just use my words in Bible studies and don't work them into your life,
you are like a dumb carpenter who built a house but skipped the foundation.
When the swollen river came crashing in, it collapsed like a house of cards. It was
a total loss.[10]

Eugene Peterson, who wrote the paraphrased verse you just read, uses such eloquent words to describe the person who uses words to proclaim what they believe but then acts in a different way: "dumb."

If our desire is to establish faith in our kids, we cannot be dumb carpenters who skip the foundation. If we're not secure in our faith, how can we expect our kids to be? I think Ravi Zacharias said it best: "I have little doubt that the single greatest obstacle to the impact of the gospel has not been its inability to provide answers, but the failure on our part to live it out."[11]

> If we're not secure in our faith, how can we expect our kids to be?

When Christi was pregnant with Kennedy, people would ask if Landon, who was almost two years old at the time, knew that he was soon getting a baby sister. In some ways he did.

He knew the crib in the other bedroom of our home was meant for—as he would say in a very affectionate tone of voice—a "baaa-by."

He also knew his mommy's belly was synonymous with the word *baby* as he patted it, saying "Gen-tle."

To prepare him for his sister's arrival, we gave him a baby doll to hold and practice with. Sometimes he was gentle with her. But sometimes he threw her across the room by her head. Fortunately, he's been batting 1.000 on gentleness since Kennedy's arrival. We doubt that will last.

Cognitively, these are the things he knew *about* his baby sister.

Did he *know* how much his little sister would take away from the attention he received around the house?

Does he *know* how much a little sister will shortchange him on his inheritance?

Did he *know* what a joy having a sibling would be?

Of course not. He hadn't *experienced* a baby sister yet.

Knowing *about* something in our heads is quite different from *knowing* something in our hearts.

I cognitively (in my head) know *about* labor pains; Christi, on the other hand, experientially (all over her body) *knows* labor pains.

Which leads me to one of the most curious verses in the Bible. In Galatians, the apostle Paul wrote: "I am again in the pains of childbirth until Christ is formed in you."[12]

How did Paul know what labor pains feel like? The truth is he didn't.

Paul wanted to convey the anguish he was feeling for how far away the Galatians were from God. So he used the analogy of childbirth to express the intensity of his passion to see them become well formed in their faith, just as a baby becomes well formed in the womb.

While standing beside my wife in labor, I witnessed the distress of a woman giving birth. Paul equated that pain with the angst of seeing others truly alive in their faith.

I pray to have an inkling of this pain. Especially for my kids.

As a mom or dad, how much do we anguish over our kids, especially that they be well formed in Jesus?

Perhaps the more practical question is, Do our kids *really* know?

Do our kids know by the way we live, experientially, that our passion, more than any other, is *for them* to be well formed in Jesus? Do our kids know by the way we pursue *our own* spiritual formation?

Or will they merely see a manger at Christmas time and say, "Ba-by."

Knowing *about* Jesus won't get them to heaven or allow them to *experience* the joy of salvation. *Knowing* Jesus will.

But we cannot assume they know.

Research found that parents are more optimistic and confident that the life messages they're giving their children are getting through more than they really are. The relational divide is highlighted by this one statistic: 59 percent of teenagers report they feel emotionally (experientially) close to their mom, but only 35 percent say that they feel relationally close to their dad.[13]

For our kids to *know,* they need us to disciple them.

For our kids to *know,* they need us to model it for them.

For our kids to *know,* they need us to relate to them.

For our kids to *know,* we need to invite them into our own spiritual journey. Established faith happens when we become the primary disciplers of our kids. We cannot expect the church to spiritually raise our kids for us. It begins with us, being smart carpenters, digging deep and working the words into our own lives.

Remember, what we do matters more than what we say. If we want our kids to *know* Jesus, not just know *about* him, they have to know we genuinely experience him and allow that relationship to spill over into our love for them.

PRODIGALS, PROVERBS, AND PROMISES

I have a dear friend and his wife who are the epitome of what emotionally safe parenting should look like. Their faith is more than words. They are living it and modeling it. They established a foundation of faith in their home from the moment they were married. What's more, they run a national ministry for helping families. Yet they have a prodigal, a child who squandered his faith-filled roots to pursue his own desires. My friend described it as the most "heartrending, painful thing I've ever experienced."

Unfortunately, there are exceptions to every rule.

The agony a parent endures about a wayward son or daughter may be the most heartrending experience in my work with families. Perhaps that's why the apostle John said there's "no greater joy than to hear that my children are walking in the truth."[14] I think God experiences that joy with us. That's why his eyes are always roaming the earth, looking for hearts undeniably zealous toward him.[15]

I think the opposite it equally true. There is no greater sorrow than to hear that your children are walking away from the truth. My friend made a list of everything he was feeling about his wayward son (if you haven't experienced a prodigal, you can see my friend's raw emotion. If you have a prodigal, I'm sure you can relate):

- hopeless
- alone
- desperate
- angry
- like I have failed at something
- thinking there are people who are enjoying watching me go through this and glad about it
- frustrated that I can't say anything that will help the situation
- wanting to scream and punch and break stuff, but knowing it won't do any good
- like I want to take my own life and just be done with it

Parents of prodigals often ask me about and question the wise words of Solomon: "Train a child in the way he should go, and when he is old he will not turn from it."[16] There are three important truths of this passage to be considered.

First, this verse is a proverb, not a promise. Many well-meaning people quote this passage as if it's a promise from God. But it's not. Nevertheless the proverb is true. If we establish an emotionally and spiritually safe foundation for our children in the early years of life, they are *more likely* to have an established faith themselves. Research shows a child's ability to verbalize the difference between right and wrong decisions and describe why they're wrong (that is, a moral compass) can be established by age twelve.[17] George Barna found that morals and values are established by age nine, relationships by age twelve, and spiritual beliefs and habit by age thirteen. One of his most intriguing findings was the importance of being intentional with our kids, especially when they're between eighteen months and two years.[18]

Why so young you may wonder? Children learn from observation, picking up the routines and practices of their parents. And since a child's brain grows more significantly during these years than at any other point, the more they see us rely on the character of God in our lives, the more likely they are to do the same. The earlier we begin, the better.

Second, the words "when he is old" can be quite scary. The trouble most parents have with prodigals is wondering if *they* will ever see their children come back. Though our children may stray, we must rely on the foundation of faith we established well enough for them to return. George Barna found teens and twentysomethings will refine and apply what they learned as preteens. Unfortunately, this may mean a season of wandering to test the foundation of faith already laid.

Wandering and testing are hard for parents to watch.

God is mysterious. I can do everything I know to do according to research and the Bible, and my kids may still stray. We pray every day for their protection and God's forbiddance. Free will is a necessity for true love to exist. God must not and cannot therefore control our kids' decisions. Nor can we. We have to trust in his character, that if we lay the foundation on bedrock, the proverb will be established in our home that, when they're old, they will come back. This, too, means we have to pray for peace with his timing, not ours. His will, not ours, be done.

I think this is the hardest prayer we ever pray—not our will.

God may want to use our prodigal to lead others to him, other prodigals that may never have otherwise come to faith or gone back home themselves. Embracing such mysteries is heartening, but no less painful. Nothing is more powerful than prayer, both to protect your kids from venturing down prodigal ways and bringing them back should they choose to wander.

Third, and this is where all of us make parenting mistakes in some fashion, the verse states to "train a child in the way *he* should go." What it doesn't say is "train a child in the way *we* want him to go." This is where our parental agendas get in the way of raising our kids to become who God created them to be. Our own fears of how our children may turn out can turn us into a master controller who tries to dictate the decisions our kids should make for themselves. But our child's faith is their faith, not ours. To establish faith in our kids means we must learn to let go of the reigns.

THE FREEDOM OF LIVING WITHIN THE FOUR WALLS

The four walls of a Safe House function the same for our kids in relationship to God just as they do in relationship to us as parents. Jesus himself is the personification of *grace* (unconditional love) and *truth* (commands).[19] But even more, he allows us the free will to *explore* and make decisions. His commands are in place not to prevent us from enjoying life but to make sure we do. He knows true freedom and joy are found in following his commands.[20]

I believe that's why we're told to "keep [God's] commandments and live; . . . write them on the tablet of [your kids'] heart."[21] Our kids are free to be fully alive when they follow God's truths. He sets his commands in place to *protect* them from spiritual and relational enslavement and possible death that can come when they choose to live outside the four walls. I love how David describes it: "I run in the path of your commands, for you have set my heart free."[22] In God's kingdom, commands equal freedom. It's weird but so true.

Obedience, however, is never as easy as it sounds. Commands seem restrictive, not freeing. Even David, the man after God's own heart, messed up quite a bit. We rebel against God because we think we know best. Our kids rebel against us because they think they know best. Apparently, we're all know-it-alls.

I can think of no better illustration to describe this process than Tim Keller used in a sermon a number of years ago. Our children, as we raise them to go in the way *they* should go and become who they were created to be are like fish in water.

A fish confined to water is free to be whoever she wants to be. The problem is when she begins to believe she is precisely that: confined, restricted, enslaved from doing what she wants to do.

"If only I could eat as much sugar as I wanted," demands the toddler, blind to the consequences of a tummy ache and possible obesity or diabetes in the long term.

"If only I could play video games instead of going to school," complains the child.

"If only I could go to that party with my buddies," asserts the teenager.

"If only I could have sex with my girlfriend tonight," wonders the prom date.

"If only I could get a pair of legs and walk out of this water, I'd be free," the fish thinks to herself.

So God allows her, in his free will, to grow a pair of legs from which she can explore outside the water. As she speedily swims for the shore, the water around her that she believes has kept her limited becomes shallower. Feelings of exhilaration, mixed with a morsel of fear, grab hold. As she steps onto the shore, she *feels* free.

Enjoying the first few minutes of self-proclaimed freedom, she begins to wonder why she can't breathe. The sun, which she used to enjoy at the surface of the water, is now hotter than ever. She gasps for air. Trying to make her way back to the water, she realizes she's too far away. Lying motionless on the beach, she blames God for her plight. Why would he allow her to grow legs to step so far out? Why would he allow her to suffer like this?

The water she saw as a restriction actually provided the oxygen she needed to live free, to become the fish God created her to be. The closer she got to the shore, the shallower the water got and the more enslaved she became—but she didn't know it.

It is fascinating that a few minutes of short-term fun to feel *happy* can have such deadly long-term consequences on those we love most. Raising our kids to write the commands of God on the tablet of their hearts is a matter of helping them understand how and why his commands are truly the oxygen to living free.

> Within reason, allowing our child to make the wrong choice can be one of the best parenting techniques we ever employ.

When our kids feel restricted by God's commands or the rules we set in the home, it's a great opportunity to teach them both the short- and long-term consequences of the decisions they want to make. Within reason, allowing them to make the wrong choice can be one of the best parenting techniques we ever employ. In so doing, we help them discover, within the safe walls of grace and truth, that they will make mistakes, explore too far, and fail. I don't want my children growing up not seeing their need for Jesus because I pampered them too much.

Instead, with pencil and eraser in hand, I want to have the privilege of helping them problem solve when they make poor decisions. I want to be the one who helps edit the false messages that are scribbled on the tablet of their heart by the culture around them. I want to teach and rewrite the commands that set them free. (Using the problem-solving techniques we discussed in chapter 7 is an effective way of doing this.)

Most important, as the coauthor of their story, you can point them into the safe and open arms of the Father who places them back into the water and shows them their role in a story much bigger than their own—his story.

WRITING LOVE

No matter your own spiritual upbringing, you can establish faith in your children. You have what it takes to write steadfast love on the tablet of your kids' hearts. But it requires intentionality.

In what arguably has become the most famous farewell address of all time, Moses communicated to the Israelites a plan for instilling the love of God on the next generation.

He essentially said, "Hey, Church, here's how we leave a legacy." Look at the first portion of his speech:

> Hear, O Israel: The LORD our God, the LORD is one. You shall love the LORD
> your God with all your heart and with all your soul and with all your might.
> And these words that I command you today shall be on your heart.[23]

Even here Moses declares the commandments of God be written on the tablet of our hearts. I don't know about you, but with so many commandments, I get confused. And so did the disciples. That's why later in the Gospels the disciples asked Jesus which of the commandments is the greatest of all. Jesus answered using Moses's words from this very speech, that is, you shall love the Lord your God with every fiber of your being. The second greatest commandment is like it. Jesus said, "Love your neighbor as yourself."[24]

I love how Jesus simplified it for us. The two most important commands to write on the tablet of our kids' hearts are to love God and love others. Truthfully, our kids can have and be anything they want, but if they don't have love, they're nothing but a "noisy gong or a clanging cymbal."[25]

This is why I'm so passionate about raising a generation of kids who learn the value of *loving better* over *feeling better.* As a parent, there's no greater legacy than writing love on the tablet of our kids' hearts, creating a generation of kids who look out not for their own #selfies but for others. The Bible tells us to crucify our #selfies with all of its passions and desires. The more we seek our own happiness, or our kids', the more self-centered we become.

Yet love releases us to experience a deeper joy than we ever imagined. But it comes with a price. Writing steadfast love on the tablets of our kids' hearts is teaching them not just what love is but also *who* love is.

> This is how we know what love is: Jesus Christ laid down his life for us. And we
> ought to lay down our lives for our brothers.[26]

My friend Larry Crabb defines love as "being committed to the wellbeing of another at any cost of my own."

Love seems restrictive, I know. But it's the very water we—and our kids—need to survive.

The Ordinary Moments of a Safe House

Having an everyday kind of faith is difficult when you're chasing toddlers, getting little sleep, working, and balancing everybody else's demands on your life. Especially now that we're accessible to anybody simply by the stress-provoking *ding* of our phone. It's no wonder we place so much responsibility on the church to establish our kids' faith.

However, in the next part of Moses's speech he provided a plan for us to write love on the tablet of our kids' hearts, not through extraordinary moments but through the mundane, ordinary ones of the day.

> You shall teach [these commands] diligently to your children, and shall talk of them when you sit in your house, and when you walk by the way, and when you lie down, and when you rise. You shall bind them as a sign on your hand, and they shall be as frontlets between your eyes. You shall write them on the doorposts of your house and on your gates.[27]

Using Moses's wisdom, here are the magic moments of the day where our faith spills over into the hearts of our kids.

- *Eating meals together.* It's an unbelievably optimal time to have focused discussion with your kids about their day, feelings, friends, and failings. Average parents only spend thirty-eight and a half minutes per week in meaningful conversation with their children. You can have one meal with your family and meet that quota. Start eating together as a family. Try to begin with at least five meals a week with your kids. And I implore you, try to do everything you can to omit technology from these special opportunities to connect with your family. It may be difficult at first, but I know, after sticking to it, you'll be incredibly glad you did.
- *Walking or traveling together.* Moses referred to it as walking "by the way." We refer to it as drive time. Take advantage of your time as a pro-bono chauffeur. Again, as you drive around town, taking your kids to school and extracurricular activities, power down the technology. There will be many days when nobody says a word. But your presence with your kids during this time opens up opportunities for the one conversation that could matter. Be creative on this one too. Our favorite moments are sing-alongs.

- *Tucking kids into bed.* Don't send your kids to bed on their own. Fight the urge to turn on the television or tackle the kitchen cleanup just yet. Take the time to walk them there and tuck them in. There is something special about the private domain of a child's bedroom that allows them to be vulnerable. Our consistent concern for and availability to our children in these quiet moments of the day create an expectation in our children that we're accessible when they need us. You never know when you'll be called on to be your child's counselor in these precious moments.

- *Getting up in the morning.* Sunrise provides a blank page for families to get a fresh start. As you're getting your kids' breakfast or helping them get ready for the day, ask yourself, From the tablet of my own heart, what encouragement am I giving to my children? Make it a point every morning—whether it's sticking a note in her lunch box, thanking him for cleaning up the kitchen, or spending an extra few minutes to read a book to the youngest—to give your kids the spiritual energy they need for whatever happens to them that day.

THE MOST POWERFUL PARENTING TECHNIQUE

The most significant way of establishing faith in our kids is to pray for and with them in every one of these ordinary moments throughout the day.

When we sit down as a family for dinner, we begin in prayer. Landon is often the first to remind us to pray, holding out his little hands and repeating, "A-men, A-men, A-men." When he was about twenty-two months old, all he wanted to do during the meal was pray. I remember at least five times in one meal, Landon held out his hands to pray. I finally said, "No, Landon, we've prayed enough."

Really? I just told my son we had prayed enough?

What message am I sending him? *It's okay, son. God's tired of hearing us talk. Besides, let's give others a turn. Lord knows they need it more than we do.*

Never did I think I would say such nonsense to my kids. But my food was getting cold.

The truth is, I hope he always has a passion for praying. I hope he grows up to challenge me to pray more, even if it means letting the food get cold.

Most of all, I hope he learns that prayer matters.

For this to happen though requires two steps:

- We, as his parents, have to believe that prayer matters.
- We, as his parents, have to act on that belief by doing it and relying on it.

How much *do you* believe that praying for your children matters? Here's a quick litmus test. Ask yourself how often you do it, both praying *for* and *with* them. Here are three ideas to get started:

1. *Pray with your kids.* We pray with Landon every night before bed. We ask him who he wants to pray for. Sometimes he answers us. Other times he just listens. As part of the routine each night, he asks us to read the verse hanging over his bed: "The LORD your God is with you, he is mighty to save. He will take great delight in you, he will quiet you with his love, he will rejoice over you with singing."[28] I hope our children learn the importance of praying Scripture.

2. *Pray for your kids.* My friend Adam Donyes's son is a few months older than Landon. Our little guys are also quickly becoming good buddies. Adam told me he bought a Bible that was designed similar to a journal. He planned to read it from cover to cover and write prayers specifically for and to his son in the journal sections as he is prompted to pray them. When his son is eighteen years old, Adam will bury it in the mountains, give his son a map, and as a rite of passage have him discover that Bible. I chose to do the same thing. And both of us are praying prayers for our sons we never thought we'd pray. I hope our children learn that these prayers for them are timeless.

3. *Circle your kids in prayer.* Christi and I pray circles around our kids based on Mark Batterson's book *The Circle Maker.*[29] We circle prayers for our kids' spouses, health, education, and especially their faith development and character. One of Batterson's insights has stuck with me: "Our prayers never die." You can pray today for your great-great-great-grandkids and those prayers won't die with you. Talk about leaving a legacy of faith in your family lineage. It begins—and ends—with prayer.

We have to believe our prayers matter and pray them. No other parenting technique has been, or ever will be, as effective.

The #SafeHouseFamily

In his speech, Moses didn't speak to atheists; he spoke to Israel, a nation who believed in God and his workings to free them from slavery in Egypt. Moses was telling the church to take responsibility for the next generation by writing the commands of God, a love that transcends every culture, on the hearts of our children.

Leaving a legacy, Moses said, requires a community.

Christi and I have a group of friends we do life with. Their kids are all around the same age as our kids. We get together with those friends on a regular basis. We talk about the struggles of raising our kids, loving our spouses better, and connecting with God. I know we can send our children to our friends' house and they will receive the same love, discipline, and values we teach in our own home. Without this safe community, our family would be on a dangerous island trying to figure out our way as we go. Instead, we have an established Safe House community—a model of what I believe the church was designed to be—the bedrock of loving communities.

Establishing faith in our children includes a community of safe people. Just as Moses described in his farewell speech, the church must come around our kids to consistently provide the same faith messages. This is where grandparents, aunts, uncles, and even church members whose families aren't living in close proximity can help young families, especially single-parent families, by being a supporting cast in writing their family stories.

Kids need a group of people who believe in them and will instill the same faith values in the same way we do as parents in our home. Kids need four key influences:

1. *A Safe House of immediate family.* As parents, establishing faith means we prioritize heavenly matters, not earthly success in our homes. Living in a culture of busyness, it's too easy to fall victim ourselves, filling our kids' schedules with activities that build their grades, athletic prowess, or musical talent, all the while allowing spiritual growth to become an afterthought. Jesus says it's no good to allow our kids to gain the whole world and forfeit their soul.[30]

   Full calendars cannot replace empty souls.

   I'm in no way downplaying the role of earthly activities for our kids. I'm as big a fan as any for the life lessons found in healthy competition. In fact, these activities are often where our kids learn how to fail. The trouble is when we prioritize them over establishing faith.

2. *A Safe House of extended family.* These adults either are or become extended family to our children. Three or four other adults who function as the child's faith team outside of the parents: aunts, uncles, grandparents, mentors, or any other supporting cast. I encourage singles to become aunts and uncles to other families to help parents have date nights. I also encourage spiritually and emotionally healthy men to mentor fatherless kids.

The church is designed to be a fellowship, a support network, a community of people who live out and reinforce the same values that parents are already instilling in the home.

3. *A Safe House tribe of social relationships.* We are who we spend time with. The Bible says "bad company corrupts good character."[31] Here's where coaches, teachers, pastors, and other parents support our children to reinforce the values we're teaching in the home. Where possible, it's essential to have another family, church, athletic team, club, or activity where a community of people becomes part of your child's faith team.[32]

How much time have you spent getting to know the people who speak into your kids' life? Their teachers? coaches? church leaders? Are you strategic about inviting them over for dinner to get to know who they are? Do you know the friends your kids spend the most time with? How well do you know their parents? In the twenty-first century, we have to be vigilant about who our kids are spending time with and what they're doing.

4. *Intergenerational activities and worship.* Involve great-grandparents and grandparents. Research shows that intergenerational worship promotes a faith that sticks.[33] We pick up our children from their classroom immediately after the sermon so they can worship with us in the main sanctuary to close out the service. These moments of worshiping with our kids create sweet memories and provide meaningful conversation for those ordinary moments, like bedtime.

Parents need a community of others to help instill faith values in an emotionally healthy environment. Using #SafeHouseFamily, these online communities are coming together to share ideas:

- church communities that produce groups of parents who can be there for one another
- groups of parents who do life together
- groups of parents who are safe for our children when nobody else is
- communities where grandparents adopt other young families who live away from their immediate families
- communities where emotionally healthy men mentor and counsel fatherless children
- communities that provide singles opportunities to help young families and become adopted aunts and uncles

There's no better example of a Safe House community than a single mother I read about a few years ago. She took empty picture frames and hung them outside the bedroom door of each of her children. She empowered her children, through the church community, to find five godly influences and mentors that they could look up to because she was a single mom.

Each time her children found somebody to be a godly influence in their life, she took a picture of her child with that person. She filled the five picture frames outside her kids' bedrooms so that every time the kids walked into their bedroom—the one place they enter more than any other room throughout the day—they could look at and remember the people who were mentoring them, the people they want to become like when they grow up.

As you build a #SafeHouseFamily in the community where you live, be sure to use the membership site we created for this book: www.joshuastraub.com/members. We have a host of creative ideas and resources. Be sure to also join the community of parents using #SafeHouseFamily when posting to social networks to share how you're building a Safe House community.

The more we unite as parents and offer support to one another, the safer our homes will be. The safer our homes are, the stronger our communities will be. And the stronger our communities are, the stronger and safer the society we leave to our kids will be.

That's a legacy worth leaving together.

The Sacrifice Is Worth It

After a recent Christmas holiday at my in-laws, Christi sent her mum a long text message that I believe is the clarion call of a Safe House. Not only does it describe what she experienced as a little girl but also what we pray our children are stepping into; namely, a lineage of emotional safety.

> Mummy, I just have to tell you what's on my heart: You have given your life creating a home, a family, a love and relationships that your children long to come back to. And now their spouses and kids long for that "home" too. It is a pure, beautiful and grounding atmosphere of love that welcomes the heart to stay, rest and be known. I think it's truly the greatest and most weighty life accomplishment. I think of all that you and Dad have done and given, and something aches inside because I fear it feels like it's gone unnoticed. Like the years of investment have rushed by and now the world has moved on. But you must know it hasn't gone unnoticed—not a day, moment, conversation, meal, selfless act, carefully selected gift, touch or nugget of wisdom.
>
> They're still felt every day in the lives of us three—accumulated into a heart bank of memories, love and acceptance that is stuffed full. And that's how I feel—full, grounded. With a confidence to walk each day in this big world. And now, I pray, we replicate it into the hearts of your grandbabies. That is my deepest desire—to create what you have for mine. To do soul work like you.
>
> Know that you have accomplished and created something so incredibly weighty and infinitely important. I burst to know the reach of it on the other side of heaven. Thank you, Mummy, for all of it. Those words seem so trite. To me, to us, you are home.
>
> How I love you so.

My prayer is that you and I one day receive a message like this from our kids. Press on, Mom and Dad. What you're doing matters.

Notes

Chapter 1 | Can Parenting Really Be This Simple?

1. Dale Kuehne, *Sex and iWorld: Rethinking Relationship Beyond an Age of Individualism* (Grand Rapids: Baker Academic, 2009).
2. Making Caring Common Project, "MCCP Report: The Children We Mean to Raise," Harvard Graduate School of Education, June 25, 2014, www.gse.harvard.edu/news/14/06/mccp-report -children-we-mean-raise.
3. Jean M. Twenge and W. Keith Campbell, *The Narcissism Epidemic: Living in the Age of Entitlement* (New York: Free Press, 2009). More in-depth analysis on this epidemic can be found in Twenge's research at http://twenge.socialpsychology.org/publications.
4. Twenge and Campbell, *Narcissism Epidemic*.
5. Jean M. Twenge et al., "Birth Cohort Increases in Psychopathology Among Young Americans, 1938–2007: A Cross-Temporal Meta-Analysis of the MMPI," *Clinical Psychology Review* 30, no. 2 (March 2010): 145–54, www.sciencedirect.com/science/article/pii/S027273580900141X.
6. Most recent results can be found at http://timss.bc.edu. Another recent analysis on the topic for further consideration can be found at Martin Carnoy and Richard Rothstein, "What Do International Tests Really Show About U.S. Student Performance," Economic Policy Institute, January 28, 2013, www.epi.org/publication/us-student-performance-testing.
7. Executive Summary, "Millennials: Confident. Connected. Open to Change," Pew Research Center, February 24, 2010, www.pewsocialtrends.org/2010/02/24/millennials-confident -connected-open-to-change.
8. Research on these aspects of technology's effect on the brain can be found in two highly recommended books: Gary Small and Gigi Vorgan, *iBrain: Surviving the Technological Alteration of the Modern Mind* (New York: Collins Living, 2008); and Nicolas Carr, *The Shallows: What the Internet Is Doing to Our Brains* (New York: Norton, 2011).
9. "2012 Online Stress in America: Survey of 2,020 U.S. Adults 18 and Older by Harris Interactive for American Psychological Association," cited by Sharon Jayson, "Who's Feeling Stressed? Young Adults New Survey Shows," *USA Today,* February 7, 2013, www.usatoday.com/story/news /nation/2013/02/06/stress-psychology-millennials-depression/1878295.
10. "2012 Online Stress in America."
11. "2012 Online Stress in America."
12. Terrance Woodworth, *Ritalin: The Fourth R in Schools: Discussing the Use of Psychotropic Drugs for Youth, DEA Congressional Testimony Before the Committee on Education and the Workforce: Subcommittee on Early Childhood, Youth, and Families* (Washington, DC: Department of Education, 2000); Public Broadcasting System, *Statistics on Stimulant Use,* www.pbs.org/wgbh /pages/frontline/shows/medicating/drugs/stats.html; and Bruce Jonas et al., *Trends in Psychotropic Medication Use in the Noninstitutionalized Adolescent Population: An NHANES Analysis* (National Center for Health Statistics, 2012), www.cdc.gov/nchs/ppt/nchs2012/SS-22_JONAS.pdf.
13. Anne Lamott, *Bird by Bird: Some Instructions on Writing and Life* (New York: Anchor Books, 1995), 28.

Chapter 2 | You Are Home: A Safe House Begins with You

1. See Psalm 34:8.
2. 1 John 4:19.
3. Daniel A. Hughes, *Attachment-Focused Parenting: Effective Strategies to Care for Children* (New York: Norton, 2009.
4. Hughes, *Attachment-Focused Parenting.*
5. Brené Brown, *Daring Greatly: How the Courage to Be Vulnerable Transforms the Way We Live, Love, Parent, and Lead* (New York: Gotham Books, 2013), 16.
6. Daniel J. Siegel and Tina Payne Bryson, *No-Drama Discipline: The Whole-Brain Way to Calm the Chaos and Nurture Your Child's Developing Mind* (New York: Bantam, 2014), xxii.
7. Psalm 103:8–10.
8. M. Main et al., "Security in Infancy, Childhood, and Adulthood: A Move to the Level of Representation," *Monographs of the Society for Research in Child Development* 50, nos. 1–2, Growing Points of Attachment Theory and Research (1985): 66–104.
9. 1 John 4:18.
10. Siegel and Bryson, *No-Drama Discipline,* xxiv.
11. S. W. Porges, "Love: An Emergent Property of the Mammalian Autonomic Nervous System," *Psychoneuroendocrinology* 23, no. 8 (1998): 837–61. Also see Daniel J. Siegel, *The Mindful Brain: Reflection and Attunement in the Cultivation of Well-Being* (New York: Norton, 2007).
12. Siegel, *The Mindful Brain,* 206 (emphasis added).
13. John Gottman and Joan DeClaire, *The Heart of Parenting: How to Raise an Emotionally Intelligent Child* (New York: Simon & Schuster, 1997).
14. Brown, *Daring Greatly,* 217.
15. Numbers 6:24–26, NIV (emphasis added).
16. Psalm 127:1.
17. See 1 John 4:18.
18. Philippians 4:7 (emphasis added).
19. See Louis Cozolino, *The Neuroscience of Human Relationships: Attachment and the Developing Social Brain* (New York: Norton, 2006), 16.
20. This is explained in more detail in Tim Clinton and Joshua Straub, *God Attachment: Why You Believe, Act, and Feel the Way You Do About God* (Nashville: Howard Books, 2010).
21. John Bowlby, *Attachment and Loss,* vol. 1, *Attachment,* 2nd ed. (New York: Basic Books, 1999). The book was originally published in 1969.
22. These are clearly stated and defined in greater detail in Mario Mikulincer and Phillip R. Shaver, *Attachment in Adulthood: Structure, Dynamics, and Change* (New York: Guilford, 2007), 17.
23. For a more complete review of how early caregiving relationships affect the brain function of an infant, see Allan N. Schore, "Effects of a Secure Attachment Relationship on Right Brain Development, Affect Regulation, and Infant Mental Health," *Infant Mental Health Journal* 22, nos. 1–2 (January–April 2001): 7–66.
24. C. B. Thomas and K. R. Duszynski, "Closeness to Parents and the Family Constellation in a Prospective Study of Five Disease States: Suicide, Mental Illness, Malignant Tumor, Hypertension, and Coronary Heart Disease," *Johns Hopkins Medical Journal* 134, no. 5 (May 1974): 251–70.
25. Daniel J. Siegel, *Pocket Guide to Interpersonal Neurobiology: An Integrative Handbook of the Mind* (New York: Norton, 2012), 20-11, 20-12.

Chapter 3 | Your Story, Your Kid's Brain, and the Science of Safety

1. Daniel J. Siegel, *Pocket Guide to Interpersonal Neurobiology: An Integrative Handbook of the Mind* (New York: Norton, 2012), 20-11.

2. Siegel, *Pocket Guide to Interpersonal Neurobiology,* 21-3.
3. M. D. S. Ainsworth, "The Development of Infant-Mother Attachment," in *Review of Child Development Research,* vol. 3, ed. B. M. Caldwell and H. N. Ricciuti (Chicago: University of Chicago Press, 1973); M. D. S. Ainsworth, "Patterns of Infant-Mother Attachments: Antecedents and Effects on Development," *Bulletin of the New York Academy of Medicine* 61 (1985): 771–91; John Bowlby, *A Secure Base: Parent-Child Attachment and Healthy Human Development* (New York: Basic Books, 1988); and L. Alan Sroufe and Everett Waters, "Attachment as an Organizational Construct," *Child Development* 48 (1977): 1184–99.
4. These brain functions are more clearly defined in Daniel J. Siegel and Tina Payne Bryson, *The Whole-Brain Child: 12 Revolutionary Strategies to Nurture Your Child's Developing Mind* (New York: Bantam, 2011). If you are interested in a more in-depth look at how your interaction with your child builds their brain, I recommend this book.
5. Siegel, *Pocket Guide to Interpersonal Neurobiology,* 20-1.
6. Siegel, *Pocket Guide to Interpersonal Neurobiology,* 20-5, 20-6.
7. This is found in more than sixty studies on the topic. The table of findings can be found in Mario Mikulincer and Phillip R. Shaver, *Attachment in Adulthood: Structure, Dynamics, and Change* (New York: Guilford, 2007), 155–60.
8. L. Matas et al., "Continuity of Adaptation in the Second Year: The Relationship Between Quality of Attachment and Later Competence," *Child Development* 49 (1978): 547–56.
9. There are numerous studies linking attachment security to identity achievement. See Mikulincer and Shaver, *Attachment in Adulthood,* 235.
10. E. T. Huntsinger and L. J. Luecken, "Attachment Relationships and Health Behavior: The Meditational Role of Self-Esteem," *Psychology and Health* 19 (2004): 515–26; and E. Scharfe and D. Eldredge, "Associations Between Attachment Representations and Health Behaviors in Late Adolescence," *Journal of Health Psychology* 6 (2001): 295–307.
11. This is found in at least nine published studies. A review of these findings can be found in Mikulincer and Shaver, *Attachment in Adulthood,* 288.
12. This is found in many studies. The seminal studies include M. Mikulincer et al., "Attachment Styles, Coping Strategies, and Posttraumatic Psychological Distress: The Impact of the Gulf War in Israel," *Journal of Personality and Social Psychology* 64 (1993): 817–26; and Gurit E. Birnbaum et al., "When Marriage Breaks Up: Does Attachment Style Contribute to Coping and Mental Health?" *Journal of Social and Personal Relationships* 14 (1997): 643–54.
13. John Bowlby, *Attachment and Loss,* vol. 2, *Separation: Anxiety and Anger* (New York: Basic Books, 1973); M. D. S. Ainsworth, "Attachment and Other Affectional Bonds Across the Life Cycle," in *Attachment Across the Life Cycle,* ed. C. Murray Parkes et al. (New York: Routledge, 1991), 33–51. Also see Mikulincer and Shaver, *Attachment in Adulthood,* 225.
14. C. Murray Parkes, "A Historical Overview of the Scientific Study of Bereavement," in *Handbook of Bereavement Research: Consequences, Coping, and Care,* ed. Margaret S. Stroebe et al. (Washington, DC: American Psychological Association, 2001), 25–45; and M. Stroebe et al., "Attachment in Coping with Bereavement: A Theoretical Integration," *Review of General Psychology* 9 (2005): 48–66.
15. This is found in many studies. The seminal studies include Pehr Granqvist, "Religiousness and Perceived Childhood Attachment: On the Question of Compensation or Correspondence," *Journal for the Scientific Study of Religion* 37 (1998): 350–67; Pehr Granqvist and Berit Hagekull, "Religiousness and Perceived Childhood Attachment: Profiling Socialized Correspondence and Emotional Compensation," *Journal for the Scientific Study of Religion* 36, no. 2 (1999): 254–73; Lee A. Kirkpatrick and Phillip R. Shaver, "Attachment Theory and Religion: Childhood Attachments, Religious Beliefs, and Conversion," *Journal for the Scientific Study of Religion* 29, no. 3 (1990): 315–34; Pehr Granqvist, "Building a Bridge Between Attachment and Religious Coping: Tests of Moderators and Mediators," *Mental*

Health, Religion and Culture 8, no. 1 (2005): 35–47; and Kara E. Powell and Chap Clark, *Sticky Faith: Everyday Ideas to Build Lasting Faith in Your Kids* (Grand Rapids: Zondervan, 2011).

16. Mario Mikulincer and Michal Selinger, "The Interplay Between Attachment and Affiliation Systems in Adolescents' Same-Sex Friendships: The Role of Attachment Style," *Journal of Social and Personal Relationships* 18 (2001): 81–106.

17. A list of twenty-three studies related to attachment security and loneliness can be found in Mikulincer and Shaver, *Attachment in Adulthood,* 282.

18. There are more than a dozen studies related to this finding, and a review of those can be found in Mikulincer and Shaver, *Attachment in Adulthood,* 283.

19. Mikulincer and Shaver, *Attachment in Adulthood,* 283.

20. Judith A. Feeney and Patricia Noller, "Attachment Style as a Predictor of Adult Romantic Relationships," *Journal of Personality and Social Psychology* 59, no. 2 (1990): 281–91; Cindy Hazan and Phillip Shaver, "Romantic Love Conceptualized as an Attachment Process," *Journal of Personality and Social Psychology* 52 (1987): 511–24; Cindy Hazan and Phillip R. Shaver, "Love and Work: An Attachment-Theoretical Perspective," *Journal of Personality and Social Psychology* 59 (1990): 270–80; C. L. Heavey et al., "Marital Conflict and Divorce: A Developmental Family Psychology Perspective," in *Handbook of Developmental Family Psychology and Psychopathology,* ed. Luciano L'Abate (New York: Wiley, 1994), 221–42; M. B. Levy and K. E. Davis, "Love Styles and Attachment Styles Compared: Their Relations to Each Other and to Various Relationship Characteristics," *Journal of Social and Personal Relationships* 5 (1988): 439–71; and Jeffrey A. Simpson, "Influence of Attachment Styles on Romantic Relationships," *Journal of Personality and Social Psychology* 59 (1990): 971–80.

21. Kim Leon and Deborah B. Jacobvitz, "Relationships Between Adult Attachment Representations and Family Ritual Quality: A Prospective Longitudinal Study," *Family Process* 42 (2003): 419–32.

22. O. Gillath and D. A. Schachner, "How Do Sexuality and Attachment Interact? Goals, Motives, and Strategies," in *Dynamics of Love: Attachment, Caregiving, and Sex,* ed. Mario Mikulincer and Gail S. Goodman (New York: Guilford Press, 2006), 337–55.

23. Mikulincer and Shaver, *Attachment in Adulthood,* 301.

24. Mary B. Eberly and Raymond Montemayor, "Adolescent Affection and Helpfulness Toward Parents: A 2-Year Follow-Up," *Journal of Early Adolescence* 19 (1999): 226–48.

25. V. G. Cicirelli, "Attachment and Obligation as Daughters' Motives for Caregiving Behavior and Subsequent Effect on Subjective Burden," *Psychology and Aging* 8 (1993): 144–55; and Aloen L. Townsend and Melissa M. Franks, "Binding Ties: Closeness and Conflict in Adult Children's Caregiving Relationships," *Psychology and Aging* 10 (1995): 343–51.

26. Brooke C. Feeney and Nancy L. Collins, "Predictors of Caregiving in Adult Intimate Relationships: An Attachment Theoretical Perspective," *Journal of Personality and Social Psychology* 80 (2001): 972–94; Judith A. Feeney, "Attachment, Caregiving and Marital Satisfaction," *Personal Relationships* 3 (1996): 401–16; Judith A. Feeney and Lydia Hohaus, "Attachment and Spousal Caregiving," *Personal Relationships* 8 (2001): 21–39; and Linda J. Kunce and Phillip R. Shaver, "An Attachment-Theoretical Approach to Caregiving in Romantic Relationships," in *Advances in Personal Relationships: Attachment Processes in Adulthood,* vol. 5, ed. K. Bartholomew and D. Perlman (London: Kingsley, 1994), 205–37.

27. B. C. Feeney and N. L. Collins, "Motivations for Caregiving in Adult Intimate Relationships: Influences on Caregiving Behavior and Relationship Functioning," *Personality and Social Psychology Bulletin* 29 (2003): 950–68; and B. C. Feeney, "Individual Differences in Secure Base Support Provision: The Role of Attachment Style, Relationship Characteristics, and Underlying Motivations" (unpublished manuscript, Carnegie Mellon University, Pittsburgh, PA, 2005).

28. Mikulincer and Shaver, *Attachment in Adulthood,* 344.

29. Mikulincer and Shaver, *Attachment in Adulthood,* 237.

30. Mikulincer and Shaver, *Attachment in Adulthood,* 234.

31. Adriana G. Bus and Marinus H. Van Ijzendoorn, "Attachment and Early Reading: A Longitudinal Study," *Journal of Genetic Psychology* 149 (1988): 199–210.

32. Klaus E. Grossman et al., "A Wider View of Attachment and Exploration: Stability and Change During the Years of Immaturity," in *Handbook of Attachment: Theory, Research, and Clinical Applications,* ed. Jude Cassidy and Phillip R. Shaver (New York: Guilford Press, 1999), 760–86.

33. Ora Aviezer et al., "School Competence in Young Adolescence: Links to Early Attachment Relationships Beyond Concurrent Self-Perceived Competence and Representations of Relationships," *International Journal of Behavioral Development* 26 (2002): 397–409.

34. Teresa Jacobsen et al., "A Longitudinal Study of the Relation Between Representations of Attachment in Childhood and Cognitive Functioning in Childhood and Adolescence," *Developmental Psychology* 30 (1994): 112–24.

35. Teresa Jacobsen and Volker Hofmann, "Children's Attachment Representations: Longitudinal Relations to School Behavior and Academic Competency in Middle Childhood and Adolescence," *Development Psychology* 33 (1997): 703–10.

36. Debra E. Felsman and David L. Blustein, "The Role of Peer Relatedness in Late Adolescent Career Development," *Journal of Vocational Behavior* 54 (1999): 279–95; Timothy U. Ketterson and David L. Blustein, "Attachment Relationships and the Career Exploration Process," *Career Development Quarterly* 46 (1997): 167–78; and H. Y. Lee and K. F. Hughey, "The Relationship of Psychological Separation and Parental Attachment to the Career Maturity of College Freshman from Intact Families," *Journal of Career Development* 27 (2001): 279–93.

37. David L. Blustein et al., "Contributions of Psychological Separation and Parental Attachment to the Career Development Process," *Journal of Counseling Psychology* 38 (1991): 39–50; Debra E. Felsman and David L. Blustein, "The Role of Peer Relatedness in Late Adolescent Career Development," *Journal of Vocational Behavior* 54 (1999): 279–95; and Donna J. Scott and A. Timothy Church, "Separation/Attachment Theory and Career Decidedness and Commitment: Effects of Parental Divorce," *Journal of Vocational Behavior* 58 (2001): 328–47.

38. Many studies have contributed to these findings; see Mikulincer and Shaver, *Attachment in Adulthood,* 228–32.

39. The list of questions is included in Marshall P. Duke, "The Stories That Bind Us: What Are the Twenty Questions?" *Huffington Post,* March 23, 2013, www.huffingtonpost.com/marshall -p-duke/the-stories-that-bind-us-_b_2918975.html.

40. Bruce Feiler, "The Stories That Bind Us," *New York Times,* March 15, 2013, www.nytimes .com/2013/03/17/fashion/the-family-stories-that-bind-us-this-life.html?pagewanted=all&_r=0.

41. This is an example of the oscillating family narrative as described by Marshall Duke in Feiler, "The Stories That Bind Us."

Chapter 4 | The Four Walls of a Safe House

1. See Hebrews 13:2.

2. Matthew 7:12, NASB.

3. Proverbs 3:13–15.

4. Stella Chess and Alexander Thomas, *Temperament: Theory and Practice* (New York: Brunner/ Mazel, 1996).

5. John Gottman, "Emotion Coaching: The Heart of Parenting," The Gottman Institute, 2013, http://emotioncoaching.gottman.com/about.

6. Walter Mischel et al., "Cognitive and Attentional Mechanisms in Delay of Gratification," *Journal of Personality and Social Psychology* 21, no. 2 (February 1972): 204–18; Walter Mischel et al., "Delay of Gratification in Children," *Science* 244, no. 4907 (May 26, 1989): 933–38; Walter Mischel and Ozlem Ayduk, "Willpower in a Cognitive-Affective Processing System: The Dynamics of Delay of Gratification," in *Handbook of Self-Regulation: Research, Theory, and Applications,* ed. Roy F. Baumeister and Kathleen D. Vohs (New York: Guilford, 2004), 99–129;

Ozlem N. Ayduk et al., "Regulating the Interpersonal Self: Strategic Self-Regulation for Coping with Rejection Sensitivity," *Journal of Personality and Social Psychology* 79, no. 5 (2000): 776–92; Tanya R. Schlam et al., "Preschoolers' Delay of Gratification Predicts Their Body Mass 30 Years Later," *Journal of Pediatrics* 162 (2013): 90–93; and Yuichi Shoda et al., "Predicting Adolescent Cognitive and Self-Regulatory Competencies from Preschool Delay of Gratification: Identifying Diagnostic Conditions," *Developmental Psychology* 26, no. 6 (1990): 978–86.

7. John Gottman and Joan DeClaire, *Raising an Emotionally Intelligent Child: The Heart of Parenting* (New York: Simon & Schuster, 1997).

8. Daniel J. Siegel, *Pocket Guide to Interpersonal Neurobiology: An Integrative Handbook of the Mind* (New York: Norton, 2012), 27-2.

9. Ross W. Greene and J. Stuart Albon, *Treating Explosive Kids: The Collaborative Problem-Solving Approach* (New York: Guilford Press, 2006).

10. Siegel, *Pocket Guide to Interpersonal Neurobiology,* A1-16.

11. Judith Locke et al., "Can a Parent Do Too Much for Their Child? An Examination by Parenting Professionals of the Concept of Overparenting," *Australian Journal of Guidance and Counseling* 22, no. 2 (2012): 249–65.

Chapter 5 | Explore and Protect

1. Juliana Negreiros and Lynn D. Miller, "The Role of Parenting in Childhood Anxiety: Etiological Factors and Treatment Implications," *Clinical Psychology: Science and Practice* 21, no. 1 (2014): 3–17.

2. Jessica Lahey, "Why Parents Need to Let Their Children Fail," *Atlantic,* January 29, 2013, www .theatlantic.com/national/archive/2013/01/why-parents-need-to-let-their-children-fail/272603.

3. Lahey, "Why Parents Need to Let Their Children Fail."

4. Proverbs 22:6.

5. Stanley I. Greenspan and Nancy Breslau Lewis, *Building Healthy Minds: The Six Experiences That Create Intelligence and Emotional Growth in Babies and Young Children* (Boston: Da Capo Press, 2000), 112–13.

6. Laura Clark, "Want Your Children to Learn? Give Them Time to Play Alone and Explore the World, Says Academic," *Daily Mail,* August 13, 2014, www.dailymail.co.uk/news/article-2724205 /Want-children-learn-Give-time-play-explore-world-says-academic.html.

7. Greenspan and Lewis, *Building Healthy Minds,* 112–13.

8. Greenspan and Lewis, *Building Healthy Minds,* 112–13.

9. These exercises are based on forty years of child development research by Stanley Greenspan. You can more specifically learn these important strategies with his book *Building Healthy Minds.*

10. Andy Chen, "Best Present: Play with Your Kids," *Straits Times* (Singapore), December 17, 2014, http://women.asiaone.com/women/parenting/best-present-play-your-kids#sthash.2lD58cAf.dpuf.

11. Greenspan and Lewis, *Building Healthy Minds,* 108.

12. Daniel J. Seigel and Tina Payne Bryson, *No-Drama Discipline: The Whole-Brain Way to Calm the Chaos and Nurture Your Child's Developing Mind* (New York: Bantam, 2014).

13. Jane E. Barker et al., "Less-Structured Time in Children's Daily Lives Predicts Self-Directed Executive Functioning," *Frontiers in Psychology,* June 17, 2014, doi: 10.3389/fpsyg.2014.00593.

14. CBS News, "Pediatricians Urge Parents to Limit Kids' 'Screen Time,'" October 28, 2013, www .cbsnews.com/news/pediatricians-urge-parents-to-limit-kids-screen-time.

15. D. Baumrind, "Rearing Competent Children," in *Child Development Today and Tomorrow,* ed. William Damon (San Francisco: Jossey-Bass, 1989), http://social.jrank.org/pages/352/Laissez-Faire-Parents.html">Laissez-Faire Parents.

16. Tim Clinton and Joshua Straub, *God Attachment: Why You Believe, Act, and Feel the Way You Do About God* (Nashville: Howard Books, 2010), 93 (emphasis added).

17. 1 Corinthians 15:33, NIV.

18. John Gottman and Julie S. Gottman, *Emotion Coaching: The Heart of Parenting Video Program* (DVD and Parenting Workbook) (Seattle, WA: Gottman Institute, 2013). For information about purchasing, see www.gottman.com/shop/emotion-coaching-video-series.

Chapter 6 | Grace and Truth

1. Henry Cloud and John Townsend, *Raising Great Kids for Parents of Preschoolers Leaders' Guide* (Grand Rapids: Zondervan, 2000), 34.
2. See Katie Davis, "Understanding the Disneyland Dad," Dads Divorce, www.dadsdivorce.com /articles/understanding-the-disneyland-dad.html.
3. Ann D. Murry, "Laissez-Faire Parents," Child Development Reference, http://social.jrank.org /pages/352/Laissez-Faire-Parents.html#ixzz3MkmsXH00.
4. Hebrews 12:5–9, MSG.
5. Michael Carr-Gregg, *Strictly Parenting: Everything You Need to Know About Raising School-Age Kids* (Melbourne, Australia: Penguin, 2014), e-book.
6. Henry Cloud and John Townsend, *Raising Great Kids: A Comprehensive Guide to Parenting with Grace and Truth* (Grand Rapids: Zondervan, 2009), 48.
7. Carole Banks, "You're Grounded for Life! Why Harsh Punishments for Children and Teenagers Don't Work," Empowering Parents, www.empoweringparents.com/Why-Harsh-Punishments -for-Children-Teenagers-Dont-Work.php#.
8. John Townsend, *Leadership Beyond Reason: How Great Leaders Succeed by Harnessing the Power of Their Values, Feelings, and Intuition* (Nashville: Thomas Nelson, 2009), 126.
9. Philippians 4:5–7 (emphasis added).
10. Philippians 4:8 (emphasis added).
11. Daniel J. Seigel and Tina Payne Bryson, *No-Drama Discipline: The Whole-Brain Way to Calm the Chaos and Nurture Your Child's Developing Mind* (New York: Bantam, 2014).
12. Murry, "Laissez-Faire Parents," http://social.jrank.org/pages/352/Laissez-Faire-Parents.html #ixzz3MkmsXH00.
13. Proverbs 24:3–4 (emphasis added).
14. James 3:17–18.

Chapter 7 | Safe Discipline

1. Jane Nelsen, *Positive Discipline,* rev. ed. (New York: Random House, 2006), 14.
2. Philippians 2:3.
3. Ephesians 6:4, KJV.
4. Ephesians 6:4, MSG.
5. John Gottman and Joan DeClaire, *The Heart of Parenting: How to Raise an Emotionally Intelligent Child* (New York: Simon & Schuster, 1997).
6. Stanley I. Greenspan and Nancy Breslau N. Lewis, *Building Healthy Minds: The Six Experiences That Create Intelligence and Emotional Growth in Babies and Young Children* (Boston: Da Capo Press, 2000).
7. For more information on emotion coaching, see the Gottman Institute website at www. emotioncoaching.gottman.com or John Gottman and Joan DeClaire, *The Heart of Parenting: How to Raise an Emotionally Intelligent Child* (New York: Simon & Schuster, 1997).
8. The following are emotion-coaching principles based on the research found in John Gottman, *Raising an Emotionally Intelligent Child: The Heart of Parenting* (New York: Simon and Schuster, 1997).
9. Haim G. Ginott, *Between Parents and Child* (New York: Macmillan, 1965) p. 110.
10. John Gottman and Julie S. Gottman, *Emotion Coaching: The Heart of Parenting Video Program* (DVD and Parenting Workbook) (Seattle, WA: Gottman Institute, 2013). For information about purchasing, see www.gottman.com/shop/emotion-coaching-video-series.

11. Ross W. Greene, *The Explosive Child: A New Approach for Understanding and Parenting Easily Frustrated, Chronically Inflexible Children*, 5th rev. ed. (New York: Harper, 2014); and David D. Burns, *Feeling Good Together: The Secret to Making Troubled Relationships Work* (New York: Broadway Books, 2008).

12. The EAR principles are outlined in Burns, *Feeling Good Together*.

13. Matthew 7:1, KJV.

14. Greene, *The Explosive Child*; and Burns, *Feeling Good Together*.

15. See Gottman and Gottman, *Emotion Coaching* (DVD and Parenting Workbook).

16. Mari-Jane Williams, "Study Says Yelling as Harmful as Spanking in Disciplining Kids. So What Should Parents Do?" *Washington Post,* October 2, 2013, www.washingtonpost.com/lifestyle /on-parenting/study-says-yelling-as-harmful-as-spanking-in-disciplining-kids-so-what-should -parents-do/2013/10/01/dcb01b74-1bf1-11e3-8685-5021e0c41964_story.html.

17. Brené Brown, *Daring Greatly: How the Courage to Be Vulnerable Transforms the Way We Live, Love, Parent, and Lead* (New York: Gotham Books, 2012).

Chapter 8 | Nurturing Our Child's Brain: From Infancy Through Adolescence

1. Matt Richtel, "Silicon Valley School Sticks to Basics, Shuns High-Tech Tools," *Boston Globe,* October 23, 2011, www.boston.com/news/education/k_12/articles/2011/10/23/school_that _educates_the_children_of_silicon_valley_eschews_high_tech.

2. Nick Bilton, "Steve Jobs Was a Low Tech Parent," *New York Times,* September 20, 2014, www .nytimes.com/2014/09/11/fashion/steve-jobs-apple-was-a-low-tech-parent.html?_r=0.

3. Rima Shore, *Rethinking the Brain: New Insights into Early Development* (New York: Families and Work Institute, 1997), 16–17.

4. Shore, *Rethinking the Brain*.

5. Stanley Greenspan and Nancy Breslau Lewis, *Building Healthy Minds: The Six Experiences That Create Intelligence and Emotional Growth in Babies and Young Children* (Boston: Da Capo Press, 2000), 1.

6. Jenn Berman, "10 Reasons Play Makes Babies Smarter," *CNN,* January 31, 2011, www.cnn.com /2011/HEALTH/01/31/play.babies.smarter.parenting.

7. Berman, "10 Reasons Play Makes Babies Smarter."

8. Jane E. Barker et al., "Less-Structured Time in Children's Daily Lives Predicts Self-Directed Executive Functioning," *Frontiers in Psychology,* June 17, 2014, doi: 10.3389/fpsyg.2014.00593.

9. Greenspan and Lewis, *Building Healthy Minds,* 112–13.

10. These exercises are based on forty years of child development research by Stanley Greenspan. These important strategies are outlined in his *Building Healthy Minds*.

11. Greenspan and Lewis, *Building Healthy Minds,* 36.

12. Greenspan and Lewis, *Building Healthy Minds,* 135.

13. Greenspan and Lewis, *Building Healthy Minds,* 256.

14. Ephesians 4:15.

15. Dimitri Christakis, "Media and Children," YouTube video, TEDxRainier, December 27, 2011, www.youtube.com/watch?v=BoT7qH_uVNo.

16. "Too much screen time can delay a child's brain development," Zee News (India), October 4, 2013, http://zeenews.india.com/news/health/health-news/too-much-screen-time-can-delay-childs -brain-development_24343.html.

17. American Academy of Pediatrics, "Policy Statement: Children, Adolescents, and the Media," *Pediatrics* 132, no. 5 (2013): 958–62, doi: 10.1542/peds.2013-2656.

18. Dimitri Christakis, "Media and Children," December 27, 2011, TedxRainer, www.youtube.com /watch?v=BoT7qH_uVNo.

19. "Generation M2: Media in the Lives of 8- to 18-Year-Olds," Kaiser Family Foundation, January 20, 2010, http://kff.org/other/event/generation-m2-media-in-the-lives-of.

20. Wendy Wang, "Parents' Time with Kids More Rewarding Than Paid Work—and More Exhausting," Pew Research Center, *Social and Demographic Trends,* October 8, 2013, www .pewsocialtrends.org/2013/10/08/ parents-time-with-kids-more-rewarding-than-paid-work-and-more-exhausting.
21. Christakis, "Media and Children."
22. Christakis, "Media and Children."
23. See Matthew 26:37.
24. Genesis 2:18.
25. See Henry Cloud and John Townsend, *Safe People: How to Find Relationships That Are Good for You and Avoid Those That Aren't* (Grand Rapids: Zondervan, 1995).

Chapter 9 | The Bible and Safe Parenting

1. The scientific data is found primarily in the area of attachment research, that the safer we feel, the more we are free to be who we are in relationships. The latest area in which this has been found to be true is Brené Brown's sociological research. See Brené Brown, *Daring Greatly: How the Courage to Be Vulnerable Transforms the Way We Live, Love, Parent, and Lead* (New York: Gotham Books, 2013).
2. 1 John 4:19.
3. For an understanding of how we relate to God based on our styles of relating, see Tim Clinton and Joshua Straub, *God Attachment: Why We Believe, Act, and Feel the Way We Do About God* (Nashville: Howard Books, 2010).
4. Psalm 46:1.
5. Hebrews 13:5.
6. John 1:14 (emphasis added).
7. Galatians 6:7.
8. Psalm 127:1.
9. 1 Kings 3:26, HCSB (emphasis added).
10. 1 Kings 3:26, KJV.
11. See 1 Kings 3:26.
12. 1 Kings 3:26.
13. 1 Kings 3:27.
14. Psalm 103:13.
15. Psalm 103:14.
16. Psalm 103:8–18.
17. Daniel J. Seigel and Tina Payne Bryson, *No-Drama Discipline: The Whole-Brain Way to Calm the Chaos and Nurture Your Child's Developing Mind* (New York: Bantam, 2014).
18. Psalm 103:8–10.
19. Margaret Feinberg, *Scouting the Divine: My Search for God in Wine, Wool, and Wild Honey* (Grand Rapids: Zondervan, 2009), 32.
20. Ephesians 6:4.
21. Feinberg, *Scouting the Divine,* 55.
22. Matthew 18:12–14, NIV (emphasis added).
23. Isaiah 40:11, NIV (emphasis added).
24. John 10:7, 11, NIV.
25. Matthew 27:46.
26. In this chapter, I owe some of the parental insights derived from Psalm 103 to a sermon by Timothy Keller titled "God Our Father," in a series titled Four Ways to Live, Four Ways to Love, delivered September 17, 2000.
27. Psalm 103:17–18.

Chapter 10 | A Safe Marriage

1. Marcia J. Carlson and Mary E. Corcoran, "Family Structure and Children's Behavioral and Cognitive Outcomes," *Journal of Marriage and Family* 63 (August 2001): 779–92, www .stanford.edu/group/scspi/_media/pdf/Reference%20Media/Carlson%20and%20Corcoran _2001_Children.pdf.

2. John Gottman, *Raising an Emotionally Intelligent Child: The Heart of Parenting* (New York: Simon and Schuster, 1997), 172.

3. U.S. Census Bureau, *Current Population Survey: Living Arrangements of Children Under 18 Years/1 and Marital Status of Parents by Age, Sex, Race, and Hispanic Origin/2 and Selected Characteristics of the Child for all Children 2010* (November 2010), Table C3.

4. Romans 12:10.

5. 1 Peter 3:1–4.

6. To go deeper than these five steps, I recommend David D. Burns, *Feeling Good Together: The Secret to Making Troubled Relationships Work* (New York: Broadway Books, 2008). In my work with couples, I use his form of cognitive interpersonal therapy. Some of these principles are explained in more depth in this book.

7. Gottman, *Raising an Emotionally Intelligent Child,* 139.

8. Gottman, *Raising an Emotionally Intelligent Child,* 139.

9. See Genesis 2:24.

10. Tim Keller, *The Meaning of Marriage* (New York: Dutton, 2012), 131.

11. You can download these resources at www.joshuastraub.com/familyresources.

12. Brené Brown, *Daring Greatly: How the Courage to Be Vulnerable Transforms the Way We Live, Love, Parent, and Lead* (New York: Gotham Books, 2013), 125.

Chapter 11 | Establishing Faith

1. Exodus 31:18.

2. Proverbs 3:3.

3. Proverbs 7:2–3.

4. Matthew 6:21.

5. See Luke 6:45; 1 Corinthians 15:33.

6. To gain a more in-depth understanding into how the Bible and research work together here, I recommend Tim Clinton and Joshua Straub, *God Attachment: Why We Believe, Act, and Feel the Way We Do About God* (Nashville: Howard Books, 2010).

7. Andreas Birgegard and Pehr Granqvist, "The Correspondence Between Attachment to Parents and God: Three Experiments Using Subliminal Separation Cues," *Personality and Social Psychology Bulletin* 30 (2004): 1122–35.

8. Angie McDonald et al., "Attachment to God and Parents: Testing the Correspondence vs. Compensation Hypotheses," *Journal of Psychology and Christianity* 24 (2005): 21–28.

9. Lee A. Kirkpatrick, *Attachment, Evolution, and Psychology of Religion* (New York: Guilford Press, 2005).

10. Luke 6:46–49, MSG.

11. Ravi Zacharias, "The Apologetic of the Apologist," Ravi Zacharias International Ministries, November 8, 2012, rzim.org/a-slice-of-infinity/the-apologetic-of-the-apologist.

12. Galatians 4:19, NIV.

13. *The Family and Technology Report: How Technology is Helping Families and Where They Need Help.* 2011 Annual Report. A study commissioned by Orange, a division of reThink Group in collaboration with Barna Group.

14. 3 John 1:4.

15. See 2 Chronicles 16:9.

16. Proverbs 22:6, NIV.

17. Stanley I. Greenspan and Nancy Breslau Lewis, *Building Healthy Minds: The Six Experiences That Create Intelligence and Emotional Growth in Babies and Young Children* (Boston: Da Capo Books, 1999).

18. George Barna, *Revolutionary Parenting: What the Research Shows Really Works* (Carol Stream, IL: BarnaBooks, 2007).

19. See John 1:14.

20. Galatians 5:1.

21. Proverbs 7:2–3.

22. Psalm 119:32, NIV.

23. Deuteronomy 6:4–6.

24. See Matthew 22:36–40.

25. 1 Corinthians 13:1.

26. 1 John 3:16, NIV.

27. Deuteronomy 6:7–9.

28. Zephaniah 3:17, NIV.

29. Mark Batterson, *The Circle Maker: Praying Circles Around Your Biggest Dreams and Greatest Fears* (Grand Rapids: Zondervan, 2011).

30. See Mark 8:36.

31. 1 Corinthians 15:33, NIV.

32. Michael Gurian, *The Purpose of Boys: Helping Our Sons Find Meaning, Significance, and Direction in Their Lives* (San Francisco: Jossey-Bass, 2009).

33. Kara E. Powell and Chap Clark, *Sticky Faith: Everyday Ideas to Build Lasting Faith in Your Kids* (Grand Rapids: Zondervan, 2011).